CONTEMPORARY MORMONISM

CONTEMPORARY MORMONISM

LATTER-DAY SAINTS IN MODERN AMERICA

Claudia L. Bushman

Westport, Connecticut
London

Library of Congress Cataloging-in-Publication Data

Bushman, Claudia L.
  Contemporary Mormonism : Latter-day Saints in modern America / Claudia L. Bushman.
     p.   cm.
  Includes bibliographical references (p.   ) and index.
  ISBN 0-275-98933-X (alk. paper)
  1. Church of Jesus Christ of Latter-day Saints—United States—History—20th century.
2. Mormon Church—United States—History—20th century. 3. Mormons—United States.
I. Title.
BX8611.B83   2006
289.3'73'090511—dc22   2005021358

British Library Cataloguing in Publication Data is available.

Library of Congress Catalog Card Number: 2005021358
ISBN: 0-275-98933-X

First published in 2006

Praeger Publishers, 88 Post Road West, Westport, CT 06881
An imprint of Greenwood Publishing Group, Inc.
www.praeger.com

Printed in the United States of America

The paper used in this book complies with the
Permanent Paper Standard issued by the National
Information Standards Organization (Z39.48-1984).

10   9   8   7   6   5   4   3   2   1

For Richard
My resident editor, critic, and co-conspirator in all things
on the occasion of our fiftieth wedding anniversary

Contents

PREFACE

"There is in Mormondom, as in all other exclusive faiths, whether Jewish, Hindoo, or other," Sir Richard Burton wrote in his book *The City of the Saints* (1862), "an inner life which I cannot flatter myself or deceive the reader with the idea of my having penetrated." Burton, a world traveler and adventurer, visited Salt Lake City with an Orientalist's eye, observing the colorful sect and its much-married leader, Brigham Young, in a generally sympathetic way, yet admitting his inability to comprehend the Mormons.[1]

Academics acknowledge the same difficulty. When Sydney Ahlstrom described Mormonism in his prize-winning *A Religious History of the American People* (1972), he stopped short of pinning the faith down. "The exact significance of this great story persistently escapes definition." The categories normally invoked to explain denominations were rendered practically useless. "One cannot even be sure if the object of our consideration is a sect, a mystery cult, a new religion, a church, a people, a nation, or an American subculture; indeed, at different times and places it is all of these."[2]

The positions of Burton and Ahlstrom point to the question and the problem of this book. Readers trust the objectivity of outside writers even though they admit difficulty in penetrating the inner life of Mormondom, while the reports of those living that inner life are often dismissed as biased and misleading. Even those who have been disillusioned by the strange life of the Mormons and broken from the faith are believed more than those who write from the inside. Latter-day Saints may be among the last groups in contemporary America not trusted to speak for themselves. At the same time, Mormons dismiss the outside appraisals for failing to describe a life that Mormons recognize. Few people try to see the Saints both from the inside and the outside.

I write from this no man's land as a third-generation member of The Church of Jesus Christ of Latter-day Saints. I attend meetings regularly and fulfill church obligations. I was married in the Salt Lake Temple to a man whose Mormon lineage dates from the 1830s. We have both held many positions of leadership. We have raised our six children as Mormons, and our four sons have also served missions and been married in the temple. But we are not Utahns. We were both raised on the West Coast and attended college on the East Coast. Although our ties are strong to Utah where many of our family members live, we have generally lived elsewhere, both as citizens in multicultural environments and as members of Latter-day Saint congregations. I understand both contemporary American culture as well as inner Mormonism. I know how Church life looks to the greater public, even as I view it from within.

By "inner" I mean the ordinary life of Mormons as they experience it. I am not describing the hidden so much as the obvious. To describe the inner Mormonism I have used examples from my own experience, the words of ordinary Mormons, and materials from print sources. My aim has been to describe the current evolving Church as it is experienced by members in a narrative that others can also understand.

Though my approach is straightforward, my subject is not. "Mormonism" is an elusive term, defying easy definition. The schismatic branches of The Church of Jesus Christ of Latter-day Saints encompass many disparate people, all claiming present or past loyalty to and descent from Joseph Smith, Jr., the Mormon prophet, generally called here Joseph Smith. Mormondom encompasses them all. By far the largest number of followers belongs to the church based in Salt Lake City that traces its history through Brigham Young who led the majority of believers from Illinois across the western plains to settle in the desert wilderness. I focus on this group. But many of Smith's followers stayed in the Midwest where they later founded the Reorganized Church of Jesus Christ of Latter Day Saints (spelled with a capitalized "D" and without a hyphen) in the 1850s. The Reorganized Church included Joseph Smith's wife and family; Smith's son Joseph Smith III became the prophet-president in 1860.

The two groups divided over the issue of plural marriage, which Joseph Smith had privately preached to a limited group in Nauvoo. The Reorganized Church denied Smith's marriages to multiple women and built up a church that focused on earlier teachings. Leadership of this group succeeded through Smith's line for 136 years until 1996. The Reorganized Church has moved steadily toward the Protestant mainstream, adopting the name The Community of Christ in 2002, a name that better explains what it is rather than what it is not. The church promotes "communities of joy, hope, love and peace." The Community of Christ, a church in its own right rather than an offshoot of the Utah church, claimed 250,000 members in forty countries in 2003.[3]

After his appointment in 1996, President W. Grant McMurray, who wanted to be known as the leader of "a prophetic people," rather than as a prophet himself, steered the group toward ecumenism and reconciliation, avoiding, as he said, "sappy sentimentality" and "stifling literalism." The Utah church and the Community, drifting farther apart, show the different possibilities of evolution within Mormondom. In 2005 McMurray resigned from his leadership of the Community of Christ, for health and personal reasons, without naming a successor. The Council of the Twelve chose Stephen M. Veazey, who had been the director of field ministries and so the leader of this church's fast growing outposts, to succeed McMurray.[4]

About 130 other groups, mostly small, have broken off from the main body of Latter-day Saints. After Smith's death in 1844, James J. Strang took a group to Beaver Island, Wisconsin, where he continued polygamy and was crowned king. Strang was shot and killed in 1856, but a small remnant of his order remains. The Godbeites, a group of intellectual converts from England, broke from the Utah church in the 1860s, favoring more interaction with the outside world. The literate members produced many documents before the group died out by 1880.[5]

Polygamy has also led to divisions in the twentieth century. After coming to the Salt Lake Valley, the Latter-day Saints lived the practice openly and announced it publicly in 1852. Polygamy continued through years of oppression and persecution by the U.S. government and was paired with slavery as one of the "twin relics of barbarism." When national laws made the extinction of the Church likely, the leaders capitulated, forswearing polygamy and renouncing involvement in local politics. A document called the Manifesto discontinued the practice in 1890, and Utah was soon granted statehood.[6]

Since that time, Mormons who felt that polygamy was the true way, discontinued for political or social reasons, have carried it on in schismatic churches of their own. Gordon B. Hinckley, president of the Utah church, has called polygamy, which was practiced for about fifty years and has been outlawed for more than 100, a past matter. "Any man or woman who becomes involved in [polygamy] is excommunicated from the Church." People who think the Church has anything to do with them are mistaken. This matter is "outside the realm of our responsibility" and has been for a very long time.[7] These dissident groups generally live quietly in Utah and other western states.

Others who may be counted among the greater Mormon family but are not directly involved in the Church are dissidents or "cultural Mormons." These "inactive" members are the "jack Mormons" who no longer attend services or have distanced themselves from the larger congregation for personal reasons. They may have been baptized but never fully integrated into a congregation. They may have been offended. They may disagree with doctrinal principles or be unwilling to live the Church's dietary guidelines, or pay the required ten percent tithing. Many descend from old church families but go their own way. These people are listed on the rolls and encouraged to return to activity. .

Others who are silent or absent have been excommunicated for moral problems, heresy, or some other cause. The most publicized of this group includes intellectuals and feminists whose activities were deemed disobedient or heretical. These articulate thinkers have been punished for writing about topics that Church leaders consider damaging and destructive. While speakers in local wards have great freedom, those who speak or write to wider audiences are carefully scrutinized and sometimes disciplined. A few well-publicized cases have given the Church a reputation for suppressing free thought. From the Church's point of view, the goal is to define acceptable doctrinal boundaries and to ensure social tranquility.[8]

The Church of Jesus Christ of Latter-day Saints, then, encompasses large numbers of people with complex histories who join for many different reasons and have chosen to relate to Mormonism in many ways. All of them are affected to some degree by the thick heritage that includes theology; a history of western frontier migration; a detailed Plan of Salvation; myths of creation; an identity built on stories of divine intervention, persecution, and sacrifice; a warm family and congregational life; and a tradition of ongoing revelation, of God leading His people as He did Israel of old. Because so many members are converts with their own histories, isolating individual beliefs is difficult. People choose the aspects of the gospel that they like best. As anthropologist Mark Leone says, the Church has a "do-it-yourself theology," which means that Mormondom is an immensely complex agglomeration of many parts.[9]

The name of the Church is also elusive. The Book of Mormon, the Scripture that Joseph Smith said he translated from golden plates, has provided the Church's misleading nickname. Mormon is a character in the book but he played no large role in Church history. He recorded the deeds of his own ancient people before his death in 385 C.E. The sect was named The Church of Christ at its founding in 1830. Eight years later, a teaching now found in Doctrine and Covenants 115:4 1981 said: "For thus shall my church be called in the last days, even The Church of Jesus Christ of Latter-day Saints," the long name by which the church is known today. Neither official name mentions the short and distinctive "Mormon." The subtitle of the Book of Mormon, "Another Testament of Jesus Christ," was adopted in the early 1980s.

In preparation for the media coverage of the Winter Olympic Games held in Salt Lake City in 2002, The Church of Jesus Christ of Latter-day Saints sent out a notice reemphasizing the centrality of Jesus Christ in its name and denying the existence of an entity called the "Mormon Church." To emphasize a Christian identity, the Church altered its logo to show the words "Jesus Christ" in larger type and urged that media accounts use the whole dauntingly long name, The Church of Jesus Christ of Latter-day Saints, in any first reference and thereafter The Church of Jesus Christ, an undistinctive name shared by other denominations. Spokesmen specifically requested that the common labels "Mormon Church," the "Latter-day Saints Church" and the "LDS Church" not be used. The word "Mormon" could still refer to individuals and to the well-known Mormon pioneers or the Mormon Tabernacle choir. Elder Dallin Oaks, of the Quorum of the Twelve Apostles, made the distinction when he said, "I don't mind being called a Mormon, but I don't want it said that I belong to the Mormon Church." But because this usage goes against a lifetime of practice, writers continue to report on the Mormon Church. The Church-owned newspaper, the *Deseret News*, still uses LDS Church, as does its weekly supplement carrying the Church's news from Salt Lake City. Later the Church distanced itself from use of the title "fundamentalist Mormon" as polygamous groups are sometimes described, as an oxymoron. "The term Mormon is not properly applied to the other . . . churches that resulted from the split after [Joseph] Smith's death."[10]

In this book, I employ a variety of titles. The word "Mormon," as I have suggested, can include the broad family of schismatic and dissident groups, but here, as the Church prefers, I use it to refer to members of The Church of Jesus Christ of Latter-day Saints, the largest Mormon group. This longer title is used from time to time, and references to LDS, the LDS Church, and to the Latter-day Saints are used occasionally. The word "Saints" implies no particular virtue, referring to everyday members. All of these terms, as well as reference to "the Church," mean The Church of Jesus Christ of Latter-day Saints. I will mostly use quotations from this main body throughout the book.

I have relied on Church and press reports on happenings of significance and from Mormons themselves who have willingly described their religious culture. A large part of the reporting has come from watching stories unfold as well as from observing ordinary occurrences in Mormon life, its meetings, its celebrations, its contentions, and its struggles. These I have approached with the eye of an amateur anthropologist observing her native people. My desire has been to depict them in their beauties and flaws. I hope it will be evident that although I see some unresolved tensions in the Church, I love the Mormons and their occasional peculiarities, eccentricities, and homely virtues. I thank here the many people who have talked to me, read chapters, and helped me to compile this record, particularly Jed and Shawna Woodworth.

ENCOUNTERING THE MORMONS

A peculiar people.

—*Gordon B. Hinckley*, 1992

The Church of Jesus Christ of Latter-day Saints, founded in rural New York in 1830 by Joseph Smith, Jr. (1805–1844), is arguably the most successful of the American religions begun in the first half of the nineteenth century.[1] The Church counted 2.9 million members in 1970. In April 2005, the Church officially listed 12,275,822 members. This fast-growing denomination increased its membership by 19.3 percent during the 1990s and rose to be the sixth largest religious body in the United States. By 2005, according to the *Yearbook of American and Canadian Churches,* the Church was the fourth largest denomination in the United States.[2]

Because many of these numbers, gathered by the Glenmary Research Center, come from the institutions themselves and represent baptized rather than active members, the figures are suggestive rather than definitive. Still, these and other figures reflect a general pattern: the growth of conservative churches such as the Latter-day Saints, while the moderate and liberal churches decline. Based on past growth figures, sociologist Rodney Stark, not a Mormon, has predicted that by 2080 LDS membership will be somewhere between 60,000,000 and 265,000,000, making it a major world religion. Stark notes that for the Mormons in the United States to have overtaken in numbers such prominent faiths as the Congregationalists, Presbyterians, Episcopalians, and even the Lutherans must be "one of the most unremarked cultural watersheds in American history."[3]

Stark also notes that Mormonism's growth does not come from high fertility, but from baptisms. In 1991, 75,000 member children were baptized; by contrast, 297,770 converts were baptized, a ratio of almost one to four. This means the majority of Mormons are first-generation members. Convert baptisms remained fairly steady during the nineties, near 300,000 a year, sinking to about 250,000 in 2004, still a substantial number.[4] Sociologists have long predicted the death of religion because of modernization and secularization. But these forces have not blunted Mormon growth. Stark dramatically noted that "after a hiatus of fourteen hundred years, in our time a new world faith seems to be stirring."[5]

Mormonism, less than 200 years old, has had many dramatic chapters, some of which have more contemporary relevance than others. The early political battles of the Church, for instance, have receded into the past. The nineteenth-century clashes with neighbors in New York, Missouri, Ohio, and Illinois do not impinge directly on the present. On the other hand, the Book of Mormon, the controversial Scripture Joseph Smith claimed to have received from an angel and to have translated from golden plates, is still very important, as is the temple building that has characterized the Latter-day Saints from the beginning. The recent proliferation of temples and the massive genealogy program the temples spawned have tremendous meaning for Church members. The pioneer trek with its covered wagons, with babies born and buried at the side of the trail, is now the stuff of myth and commemoration, but the city that rose at the end of the trail beside the Great Salt Lake is of considerable current interest. Salt Lake City's hosting of the 2002 Winter Olympics brought national media attention to Mormondom.

Distinguishing between issues of contemporary importance and those that have receded governs the story told in this book. Each chapter focuses on a segment of LDS life, offering background narrative when called for but emphasizing the experience of being a Mormon today.

History is still important, but because of the long-standing belief in current and ongoing revelation from God to modern-day prophets, Mormons are less fettered by their past than other groups. They dwell on the heroism of the founders and remain loyal to their prophet Joseph Smith, but their beliefs allow for sharp departures from past practices. The reversals on polygamy and the bestowal of the priesthood to a wider group are examples of practices not so much foresworn as revised or reinterpreted as God's will for His people at the current time. The history of the Church may seem to be an accumulation of past precedents, but sudden changes show that Church history is really the unfolding present. Different aspects of a broad range of teachings are introduced or emphasized at different times.

Even as Mormons cling to their fundamental doctrines, the expanding of the Church into new languages and countries has forced the creation of a new Christ-centered simplicity. Joseph Smith always moved forward with new ideas and conceptions, elaborating or expanding on them. Had he lived longer, he would probably have introduced more new doctrines. For now, many of his complex doctrines such as eternal progression, the Great Apostasy, the "only true church," and the Gathering of Israel, which have been debated over the years, have receded in importance in Church teachings. They either do not appear in lesson manuals or are toned down. The Church presents a simple, unified message taught simultaneously in many countries.

Mormons believe that God communicates His will through prophets, that Joseph Smith got direct instruction from heaven, and that succeeding prophets receive divine counsel. They believe in the perfection of man to a Godlike state through ages of afterlife. These claims are too much for other Christians to accept. Many Protestants have defined Mormons as separate from Christianity, citing a failure to assent to traditional Christian creeds and other accepted criteria. Yet Mormons pray to God through Jesus Christ, believe in the Atonement and the Resurrection, and partake of sacraments in His name. Mormons, who see themselves as neither Catholic nor Protestant, do not understand how other churches can deny their Christianity. Seeing themselves as the restored Christian church, they believe that their church is the current embodiment of the Church that Jesus Christ organized on earth.

The Church is authoritarian, being run from headquarters in Salt Lake City. Yet within that hierarchical mold, it is also congregational and remarkably democratic, led by local volunteers. This lay church has no paid ministry outside of headquarters except for a small corps of employees stationed throughout the world. One of the Church's great strengths is its ability to meet the needs of large numbers of ordinary people who belong to and participate in a community through a complex network of lay offices and group obligations. Church work is seen as part of membership as well as an opportunity for service.

Virtually all "active" or participating Church members, men and women alike, take on short-term administrative and teaching assignments in their congregations. Each person who accepts a responsibility has jurisdiction or stewardship over that area. Leaders, having been followers themselves, and having no real sanctions over other people, try to lead with positive reinforcement rather than bossing people around or correcting them. Twenty years of Church service might bring a dozen different jobs to these amateurs.

The high leadership of the Church, called "general authorities," tends to be made up of old men seasoned by years of service. The Church President and Twelve Apostles remain in office until they die. Of the ten deceased presidents of the Church in the last century, five died in their eighties and four in their nineties. The wards or congregations, however, are generally run by younger adults. Many ward leaders, called bishops, are in their thirties and forties. Youth also serve, and even children speak from the pulpit. A bishop will put in twenty or more hours a week counseling members, administering relief to the poor, and calling people to assignments in the congregation.

The current Church spends considerable effort strengthening and preserving the family against contemporary forces in a difficult world. Wary of the many things that can go wrong with family life today, the leaders preach a warm and sentimental message about family importance and longevity. Mormons believe that "families are forever." The Church takes a conservative stand on family issues, marriage, and all the aspects of human reproduction including child-rearing, abortion, and adoption. Leaders would like to consider polygamy or plural marriage a closed chapter, but this story will not die. The legacy remains in large Mormon families and in the schismatic fundamentalist groups that still practice "the principle." Although an estimated 20,000–50,000 people still live in polygamy, mainly in Utah, Arizona, and Idaho, The Church of Jesus Christ of Latter-day Saints repudiates the practice and consistently denies connection to any who do.[6] The Church has redefined itself as a protector of the traditional family, a conservator of traditional values, reversing the role it played in the nineteenth century.

Missionaries are one of the primary points of contact with the greater culture. The huge missionary workforce is made up of about 45,000 mainly young men and women who search out people who are willing to change their lives to become Latter-day Saints. As important as the converts made by these efforts, the year and a half or two years in the mission field discipline the missionaries themselves, adding immense strength to LDS society. Although the convert yield varies from country to country, and different places are the focus of greater effort at different times, Church doctrine requires that the gospel be preached everywhere, to all persons in all places. "Go ye unto all the world, and preach the gospel to every creature," Mark 16:15 KJV said Jesus. The Mormons add that the gospel must be preached "unto every nation, and kindred, and tongue, and people." Doctrine and Covenants 133:37 1981.

Dramatic growth of the Church at home and abroad is one of several dominant themes of the recent period. International growth has dramatically affected the Church's programs through simplification, standardization, and correlation, including the bestowal of Church authority on all nations and races. Whereas a major challenge of earlier years was the gathering of the converted Mormons to the Salt Lake Valley—leaving behind countries, families, and customs—the issue of the current day is the globalization of the Church in places where new converts are encouraged to build up congregations in their homelands. Besides training new members in Mormon ways, the Church is concerned with helping those new members, often converted from the poorer classes, to rise economically and educationally to become strong citizens and future leaders.

An unresolved issue is in knowing the extent to which international congregations should reflect the flavor of nineteenth-century Mormonism. Will vestiges of the American West remain? Will the Church adapt to local indigenous styles? Will American culture define the worldwide church? For now, the Church closely supervises its distant outposts by training local leaders and providing a basic curriculum translated into 175 local languages, casting its net ever wider. In 2005, the Book of Mormon was available in 104 different languages, seventy-four full editions and thirty editions of selections. Since its initial printing in 1830, it is estimated that more than 100 million copies have been distributed. The Book of Mormon is available from www.ldscatalog.com and from bookstores. The Doubleday company published a hardcover edition in 2004.[7] The growth of the international Church takes on larger significance now that most Church members live outside the United States and as both the nation and the Church tilt toward Spanish-language dominance.

Temples, one of the most visible and exotic manifestations of LDS culture, continue to rise on the national and international landscape. After dedication, these building are closed to all but "temple worthy" Mormons who participate in ordinances they believe can link families over time. Activities in these buildings contrast dramatically with the wholesome and noisy family gatherings in chapels. In the temples, religion is pure and mysterious. The proliferation of temples in recent years is the surest sign that Mormons will not blend into the general Christian background but remain a distinct faith with unique beliefs.

Revelation, church service, families, missionary work, and temples all come out of Mormon beliefs and indigenous practices, but another set of issues are thrust on the Church by the society around it, which is made up of people diverse in race, class, ethnicity, gender, and sexual orientation. These issues of cultural diversity are receiving a vast amount of historical and political attention these days. In each issue there is a distinctive LDS story to be told, one that illuminates stress and tension across a contested boundary. In the Church, all of these topics have been areas of tense interaction, and some of them have been resolved more successfully than others. In every case, future difficulties will force further negotiations.

All these contested relationships affect the Church's efforts to interface with the general culture and assimilate into American life. This onetime outlaw sect has accommodated in many respects to the standard norms of the United States, allowing one recent commentator to call the Mormons "quintessentially American," [8] even as they seem strange and distant to others. In this dance of opposites, the Church has moved closer to and then farther away from American society, emphasizing areas attractive to the mainstream, while guarding and pointing out the Church's effort to live out ancient, scriptural injunctions in modern society.

The Church has created its own intellectual culture in large part to deal with the dilemmas and challenges of modernity. The confrontation of religious absolutism and modern relativism defines identities and attitudes for many Mormons. Some hew strictly to orthodox doctrine and the teaching of Church leaders; others are more questioning. The basic split between the mystical religion of magic and folklore against the rational world of college-educated members generates endless discussion and debate.

The political tensions with modern life can be seen in Salt Lake City, Church headquarters and the last in a series of Mormon cities. Joseph Smith tried repeatedly and unsuccessfully to organize a City of Zion in Missouri, Ohio, and Illinois. His most enduring settlement was Nauvoo, Illinois, where the Saints managed to live for seven years. Later Brigham Young built Salt Lake City. In its 150 years of settlement, the city has undergone phases of isolation and assimilation, of integration and polarization. Currently polarized along the Mormon/non-Mormon or "Gentile" line, the city is a contested realm. Salt Lake, once the outlaw outpost, remains an indigestible lump in the public craw.

These are the contents of modern Mormonism as surveyed in the pages that follow. The final chapter evaluates the Church as it approaches its 200th anniversary. Where is it now and where will it go? An unlikely success, the Church has managed to negotiate many serious difficulties over its 175 years. At times when it seemed that ruin was inevitable, the Church adapted and survived. Now stronger and larger than ever, even as problems remain, the Church will likely sail on successfully into the future. What is its secret? One answer is that the Church mixes strong demands and expectations with encouragement for finding one's own way in the world and for the individual interpretation of scriptures. Although some general actions may seem clumsy and harsh, the Church is full of people of good will who do their best. For new converts, it is a community for lost and lonely souls. For all, it provides an answer to the question of what life is for and offers assurance that in the end the humble and faithful will find God.

This book will visit events and people as well as documents to bring this group closer to view. The words of many real Mormons will be quoted and Mormon rituals will be observed. The traditional Fast and Testimony Meeting serves as a good introduction to ordinary Mormon life. On the first Sunday of every month, Mormons in every local congregation, or "ward," gather for a seventy-minute meeting where congregants and visitors come to the pulpit to speak "from their hearts." Every Sunday has a "sacrament meeting," but on this Sunday, most come in the old Puritan tradition of fasting, having refrained from eating and drinking for two meals. They donate the cost of the missed meals as "Fast Offerings" to help the poor, a tradition dating from hard pioneer times.

FAST AND TESTIMONY MEETING

We visit a meeting in the third floor chapel of a congregation that meets near Lincoln Center in New York City. About 250 Mormons of all ages attend. They share the building each Sunday with another "family ward," a Spanish-speaking congregation, and a congregation of young singles. Five congregations meet in this building for three-hour blocks staggered throughout Sunday. A Korean-speaking group met there until recently, and multiple groups in Harlem, Chinatown, Union Square, Inwood, The Bronx, Brooklyn, and Queens meet elsewhere in the City.

An elevator carries people to the third-floor lobby where they greet each other and transact Church business. Congregants are neatly dressed in suits and dresses. The space is crowded with strollers for the noisy young children Mormons bring to services. The missionaries, ten or twelve young men and four young women, wear name badges. The pre-meeting tone is lively, even raucous, as members compete with the chapel's loud organ prelude music. There is no assigned seating.

The chapel itself is a plain auditorium in natural wood tones with no religious symbols. The ward leaders—the bishop and his two counselors—sit "on the stand," a dais at the front. People gradually fill the chapel, and a few minutes after the appointed time the bishop warmly welcomes them with announcements, many already written on a program.

The congregation sings a rousing LDS hymn. Mormons take pride in their group singing, and this congregation includes some professional singers. A chorister conducts the congregation, and the organist impro-vises interludes and key changes. Many consider this excellent music, not characteristic of all wards, the high point of the service. People fold their arms and bow their heads for the opening prayer delivered by a member of the congregation. The prayer, addressed to "Heavenly Father" in the name of Jesus Christ, closes with an "Amen" echoed by the congregation.

In the business part of the meeting, necessitated by the constant turn-over of lay workers, new assignments are announced. The newly assigned people stand, are introduced, and "sustained" in office by the congrega-tion raising their hands in support. Those "released" are thanked in the same way. This action is not a vote but an approval of decisions already made, representing a willingness to support the leaders who make the assignments.

The bishop or a counselor conducts the business. The young leaders in this congregation have families and demanding careers in finance and business; none works for the Church, although they certainly work in it. They tolerate noise because their own children often cry. Some parents take noisy children out, but infant chirping and wailing provide a steady background drone to the meeting.

Ordinances take place next. Baptism, always by immersion, usually at age eight, occurs elsewhere, but new members are often "confirmed" in Sacrament meeting with a special prayer that confers Church membership and bestows "the gift of the Holy Ghost." The newly baptized person sits in a chair while several male priesthood holders put their hands on her head, and one of them speaks the prayer. A more common ordinance, par-ticularly in this congregation, is the blessing of new babies. Male family members and friends circle the infant, each putting a hand beneath the baby and the other on the shoulder of the next man. The circles may have three to twelve men. Someone holds a microphone while the father, or another man, gives the infant "a name and a blessing." In this case, friends of the law-student father participate as he prays for wisdom in raising his son. The men gently rock the baby, and most babies are quiet through their blessings. When the prayer is completed, the beautifully dressed, handsome child is held aloft for the congregation to admire.

Efforts to include mothers in the blessings have been unsuccessful. One young father commented on this practice. "In the family, the woman has the baby, carries the baby, struggles with it, nurses the baby. The only role a man has is to bless the baby. I think it's appropriate that the man has that role. It gets him involved in the family." [9]

Next comes the Lord's Supper, or the "Sacrament," with bread and water arranged on a table at the side front and covered with a white cloth. A more solemn congregational song refers to the Crucifixion. Two young men read ritual prayers, first over the bread and then the water. These are among the few set prayers in Mormondom and are found in two books of Scripture, the Doctrine and Covenants and Book of Mormon. [10] If the young men stumble while reading these prayers, they must repeat them. The Sacrament is the high point of congregational ritual in an informal Church meeting. This Sacrament promises a forgiveness of sins. Members reflect on their "baptismal covenants" and take upon themselves Christ's name so that God's Spirit will be with them. Silence is encouraged, and the congregation is thanked for reverent behavior.

Now come the testimonies of the people who choose to come to the pulpit and speak, a voluntary and often spontaneous decision. Not even the bishop knows who will bear testimony. Speakers are told to say their names and be brief, but they often forget. Occasionally the bishop may stop a speaker if he or she drags on too long, but most say whatever they wish, as in Quaker meetings, and the audience is tolerant. Speakers testify about their personal blessings, relate faith-promoting experiences, or expound on the Scriptures. Sometimes a testimony will have a confessional aspect. In this New York City ward, many people speak during the allotted twenty-five minutes. In smaller congregations, minutes of silence may tick by. No one worries too much about these silent times. On this day, one of the bishop's counselors opened with his gratitude for the help and service of the members. During the time his young son had been hospitalized with a bone infection, the doctors had been amazed by the Church support system.

Members, new people as well as old friends, had provided meals and childcare. He thought that his family would be moving soon, and people at work were surprised that he was willing to relocate. They didn't understand that he had a community of LDS friends wherever he went. He testified that the Book of Mormon was the word of God, that Joseph Smith was a true prophet, and that Jesus Christ lived, a familiar coda. The congregation echoed his "Amen." The counselor then invited all who wished to speak to come forward and sit on the stand, reminding them of the meeting's closing time.

The speakers this day represent the diversity of this congregation. Elijah, a lively convert from Nigeria, speaks frequently, regretting the need to be brief. He is followed by a Latino convert, a divorced, single father who testifies about the power of God in his life. He had prayed for help and found the Church. Since then, things had worked out well for him and his daughter. When he sits down, a young missionary from Russia, a convert herself, translates the comments of a Russian woman who has joined the church, though she cannot yet speak English. Next a young couple introduce themselves. She is a convert, an aspiring actress, and he is a life-long member. They are glad to have this church community to join and involve themselves with. "We all have missions to accomplish," he says.

Parents and family of newly blessed babies often speak. The father who blessed his baby is grateful for friends who have participated in the blessing and for his Native American descent. His mother, visiting to help, next takes the stand. She is proud of her worthy children and her ninth grandchild. She is grateful for the Atonement of Christ. A television news anchor, a local celebrity, says she is grateful for her strong grandparents and for the good example of her family. She testifies that "we come to where we are for a reason." A lively, outspoken young man notes that he would be a "real slacker" if he did not acknowledge the three big blessings in his life: The Lord, his wife, and the ward—particularly for the love and compassion of the members and their mutual service. He has spent his best years in this ward and particularly likes the music. He testifies that the Book of Mormon is true and that Joseph Smith and the Church's current president, Gordon B. Hinckley, are both "true prophets."

The twenty-five minutes allotted for testimonies is over. A few members now awake from naps. The counselor makes a few more announcements, followed by a rousing congregational song. An organ interlude before the final verse raises the key half a step upward for a climactic finish.

The spouse of the person who opened the meeting pronounces the benediction. Fast meeting is over. But it is not time to go home. This meeting is the first of three in the regular three-hour meeting block. Sunday School comes next, and the congregation divides into smaller groups for gospel study, the largest group studying this year's text, the Old Testament. The third meeting divides women and men, instructing them separately. Additional classes provide instruction, music, and gospel activity for the children and the young people.

The Fast and Testimony meeting includes many elements of contemporary Mormon worship. Visitors and new people are very much at home because people are friendly and the programs are universal throughout the Church. Paradoxically, individual, public, personal expression is a regular part of this authoritarian church. The meeting is both structured and free. Gratitude for family, for Church connections, for religious foundations, and for sacred works and leaders are basic beliefs. Although the people are very different from each other, and without the Church would be unlikely to meet, they are comfortable together, bonded by common beliefs and commitments. Some permanent New Yorkers, some transient people, some life-long members, some new converts, and some natives of distant countries come together for a religious service. They tell stories of divine intervention in common phrases. They believe God has restored His church to the earth. Far from their childhood homes, in a tall building in the world's megacity, they find community and friendship in their ward family.

Leaders are fond of noting the differences between Mormons and others by quoting 1 Peter 2:9 KJV where the apostle says to Christians, "Ye are a chosen generation, a royal priesthood, an holy nation, a peculiar people; that ye should shew the praises of him who hath called you out of darkness into his marvelous light." Mormons feel equally chosen, peculiar in good ways, clinging to virtues of the past in obedience to moral doctrines and principles. President Hinckley tells young people of this "chosen generation," members of "this peculiar people," that they "cannot with impunity follow practices out of harmony" with what they have been taught. He challenges them to rise above the "sordid elements of the world" and remain peculiar.[11]

IDENTITY, BELIEFS, AND ORGANIZATION

If there is anything virtuous, lovely, or of good report or praiseworthy, we seek after these things.

—*Joseph Smith*, 1842

Three of the great world religions, Judaism, Christianity, and Islam, began with miraculous events: the deliverance of Israel from Egypt, the resurrection of Christ, the visions of Muhammad. Mormons, like all Christians, base their faith on the Old and New Testament miracles, but they also believe that God entered human affairs in the nineteenth century. They believe that divine events occurred less than two centuries ago that renewed divine authority and religious devotion in a Christianity that had lost some of its essential powers. Joseph Smith saw visions as Abraham, Moses, and Jesus had centuries before, making him the "prophet" of a new dispensation of the gospel.[1]

Smith's religious experiences began in 1820 in a time of religious revival in upstate New York. Confused by the cacophony of preaching, he wondered which church to join. A minimally educated, fourteen-year-old farm boy, he found in James 1:5 KJV encouragement to pray for knowledge. Kneeling in the woods near his father's farm, Smith experienced "thick darkness," then a pillar of light around "two Personages" of great brightness. Smith said one person introduced the other: "*This is My Beloved Son. Hear Him.*" Smith was told that no church was correct, that they were "all corrupt." They had a "form of godliness, but they deny the power thereof." Smith was ridiculed when he described his vision, but he clung to his story. "I had actually seen a light, and in the midst of that light I saw two Personages, and they did in reality speak to me; and though I was hated and persecuted for saying that I had seen a vision, yet it was true."[2]

Stung by early ridicule, Smith said little about his visionary experiences. Several years before his death, he published an account of this early vision. By 1900, when polygamy receded as the sect's defining doctrine, Smith's early experience received new emphasis, becoming the First Vision, defining Mormons against standard Protestantism. Latter-day Saint children learn this central story of the Church. Missionaries tell "The Joseph Smith Story" using Smith's words published as Scripture in The Pearl of Great Price. Congregations sing "Oh, How Lovely Was the Morning," a hymn describing the day when the heavens parted. For Latter-day Saints, the First Vision indicates God's interest in man. If He answered the prayer of a young farm boy, He can speak to anyone.[3]

Three years later, Smith had another vision. During an evening prayer, a bright light filled the room, and a messenger who said he was an angel of God appeared. The angel reported that the second coming of the Messiah was near and that Smith would help in bringing about some of God's purposes in the last days. The angel described historical records on gold plates written by ancient inhabitants of America buried in a hill near Smith's home. He was directed to the records, brought them home, showed them to eleven witnesses, "translate[d]" the story "by the gift and power of God," and published it as the Book of Mormon.[4]

Smith described the gold plates as six inches wide and eight inches long, with individual plates "not quite so thick as common tin." The plates were bound into a six-inch volume by three large rings. Smith said they were "beautifully engraved" with small Egyptian characters. The book showed "many marks of antiquity in its construction and much skill in the art of engraving."[5] Smith published the Book of Mormon in March 1830 and on April 6 of that year organized a church.

A cornerstone of Mormon beliefs is that Christianity, as originally established by Jesus Christ and his immediate followers, had gone through an apostasy in which the original authority—the priesthood—was lost. Mormons have taught that Protestant reforms, the American Revolution, and the rise of democracy allowing freedom of religion, all prepared the world for the reintroduction of Christ's gospel. Smith, whose First Vision told him that no current churches were true, claimed to have restored the original Christianity by divine authority. Mormons call this "the restoration," or the "restoration of all things," referred to by Peter in Acts 3:20-21 KJV. When Mormons testify to their belief that "the Church is true," they mean that Joseph Smith restored the Church of Jesus Christ.

The Church of Jesus Christ of Latter-day Saints is based on Smith's story and the miracles associated with it. Belief in the validity of the Book of Mormon as a historical document has been and continues to be a test of faith. Converts are told to read the book and pray for confirmation that it comes from God. Belief that God lives, that Jesus is the Christ, and that Joseph Smith was a true prophet is the basis of a "testimony," a personal statement of conviction and conversion. Observers, then and later, thought Smith was an imposter, a fraud, and a charlatan. Still, his writings suggest that he believed what he taught others, and he suffered a great deal for his beliefs.[6]

Joseph Smith lived only fourteen years after he organized the Church in April 1830. During that time, his primary goal was to establish the City of Zion, sometimes called the New Jerusalem. He designated a small site in Independence, Missouri, as this promised land, a place for a city and the construction of a temple. He sent out missionaries in search of converts to gather to this city, which would be a place of refuge from the calamities of the last days before the Second Coming. He laid out a plat for 15,000 to 20,000 people. When that city filled, another was to be laid out. Hundreds of converted Mormons assembled, frightening the local residents who feared the government would be hijacked by religious fanatics. The citizens forced out the Mormons, compelling Smith to find a new "Zion." He established one in Ohio and another in Far West, Missouri, with the same result: Numbers led to expulsion. Finally at Nauvoo, on the Illinois side of the Mississippi, he established a Mormon city of 10,000 converts drawn from the United States and England.

Nauvoo came to the same painful end as the previous Zions. Mormons in Nauvoo who had turned against Smith published a newspaper condemning him. Fearing the paper would ignite another round of persecution, Smith declared the copy libelous and had the press destroyed and the type scattered. Arrested on the charge of riot and, later, treason, Smith was awaiting trial in nearby Carthage, Illinois, when a mob stormed the jail and shot Smith and his brother Hyrum dead. Out of the various claimants who stepped forward to lead the Church, Brigham Young emerged to lead the main body on a 1,300-mile trek to the Salt Lake Valley, the next "Zion."[7]

To Mormons, "Zion" refers both to the "pure in heart" who follow God and to the place where they gather. Mormons attempted to create a Zion in each settlement, from Independence to Salt Lake City. This Zion identity is why Mormons consider themselves to be the restored Israel, seeing themselves akin to the original Jewish people and Christian church. Remnants of

Old Testament lore abound. Patriarchal blessings, of the sort that Isaac bestowed on Jacob and Esau, are given to Saints as direction for their lives. Mormons invoke "Redeemer of Israel" in song, calling themselves "children of Zion," and singing "How long we have wandered / As strangers in sin, / And cried in the desert for thee! / Our foes have rejoiced / When our sorrows they've seen, / But Israel will shortly be free."[8] Even the practice of polygamy comes from this connection to Abraham. Polygamists believed they were doing the "works of Abraham." Mormons feel close to Jews and more recently to Muslims, their fellow Israelites. They believe that Zion, the New Jerusalem, will be built in America. The themes of Zion, Israel, and gathering justify and explain their persecuted wanderings.

Picking up on Mormon affinity for Jews, Mormon U.S. Senator Orrin Hatch (R-Utah) wears a Jewish mezuzah around his neck. These small, biblically inscribed parchment scrolls are mounted at the entrance of Jewish homes as reminders of faith. Hatch sees connections between Mormons and Jews whose persecution confirms their chosenness. "I wear a mezuzah just to remind me, just to make sure that there is never another holocaust anywhere. You see, the Mormon church is the only church in the history of this country that had an extermination order out against it, by Governor Lilburn Boggs of Missouri. We went through untold persecutions."[9]

Along with the Old Testament connection, Mormons accept the New Testament as do all Christians and worship Jesus Christ as Savior of the world. These biblical strains are braided into the cheerful, optimistic Mormon style. The conservative, western style reflects the Church's origins in the United States. These strands in turn are being woven together now with the international, largely Latino cultures that are providing the bulk of Mormon converts. The biblical heritage, the early supernatural church founded by Joseph Smith, the frontier spirit of Brigham Young's mountain empire, modern American social conservatism, and a global multiculturalism all contribute to contemporary Mormon identity.

BELIEFS

What do the Latter-day Saints believe? The Church has a group of "distinctive doctrines" and teachings, but this is not a creedal church. There is no definitive formulation of Mormon religious beliefs. The most fundamental tenet, the belief in revelation from God to Joseph Smith and his successors, requires that doctrine be open-ended as more Scripture may be forthcoming. Joseph Smith condemned strict formulations, which, he thought, restricted the reception of truth. He said "Latter-day Saints have no creed, but are ready to believe all true principles that exist, as they are made manifest from time to time."[10]

Mormons believe that divine revelation for the direction of the entire Church comes from God to the president of the Church who is regarded by Latter-day Saints as a "prophet, seer, and revelator," a prophet like Abraham, Moses, or Peter. Mormons believe that every person may seek and receive revelation to guide his or her life. Parents may seek divine assistance to raise their children; students may pray over their studies; farmers may pray for their crops. Inspiration comes in answer to prayer. This principle of revelation saturates the body of the Church.

This principle becomes a problem when disturbed individuals cloak themselves in Church doctrine to validate questionable actions. David Brian Mitchell, a former Church member who kidnapped Salt Lake teenager Elizabeth Smart in 2002, wrote a "revelation" that justified his illegal actions. Best-selling journalist Jon Krakauer tied together several violent incidents perpetrated by fundamentalist, excommunicated Mormons to illustrate the violent potential of supposed revelations. Richard E. Turley, Jr., a Church official, noted that, "Over the last few years there have been a number of individuals we considered deviant with practices they ascribe to religious beliefs." They "embrace only selective elements of church teachings," Turley said, to justify their actions. Robert Millet, a BYU religion professor, considered personal revelation the blessing and the burden of the Church. It can "enhance a person's spirituality." But "revelation" also leads people to "plain lunacy."[11]

The best short account of Latter-day Saint belief is "The Articles of Faith," a list of thirteen principles Joseph Smith wrote in 1842 in response to the inquiry of a Chicago journalist. This list omits many key doctrines but remains the closest thing to a list of basic beliefs. The Articles of Faith was written when the Church was only twelve years old and still somewhat amorphous. Even this list would probably not exist if Smith had not been asked about the beliefs of the Church.[12]

The Articles of Faith

1. We believe in God, the Eternal Father, and in His Son, Jesus Christ, and in the Holy Ghost.

2. We believe that men will be punished for their own sins, and not for Adam's transgression.

3. We believe that through the Atonement of Christ, all mankind may be saved by obedience to the laws and ordinances of the Gospel.

4. We believe that the first principles and ordinances of the Gospel are: first, Faith in the Lord Jesus Christ; second, Repentance; third, Baptism by immersion for the remission of sins; fourth, Laying on of hands for the gift of the Holy Ghost.

5. We believe that a man must be called of God, by prophecy, and by the laying on of hands by those who are in authority, to preach the Gospel and administer in the ordinances thereof.

6. We believe in the same organization that existed in the Primitive Church, namely, apostles, prophets, pastors, teachers, evangelists, and so forth.

7. We believe in the gift of tongues, prophecy, revelation, visions, healing, interpretation of tongues, and so forth.

8. We believe the Bible to be the word of God as far as it is translated correctly; we also believe the Book of Mormon to be the word of God.

9. We believe all that God has revealed, all that He does now reveal, and we believe that He will yet reveal many great and important things pertaining to the Kingdom of God.

10. We believe in the literal gathering of Israel and in the restoration of the Ten Tribes; that Zion (the New Jerusalem) will be built upon the American continent; that Christ will reign personally upon the earth; and, that the earth will be renewed and receive its paradisiacal glory.

11. We claim the privilege of worshipping Almighty God according to the dictates of our own conscience, and allow all men the same privilege, let them worship how, where, or what they may.

12. We believe in being subject to kings, presidents, rulers, and magistrates, in obeying, honoring, and sustaining the law.

13. We believe in being honest, true, chaste, benevolent, virtuous, and in doing good to all men; indeed, we may say that we follow the admonition of Paul: We believe all things, we hope all things, we have endured many things, and hope to be able to endure all things. If there is anything virtuous, lovely, or of good report, or praiseworthy, we seek after these things.[13]

These articles locate the Church as a Christian religion but not in the Calvinist wing. Mormons believe that Jesus Christ took on himself the sins of mortal men, but unlike other Christians, they consider themselves free from the original sin that degraded mankind. Adam's fall brought death to humankind, but men will be punished for their own sins, forgiven by Christ's atoning sacrifice. As a restored church, Mormonism structures itself according to biblical patterns, preaching a gospel culminating in a millennial Second Coming of Christ. The Church claims tolerance and offers it to others, embracing good wherever found, praising all virtuous activities in a broad final article.

In addition to the Articles of Faith, the Church has a huge inventory of doctrines coming from Joseph Smith and from the rest of its history. In each period, the Church emphasizes particular messages to suit the times. In the past thirty years, leaders have stressed continued revelation, temple culture, belief in Christ, and the traditional family, among others. These fit into the larger "Plan of Salvation," or "Plan of Happiness," Book of Mormon phrases referring to life before and beyond mortality and plotting a successful journey through life.[14]

The Plan of Salvation underlies all other Latter-day Saint doctrines as the master narrative. The Plan is taught in the missionary lessons and the temples. The Plan says every person on earth is a child of God. Mortals lived with Him in a premortal existence. Through His divine plan, His spirit children come to earth to receive physical bodies, gain experience, and prove themselves worthy of the Father's greatest blessing: to live with Him forever. Through the Resurrection of Jesus Christ, all God's children will live after death as embodied beings. Through His Atonement they can be forgiven their sins. The Plan teaches about the origin and purpose of life, answering the following questions. Where do I come from? Why am I here? Where am I going?

Members find these principles moving. As Tom Robinson, a young convert said, "When the missionaries flipped the chart over and started talking about eternal marriage, that was it—preexistence, earth life, and afterlife—like a light bulb coming on." He and his wife were soon baptized. Brushes with death make this plan meaningful. Ingrid Adams, married to a Mormon, had already dismissed seven sets of missionaries when she miscarried an expected child. "It made me think. I had a husband and two children, whom I loved dearly, but I had lost someone that I had never known and it devastated me. I just wanted to make sure that I would have my husband and two kids for eternity. I fasted for two and a half days and told John that I was joining the church for his Christmas present."[15]

From the Plan of Salvation comes the doctrine of eternal marriage, performed in the temples. Family unity on earth and the potential for eternal relationships are core doctrines. Mormons believe that temple marriages continue forever, contingent on worthiness. As Joseph Smith said, the "same sociality which exists among us here will exist among us there, only it will be coupled with eternal glory."[16]

Latter-day Saints are best known for doctrines where belief merges with practice. The Word of Wisdom is their defining health code, generally interpreted as abstaining from tobacco, alcohol, tea, and coffee and the misuse of drugs. Stemming from a revelation of 1833 found in Doctrine and Covenants 89, the Word of Wisdom also emphasizes eating healthy foods. In practice, the commandment limits the LDS participation at social events where proscribed items are served. Mormons think twice before attending drinking parties, gatherings after work, or even coffee klatches; at dinners they upend their wine glasses and coffee cups. The Word of Wisdom accounts for the Mormons' clean-living reputation.[17]

The Word of Wisdom is also the clearest boundary between active, observant Mormons and those who distance themselves from the Church. Adherence to the Word of Wisdom means identity as much as health. Michelle Nevada, a Jewish writer, reported a visit she had with Mormon neighbors. She was interested in their eating laws, not unlike the kosher rules she followed. The writer was drinking coffee as the Mormon woman was drinking herbal tea. The Mormon woman's son asked his mother, "Why can't I just try some coffee? It smells so good." The mother replied, "Because you need to remember who you are."[18]

Still, there are health advantages. Mormons live long lives. Utah's percentage of smokers is the nation's lowest at 12 percent. Kentucky, the highest, is 31 percent, with the nation at 22.1 percent in 2003. Often cited is a fourteen-year study by James Enstrom, a non-LDS professor at UCLA, published in 1989. Enstrom followed mortality rates and health practices of nearly 10,000 California Church leaders and their wives and concluded that the Word of Wisdom increased life expectancy between eight and eleven years. Another study showed Utah with the nation's lowest cancer rates and heart disease.[19] Utahns smoke less and drink less alcohol than other Americans, and they stay healthy although they are low on exercise and high on hearty dining.

Tithing is the biblical principle of giving to the Lord 10 percent of earnings; and tithing by faithful Latter-day Saints accounts for the Church's prosperity. Other churches have tithe payers and encourage their members toward this goal. The average Christian church donor, about 61 percent of the population in 2000, gave $649 to churches that year, down from $806 in 1998. This comes to less than $15 a week. By contrast, many Mormons, certainly not all, give a full 10 percent to the Church; they are encouraged to pay their tithing before any other obligations, even in bad times. Paying tithing is a prerequisite to entering Mormon temples.

Brad Chadwick, one young missionary from Arizona serving in Milwaukee, said he considered the 10 percent no sacrifice. "You're helping the church's work go forward," he said. "And when you do that, you're doing God's work." Steve Young, former quarterback of the San Francisco Forty-Niners and a descendant of Brigham Young, said, "I don't really look at it as my money. You know, in my terms, it's the Lord's money, and I'd be, you know, in effect stealing from him if I didn't [pay tithing]."[20]

Some members wrestle with tithing. One family decided to forgo tithing to pay off their debts. After a year of not having one moment of good feeling, the family sat down for a council meeting and made a firm commitment to pay tithing. "I'm not anticipating a new car or a bag of money falling out of the windows of heaven," said the father, "yet I do feel much more comfortable kneeling down and saying to the Lord, 'Lord, I'm paying a full tithe. I'm doing all that I understand I should be doing, won't you help me?'"[21]

Members go without food or drink for two consecutive meals, called fasting, a day out of every month. They donate the cost of those meals to the Church to help those in need. Tithing and fast offerings have remained constant requirements of faithful Latter-day Saints, but in recent years, the financial burdens of members have sharply decreased. For most of the twentieth century, members paid substantial additional amounts in the form of "budget," "welfare," and building funds. Tithing funds, then devoted heavily to building construction, were insufficient to pay more than about 70 percent of upkeep costs. Members were asked to make an additional "budget" payment to cover the remainder. In those days, the bishop negotiated between what ward members were likely to be able to afford and what they would be willing to pay and assessed amounts based on their income and tithing receipts. Other contributions were requested to finance the support of farms and canneries producing food and supplies for the poor. A faithful member contributed about 12 percent of annual income rather than the basic 10 percent.[22] In 1990, as tithing funds grew, budget and welfare payments were phased out.

Chapel construction, a frequent occurrence in a fast-growing church, once put huge burdens on members. A new chapel could not be used or dedicated until paid for. Although Church headquarters once paid 50 percent and later 70 percent of construction costs, it now funds complete construction and maintenance. Paying these costs out of central accounts channels revenues from wealthier wards to poorer congregations.

Morality is another basic belief. The Church teaches honesty, integrity, obedience to law, abstinence from premarital sexual relationships, and complete fidelity within marriage. Adultery, abortion, abuse, pornography, and gambling are defined as evil.

Members are taught to care for their own temporal well-being. They should get adequate education, save money, and avoid debt. The Church instructs members to store a year's supply of food, fuel, and funds, as circumstances allow. Members should care for themselves and for family members; those still in need may apply to the church for assistance. Extensive programs help those whose self-reliance fails. Like the Boy Scouts, the message is: Be Prepared. As the Scriptures say, "If ye are prepared, ye shall not fear." Doctrine and Covenants 38:30 1981.[23]

Other basic LDS beliefs and practices include genealogy, family home evening, and temple work for the living and the dead. These diffuse and complex structures amount to an individual culture with broad beliefs, a unique vocabulary, and an extensive schedule. Members sometimes despair when they list the many good works they are expected to do; they prefer to think of the whole package.

A young woman, on the fringes of the Church, still felt close. "When everybody else went away to college, I felt like one of the lost sheep in my own [congregation]. I just stopped going to church and became inactive for about four years." After she married, her husband's children, with no religious beliefs or training, came to live with them. She thought it was important that the children go to some church, and she wanted them to go to her church. "Just because I had become inactive, I didn't feel that I had fallen away. I wanted the children to grow up hearing the lessons that we had learned. Looking back, I can see that my testimony was important to me."[24]

Simple answers to gospel questions can be found on a Church-maintained website, www.Mormon.org. This extensive, interactive site is the Church's effort to streamline doctrine and practice, showing how the Church wants to be represented. This emphasis at least partially results from challenges to a Mormon fundamental: belief in Christ. When Joseph Smith was asked for the Church's fundamental principles, he replied, "The fundamental principles of our religion are the testimony of the Apostles and Prophets, concerning Jesus Christ, that He died, was buried, and rose again the third day, and ascended into heaven; and all other things which pertain to our religion are only appendages to it."[25] The Godhead consists of God the Father; His Son, Jesus Christ; and the Holy Ghost, defined as one in purpose but separate in being.

Protestant groups have denied Mormon admittance to their Christian counsels, and a few denominations have passed official statements denying Mormonism's Christianity. On their Internet site, the Lutheran Church-Missouri Synod, says that "together with the vast majority of Christian denominations in the United States, [the Lutheran Church] does not regard the Mormon church as a Christian church. That is because the official writings of Mormonism deny fundamental teaching of orthodox Christianity."[26]

The Mormons' belief that Jesus Christ's original church was lost and only restored with Joseph Smith divides them from traditional Christianity. But the central difference is the doctrine of God rather than of Jesus Christ. Mormons believe in eternal progression and have taught that men may become the gods of other worlds. This doctrine implies that God, although omnipotent, continues to improve in His current eternally self-surpassing state. This doctrine is deemed heretical by other Christians. Although currently played down, this idea remains powerful in Mormon thought. Along with this conception, Mormons believe that God and the resurrected Jesus Christ have physical bodies. Evidence for this idea is the "two personages" Joseph Smith saw in his First Vision. The separateness of the Mormon Godhead, unlike traditional Christianity's notion of three in one, belief in continued revelation, and belief that their church is more truly Christian than other churches are points of tension.[27]

Another objection is to the Church's expansion of Scripture. Mormons are people of the book, like Christians, Muslims, and Jews, but instead of one book they are people of four books. The Mormon canon is the Bible, the Book of Mormon, the Doctrine and Covenants, and the Pearl of Great

Price. The Church uses the King James Version of the Bible with its own extensive notes, cross references, and definitions. Joseph Smith's revisions of the Bible, which supplement and provide variations of some verses, appear in footnotes and an appendix. The other three official books claim to be products of revelation, either translations of ancient documents or a collection of contemporary revelations. Mormons are urged to read scriptures for inspiration and strength, and they piously search the books for personal guidance. These scriptures are available via modern technology on CD-ROM as well as Palm Pilots, allowing readers to search, print, or copy them.[28]

The Book of Mormon, 584 long pages of text published in 1830, is written in biblical style as translated by Joseph Smith from the gold plates he found in the Hill Cumorah. The book purports to be the history of immigrants from Jerusalem who sailed to the Western Hemisphere before the Babylonian captivity in 600 B.C.E. Those who dismiss claims that Joseph Smith translated the book "by the gift and power of God" must still be impressed that he dictated this long manuscript steadily, without correction, in fewer than ninety days.[29]

The Book of Mormon is a complicated religious history with more than 200 characters covering more than a thousand years. Nephi, one of the immigrants, is the first narrator. Moroni, the last record-keeper, finishes up about 420 C.E. The book is primarily the work of Mormon, Moroni's father, a military figure from about 327–385 C.E. who wrote the central narrative, condensing and excerpting the records of previous chroniclers. Like the Bible, the book has some high flights of rhetoric and many interesting passages, but because it is so far removed from common experience, it remains bewildering to many readers. Mark Twain called the book "chloroform in print." Because of its claims, its length and complication, and because it is an anomaly in American culture, the Book of Mormon is seldom taken seriously. Still, it was included on a list in 2003 among twenty significant books that had "changed America."[30]

The dynamic of most of the Book pits descendants of Nephi, the good brother, against those of his wicked brothers Laman and Lemuel. The tribes that spring from these brothers remain at odds for generations. The basic operating assumption is that obedience to the Lord brings happiness and prosperity whereas pride and disobedience bring destruction. This morality frames chronicles of migration and war. Jesus Christ is a notable presence in the book, and the words of a Book of Mormon prophet establish His importance in the lives of Church members today: "We talk of Christ, we rejoice in Christ, we preach of Christ, we prophesy of Christ, and we write according to our prophecies, that our children may know to what source they may look for a remission of their sins." 2 Nephi 25:26, The Book of Mormon 1981. His birth is foretold, and after the crucifixion, He appears as the resurrected Christ and teaches biblical doctrine. This visit results in 200 years of peace before society deteriorates again, rushing toward its conclusion when the record-keeping peoples are destroyed, and Moroni buries the gold records in a hill. The survivors live to become, presumably, the ancestors of some Native Americans.

Joseph Smith and The Book of Mormon puzzled his contemporaries. Many believed he had plagiarized the text, which seems a reasonable conclusion under the circumstances. But no original source has ever been found. Other readers, noting republican passages, information on the origin of Native Americans, and similarities to anti-masonic furor, assumed the book was the fruit of his nineteenth-century imagination. But no outsiders have accounted for the book's complexity. Some consider the book to be fiction, but the rustic and unlearned Joseph Smith seems unlikely to have created such a complex narrative.[31]

As a starting point for conversion, missionaries direct readers to Moroni 10:4:

> And when ye shall receive these things, I would exhort you that ye would ask God, the Eternal Father, in the name of Christ, if these things are not true; and if ye shall ask with a sincere heart, with real intent, having faith in Christ, he will manifest the truth of it unto you, by the power of the Holy Ghost.

When members say the Book of Mormon is the true word of God, they mean that Joseph Smith translated an historical record from golden plates with divine help and that they feel the inspiration of God when reading it. In 1986, the Book of Mormon received renewed emphasis when Church president Ezra Taft Benson encouraged members to "flood the earth" with the book and read it with new devotion. He said to study the book constantly, that it would, quoting Joseph Smith, get people "nearer to God by abiding by its precepts, than by any other book."[32]

The Doctrine and Covenants, very different from the Book of Mormon, is mainly a collection of 138 revelations, meeting minutes, and letters called sections, on Church governance and doctrine; the book is, in theory, an open canon. The revelations generally speak in the voice of the Lord. "Hearken, O ye people of my church," the first verse of Section 46, is a common opening. The first section, dated 1831, is an introduction to the others, but some date back to 1823. Joseph Smith is responsible for more than 130 sections of the compilation. Brigham Young is credited with only one. The most recent addition, the official declaration extending the priesthood to all worthy males, is dated 1978. Most Church doctrines are found here somewhere.

The Pearl of Great Price is an anthology of short works accepted as Scripture. It includes "Selections from the Book of Moses," revelation given to Joseph Smith as he was reworking the Bible; "The Book of Abraham," a narrative influenced by an ancient Egyptian document that fell into Smith's hands in 1835; "Joseph Smith—Matthew," an expanded version of Matthew 24, as rewritten by Smith in 1831; "Joseph Smith—History," a relation of his early visions and translations; and "The Articles of Faith," Smith's own doctrinal summary. The book was first published in England in 1851, in the United States in 1878, and accepted as Scripture in 1880.

In 2002, the official Church website, www.lds.org, listed four documents under "Basic Beliefs." After the Articles of Faith and an edited version of Joseph Smith's account of his First Vision were two non-scriptural documents that show recent Church developments and are notable for emphasizing contemporary concerns. "The Family: A Proclamation to the World" is discussed in Chapter Three. The other, "The Living Christ: The Testimony of the Apostles: The Church of Jesus Christ of Latter-day Saints," is undated, but was issued on 1 January 2000 and signed by the First Presidency and the Quorum of the Twelve Apostles, the fifteen highest Church leaders. This reaffirmation of faith in the mission of Jesus Christ features such comments as "We solemnly testify that His life, which is central to all human history, neither began in Bethlehem nor concluded on Calvary. He was the Firstborn of the Father, the Only Begotten Son in the flesh, the Redeemer of the world." The document quotes significant scriptures and ends with this paragraph: "We bear testimony, as His duly ordained Apostles—that Jesus is the Living Christ, the immortal Son of God. He is the great King Immanuel, who stands today on the right hand of His Father. He is the light, the life, and the hope of the world. His way is the path that leads to happiness in this life and eternal life in the world to come. God be thanked for the matchless gift of His divine Son." The document may have been created to strengthen LDS Christian claims.

How do insiders feel about the Church? Responses range from the cool to the lyrical. One person says that the Church is the "fountain of hope, comfort, grace, courage, and blessings!" Through its doctrines and programs she has found purpose and help, the world's truest friends, and worthy models to emulate. A law student considers the Church God's true councils on this earth. His faith resides in spiritual answers to questions through prayer. Another feels that the Church requires her to follow Christ. Whatever has been commanded by Him or His servants, she is bound to do. Another person considers the Church an inspired vehicle, something God works through. He notes that the Church has sometimes tested his patience, but not his faith. Another said that the Church is an alternate source of meaning, apart from academic learning, a complex place where his secularism is uncomfortably incongruous.[33]

When asked to comment on some of the Church's doctrines, this same group identified the promise of forgiveness through the Savior's atonement, which allowed a person to endure and strive for perfection. Another valued the concept of the eternal family and that of Zion—a condition where evil was overcome by love. Another said that the LDS conception of progression toward godhood makes him focus on life as a place to learn "how God thinks." Another marks the Word of Wisdom and the Law of Chastity as areas of struggle in Church life. She thinks that the health of future Church life depends on the successful navigation of these issues by young people. Another sees the Word of Wisdom as kosher law, accidentally right about tobacco. He thinks that the lesson is not really about health but about defining a community. He is moved by the notion of eternal personality and the literal childhood of humanity to God.[34]

ORGANIZATION

The LDS Church is a lay church. No one at the congregational level is paid. Bishops, leaders of congregations, are called from the laity, keeping day jobs while serving in church office. After about five years, a bishop is rotated out and another man called from the congregation. Leadership is generated by an established priesthood hierarchy involving most boys and men. All LDS males are expected to be ordained into the priesthood at age twelve. Women work as Church leaders but are not ordained.

Mormon organization is shaped in the "wards," or local congregations, a term originating in early American voting districts and reflecting the original gathering into cities of Zion. Smaller groups are called branches. A ward, similar to a Catholic parish, includes members who live within a geographical area. Wards range in size from about 150 members to upwards of 800, several hundred of whom may actively participate. Some wards are organized thematically for unmarried adults, for speakers of certain languages, or for those with physical challenges such as deafness. When the ward outgrows the chapel, the boundaries are redrawn, creating two workable units.[35]

The bishop and his two counselors supervise and manage all the social, religious, educational, and cultural functions of the congregation. These include teaching classes, monthly visits to ward members, organizing programs, concerts, sports, dinners, plays, service projects, and other miscellaneous chores. The bishop oversees the welfare of his flock, comforting the afflicted and afflicting the comfortable, as the saying goes. He "calls" individuals to take on specific tasks and "sets them apart," that is, gives them blessings to carry out the tasks. Members have "free agency" to decide whether to accept the positions. Everyone is moved around. A teacher may work with the young women, then be moved to the nursery, and then be named drama director. The Relief Society president may become the pianist for the children's organization, the Primary. A man may go from bishop to Boy Scout leader.

As a young man noted, "I've heard a couple of bishops who have Ph.D.'s and master's degrees say they have never learned as much anywhere as they have in the church. You learn a little bit about accounting because of financial problems. You learn about psychological problems. You get drawn into everything that's involved in life." Another young man, before joining the Church, had always felt left out of religious activities. "I always pictured in my mind that ministers and pastors, who had never, ever had their hands dirty, never committed any of these sins, were the only ones who would be able to go to heaven. It was a real comfort to me to know that the bishop and the people giving talks in sacrament meeting or teaching classes are just like me. They work every day, supporting themselves. What they stood up and said, they said because they believed it—not because someone was paying them."[36]

This sharing of power is Joseph Smith's legacy. He gave priesthood power to all converted males, assigning out leadership positions. The Church often operated without his direction. He called himself "prophet, seer, and revelator," and gave the administration to others. That the Church is demanding, there is no doubt. Members are sometimes told to "magnify their callings," to do more than they are told. But others complain that we try to create "too many supermen," browbeating people into doing their jobs. A convert, who left the Church, was surprised at the expectations of membership. "There are a lot of things that I admire and think are great about the Mormon church and the Mormon religion. There are a lot of things that I think our society needs and that I need as an individual. I also think there are an awful lot of expectations that are hard. I wasn't used to the whole idea that you have to do all these things or you're not going to be sent to [heaven]. Having come into the church at twenty-five and progressing from there, I feel it is insurmountable—to the point of feeling, 'I'm never going to get there so why should I even try?' I do think there's a lot of love taught in the Mormon church. Besides the belief that God cares about each one of us, we were impressed by the concern of the people for each other."[37]

A man from a bishopric described reasons for inactivity. "In our ward we have 482 members and an average attendance of 165. Periodically I'm assigned to go find certain individuals. We ask the person, 'Tell me what happened. Why did you stop coming to church?' I run into: 'I couldn't be a perfect Mormon, so I didn't feel as if I belonged there. I couldn't pay my tithing every month. I didn't feel as if I could take the sacrament every Sunday. I didn't agree with that gospel doctrine teacher. At times I didn't feel that I had the spirit of the Holy Ghost with me. I didn't feel I was in tune with what the home teachers were saying when they came and presented a program. When somebody called me to do something, I didn't respond with the degree of perfection that was expected. I can't walk on water for you people and I don't hear trumpets every morning. My husband and I fight like cats and dogs.'"[38]

Most ward religious activities take place in the three-hour time block on Sundays with additional meetings as required. The number of meetings has dwindled since the 1980s. Earlier, Mormons gathered on Sunday morning and again later in the afternoon, necessitating two trips to Church each day. Additional meetings took place during the week. The meetings plus socials and fund-raising projects meant that Mormons were in isolationist mode and lived much of their lives at church. Worthiness was measured by faithful attendance. In 1980, to save energy during gasoline crises, but also to allow more family time, the schedule was consolidated to its present abbreviated form. Three hours of meeting on Sunday is still a lot, and Mormons frequently spend additional time at Church, but the previous pressure has been relieved. Now the Church is primarily a place for worship and religious instruction. Time commitments, such as financial ones, have decreased over the past few decades.

The Church "auxiliaries" include the Sunday School, the Relief Society (or women's organization), the Young Men and Young Women (for teenagers), and the Primary (for children). These all have individual presidencies of three plus a group of teachers. Each auxiliary holds its own meetings, teaches its own classes, plans its own social events, and keeps its own records.

These organizations are auxiliaries to the priesthood, the spiritual and administrative power conferred on males. The priesthood is divided between the lower or Aaronic Priesthood for those twelve to eighteen and the upper or Melchizedek Priesthood for men nineteen and up. The Aaronic Priesthood is divided into Deacons, Teachers, and Priests; the Melchizedek Priesthood consists of Elders and High Priests. The intermediate level of Seventy was phased out at the local level some years ago. Each priesthood group, or "quorum," has its own presidency and teachers.

Other organizations also exist, including the Institute, a religious, educational, and social program for LDS young adults ages eighteen to thirty. Institutes, managed by the Church Education System or CES, grow quickly worldwide, providing centers for young adults to make friends. Young adults constitute 60 percent of baptisms in the Church, and converts are more likely to remain active if affiliated with Institute.

Teenagers have a similar program called "seminary." Many rise at 5 A.M. for an hour-long class at 6 A.M. These fourteen to eighteen-year-olds meet weekday mornings with a teacher at a home or chapel to discuss and memorize scriptures. The four-year curriculum follows the Bible, the Book of Mormon, and the history of the Church. Families encourage their children to attend seminary, but some go faithfully without any family support.

One high school junior, an unknown transfer student who was elected student body president, talked about how Church identity brought him success. Older Mormon students came to him and said he had to run for the school office, the Mormon tradition. This young man was not on any teams, not in clubs, and he didn't know anyone. But he took the idea of duty seriously. "I went home and prayed about it. I thought, 'Well, I will do it for the honor of God.'" He had no campaign manager, no posters. He knew that everything depended on giving a funny talk, and he'd had experience talking in church. He thought about the talk and looked for jokes. "My talk was pretty funny with a nice little twist at the end. The other guys had not prepared. I got a majority in the first round because the freshmen and sophomores voted for me." The experience changed his life.[39]

Living in an LDS ward is often described as living in a large family. People frequently say how much they love everyone in the ward, even the people they don't know at all. "The Sugarhouse Ward is to me like my extended family. I cry with them, I laugh with them. We are all together for good things and bad things." Or, "When I got here the first time I felt welcomed, and I felt like I already knew the people from a long time, like they were relatives I was visiting after a long time spent far away." Another said, "this ward is in essence, my family. [They] made me feel I belong, that I'm one of 'theirs.'"[40]

When a young Pasadena, California, bishop was struck with a terminal blood cancer, his flock rallied to his aid. People gave blood in shifts. They filled the refrigerator with food. Such an energetic group came to paint, repair, prune, dig, and plant, that a neighbor thought the family would be on a television home show. One friend made daily lunches for the young daughter. The choir director, sitting one night with the nearly unconscious bishop, began to sing, bringing him briefly back to his former jocular self. His eventual funeral was a celebration of his life attended by hundreds of ward "family" members. His wife said she knew the measure of true friendship and love.

A group of wards is a "stake," which may include four to a dozen wards. A corps of stake leaders, led by the stake president, his two counselors, and a twelve member High Council, supervise programs and activities for the larger group. A group of stakes is an "area."

The Church is governed by a First Presidency and Twelve Apostles. The members of this fifteen-man group were called in their maturity to serve as apostles for life. They rise by seniority. President Gordon B. Hinckley, born in 1910, became a member of the Quorum of the Twelve in 1961 at the age of fifty-one. He was eighty-five when he became the Church's fifteenth president in 1995. Because of infirm predecessors, he had already been the operating head for years, dedicating twenty-two temples before he became president. He remains remarkably effective in his mid-nineties. At his first meeting with the press, he declared himself a steady leader rather than an innovative one with a theme of "Carry on the great work of those who have gone before." He called for "an increased spirit of civility" among different American faiths.[41] Yet his legacy as a builder was soon clear. On his watch thousands of new chapels have risen, and more dramatically, the number of temples has risen from forty-seven to well over 100.

When Mike Wallace interviewed President Hinckley on *Sixty Minutes,* he broached the idea that the Church was a gerontocracy, a church run by old men. Hinckley, without missing a beat, replied, "Isn't it wonderful? To have a man of maturity at the head, a man of judgment, who isn't blown about by every wind of doctrine?" Such exchanges show Hinckley as a skilled public relations man and humorist. A small man, with a croaking voice, he projects a warm and informal presence even when speaking to huge crowds. He has spoken to the Press Club, to the World Affairs Counsel, and on television. He has written books on ethical topics, which sell well in the national market. But Hinckley, the entertaining speaker, has also been the wilderness prophet. When Larry King asked him to outline his role, Hinckley replied, "My role is to declare doctrine. My role is to stand as an example before the people. My role is to be a voice in defense of the truth. My role is to stand as a conservator of those values which are important in our civilization and our society. My role is to lead people."[42]

Thomas S. Monson, President Hinckley's first counselor and heir apparent, entered the Quorum of the Twelve Apostles in 1963 at the early age of thirty-six. Next in seniority is Boyd K. Packer, now serving as President of the Quorum of the Twelve, who joined the Quorum in 1970 at the age of forty-five. All three of these senior leaders had had long careers working for the Church. Hinckley worked with the published materials and public relations of the Church. Monson worked with the Church-owned newspaper, the *Deseret News.* Packer supervised the seminaries and institutes in the Church Education System. Other apostles have worked in business, education, medicine, law, and engineering. The two Apostles called in 2004 were Dieter F. Uchtdorf, a native German business executive, formerly chief pilot for Lufthansa German Airlines, and David A. Bednar, a business educator. None studied at divinity school; none know ancient languages or Christian history. The author and Mormon observer William J. Whalen, although lamenting their lack of religious training, described them as "intelligent, shrewd, personable, well-to-do and energetic."[43] They meet privately and speak with one voice.

The First Presidency and the Twelve are assisted by the Quorums of the Seventy. Together, these men are called the "General Authorities." The Seventy provide supervision for growing international activities. These quorums, which in the 1990s were reorganized and enlarged, potentially consist of seven presidents and as many quorums as needed. In 2005 the Seventy consisted of seven presidents and eight quorums, with more likely on the way. They presided over the "areas" into which the world was divided for middle-level supervision. As Church population grows, more Seventies are called into this vast pool of experienced leadership. The First Quorum of thirty-eight was composed of permanent leaders who served until age seventy when they were retired as Seventies Emeriti. The Second Quorum of thirty-four were proven leaders who signed on to work for a specified period, usually five years. The Third Quorum resided in Europe and Africa. The Fourth Quorum included Area Seventies in Mexico, Central America, and South America. The Fifth and Sixth Quorums supervised North America. The Seventh Quorum consisted of Area Seventies in Brazil and Chile, the Eighth Quorum of leaders in Asia, Australia/New Zealand and the Pacific Islands. In 2005, there were 195 Seventies, allowing for expansion as the Church grows.[44] Numbers and names change rapidly, underscoring the need to identify, season, and call into position a steady and increasing group of new leaders.

Also at this high administrative level are the General Auxiliary presidencies of the Sunday School, the women's Relief Society, the Young Women and the Young Men's organizations for young people, the children's Primary and their board members. These women and men are experienced leaders. Each auxiliary presidency conceives its own agenda, under leadership from priesthood leaders, planning events and traveling to distant outposts of the Church to speak and train leaders. They do not, however, supervise the curriculum. All unified study manuals are supervised by "Correlation," a committee that reviews Church messages and publications. Auxiliary leaders are not paid. General authorities and mission presidents receive allowances.

A bureaucracy of career employees is paid. They work for Church institutions such as the Family History Library, the Church Museum, the building committee, the welfare program, and the Church Educational Services (CES). Some occupy the tall office building adjacent to Temple Square in

Salt Lake City; others supervise activities around the world. The Church is the largest employer in Utah, with about 7,000 more employees than the government, the second-largest employer. The state estimated in 2003 that the Church employed about 29,500 people, including 7,000 in downtown Salt Lake City—about one in eight workers in the central business district—and 18,000 at Church-owned Brigham Young University. The Church also employs administrators and teachers in the worldwide CES. Estimated wages for these employees amounted to about $250 million annually. These are state estimates as the Church does not disclose such figures.[45]

The extensive, complex organization is effective. That councils must meet and agree imposes checks on power. Though a strong-minded leader dominates some decisions, he cannot always have his way against the council as a whole. Brigham Young, President of the Quorum of the Twelve at the time of Joseph Smith's death, succeeded to the leadership of the Church, not immediately and not without competition, because he was the senior apostle. All presidents of the Church since then have risen through the Quorum to senior member. The orderly rise to power strengthens the institution by preventing competition among potential leaders. Where is the power in an organization like this? Clearly the leaders are loved and respected. People listen to them and try to follow their guidance. Within the Church they are all-powerful leaders. The members have no say in decisions made at the top. They "vote" only to approve the decisions of those above them. Intellectual leadership has no power against the Church leadership, and the last two presidents of Brigham Young University, although both had experience as academics, have been chosen from among the General Authorities rather than from universities. But do the leaders have any real power over people who are free to drop out if they wish? The leaders influence debate in the Church, but there is usually no money at stake. Leaders can excommunicate members or withhold temple privileges, which is painful. However, as in a democracy, the power of the leaders is derived from the consent of the governed who are free to follow the leaders or not. Meanwhile responsibility over each smaller grouping is dispensed widely to local leaders. Administration of the congregations is in the hands of the members. They are like shareholders in a large corporation with a stake in the company. They own it.

The scriptural admonition against unsuitable power can be found in Doctrine and Covenants 121:30, 41 1981. "We have learned by sad experience that it is the nature and disposition of almost all men, as soon as they get a little authority, as they suppose, they will immediately begin to exercise unrighteous dominion. . . . No power or influence can or ought to be maintained by virtue of the priesthood, only by persuasion, by long-suffering, by gentleness and meekness, and by love unfeigned." This scripture recognizes and disapproves of oppressive power.

Mormon identity satisfies a huge number of people, young and old, educated and not. Mormon identity has proved surprisingly pliable and enduring in a society that is often hostile to Latter-day Saint belief and practice. When Mike Wallace asked President Gordon B. Hinckley about the appeal of the Church, Hinckley acknowledged difficulties. He called it the most demanding religion in America. But he ticked off some attractions. "One, we stand for something. We stand solid and strong for something. We don't equivocate. We don't just fuss around over this and that. People are looking for something in this world of shifting values, of anchors that are slipping. . . . That's one thing. Two, we expect things of our people. . . . We expect them to measure up to certain standards. . . . But it's wonderfully fruitful and has a tremendous effect upon people."[46] More than a religion, members believe, Mormonism is a lifestyle, an island of morality in a sea of moral decay.

FAMILIES

No Other Success Can Compensate for Failure in the Home.
—*David O. McKay*, 1964

"It isn't easy being 26 and single in Happy Valley," wrote a young woman living in the Provo-Orem area in Utah. "One is considered an old maid at that point and I was getting awfully nervous about having potentially missed my prince charming!" She went on to tell how she met her future husband in a dance class at Brigham Young University. "The first time we danced together in class we had a blast and hit it off really well." The two considered dancing together in a competition and "ended up being partners for eternity." Since then there have been two college degrees and two children with more of both in the future. "Until then we will stay here and enjoy our cute house and all the time we get to be together as a family!"[1]

This brief biography, taken from a ward newsletter designed to introduce the family to the congregation, tells much about Latter-day Saint marriage. Although apparently confessional, the column is really a triumphant account of marital success. Beginning with the anxiety women feel as they grow "older"—middle twenties, in Mormon culture—without marrying, the vignette moves toward blossoming romance and proceeds toward marriage in an LDS temple, not just for a lifetime but forever.

Families, the goal of all temple work, are important in this society. Marriage and parenthood, carrying on the eternal family chain, are thought to be essential for spiritual growth and sanctification. Church leaders would like to see all members secure in happy families, intensifying the pressure to marry. Young men and women alike feel like failures if they are not married by their late twenties.[2]

When Steve Young was still single at thirty-four, he said he felt his great-great-great-grandfather Brigham Young was telling him to find a girl. "Do you wanna talk about the pressure I feel? Brigham Young once said, . . . that anyone over 27 years of age that's not married is a menace to society. So here's my grandfather telling me to get with it. You don't think that I feel the pressure? I guarantee it."[3] When Mormons do settle on an "eternal companion," they feel exhilaration. Marriage puts them on the road to happiness, stability, children, and future exaltation.

In many respects, the family, not the individual, is the unit of society in Mormon culture. Latter-day Saints see life after death as a continuation of life on earth. Those who have married in the temples will continue their families in the great hereafter. To create families worthy of maintaining, leaders promote loyalty and fidelity. Unlike the Abrahamic line, which produced descendants like unto the sands on the seashore but with a considerable amount of intra-family stress, the ideal contemporary LDS family is stable, happy, and fulfilled. Mormons aim toward a nuclear family of parents and children, with a stay-at-home mother, not unlike the traditional nineteenth-century family. They strive toward this ideal, as do many others in the greater culture, but in fact a large proportion of Mormon households fall short of this goal. Mormons are much like other American families, though there are some notable, if subtle, differences.

In this chapter, three family styles will be considered: the ideal family, as seen in *The Family: A Proclamation to the World*, the actual LDS family, as seen in statistical studies and in the comments of real people; and the "shadow family," the remains of the polygamous lifestyle abruptly discontinued a century ago.

THE IDEAL FAMILY

The Church issued the proclamation on the family in 1995. Speaking to Church members as well as to the world, written in the solemn tones of Old Testament prophets, the proclamation lays out the ideal family style and warns against other options. Missing are the sentimental tones of the usual Mormon teachings about home; this is serious business. President Gordon B. Hinckley read the Proclamation aloud as part of his talk at a General Relief Society meeting on September 23, 1995. Speaking against family disintegration, same-sex marriage, and abortion, declaring gender to be an eternal characteristic, the policy is more conservative than anything found in the

Scriptures. The document restates the desirability of eternal marriage, the equality of partners, and the need for loyalty and faithfulness.[4]

This document and its emphasis on the stability of family life have led the Church into politics. The finances and the energies of Church members have been mobilized to fight the Equal Rights Amendment and same-sex marriages, to lobby the United Nations for family-friendly policies, and to fund various legislative battles. Some might question whether the Church, with its historical defense of polygamy against the law of the land, is the best champion of the nuclear family. That criticism highlights the importance of continuing revelation. The Church is able to free itself of historical precedent if change is revealed to the Prophet. The Church now backs conservative family values. Moreover, the principles in the recent statement reformulate values underlying Mormon family life even under polygamy.

The Family: A Proclamation to the World

We, the First Presidency and the Council of the Twelve Apostles of The Church of Jesus Christ of Latter-day Saints, solemnly proclaim that marriage between a man and a woman is ordained of God and that the family is central to the Creator's plan for the eternal destiny of His children.

All human beings—male and female—are created in the image of God. Each is a beloved spirit son or daughter of heavenly parents, and, as such, each has a divine nature and destiny. Gender is an essential characteristic of individual premortal, mortal, and eternal identity and purpose.

In the premortal realm, spirit sons and daughters knew and worshiped God as their Eternal Father and accepted His plan by which His children could obtain a physical body and gain earthly experience to progress toward perfection and ultimately realize his or her divine destiny as an heir of eternal life. The divine plan of happiness enables family relationships to be perpetuated beyond the grave. Sacred ordinances and covenants available in holy temples make it possible for individuals to return to the presence of God and for families to be united eternally.

The first commandment that God gave to Adam and Eve pertained to their potential for parenthood as husband and wife. We declare that God's commandment for His children to multiply and replenish the earth remains in force. We further declare that God has commanded that the sacred powers of procreation are to be employed only between man and woman, lawfully wedded as husband and wife.

We declare the means by which mortal life is created to be divinely appointed. We affirm the sanctity of life and of its importance in God's eternal plan.

Husband and wife have a solemn responsibility to love and care for each other and for their children. "Children are an heritage of the Lord" (Psalms 127:3). Parents have a sacred duty to rear their children in love and righteousness, to provide for their physical and spiritual needs, to teach them to love and serve one another, to observe the commandments of God and to be law-abiding citizens wherever they live. Husbands and wives, mothers and fathers, will be held accountable before God for the discharge of these obligations.

The family is ordained of God. Marriage between man and woman is essential to His eternal plan. Children are entitled to birth within the bonds of matrimony, and to be reared by a father and a mother who honor marital vows with complete fidelity. Happiness in family life is most likely to be achieved when founded upon the teachings of the Lord Jesus Christ. Successful marriages and families are established and maintained on principles of faith, prayer, repentance, forgiveness, respect, love, compassion, work, and wholesome recreational activities. By divine design, fathers are to preside over their families in love and righteousness and are responsible to provide the necessities of life and protection for their families. Mothers are primarily responsible for the nurture of their children. In these sacred responsibilities, fathers and mothers are obligated to help one another as equal partners. Disability, death, or other circumstances may necessitate individual adaptation. Extended families should lend support when needed.

We warn that individuals who violate covenants of chastity, who abuse spouse or offspring, or who fail to fulfill family responsibilities will one day stand accountable before God. Further, we warn that the disintegration of the family will bring upon individuals, communities, and nations the calamities foretold by ancient and modern prophets.

We call upon responsible citizens and officers of government everywhere to promote those measures designed to maintain and strengthen the family as the fundamental unit of society.[5]

This short document, although it has not been presented or accepted as Scripture, is treated as having near-scriptural authority. Here we see basic assumptions of contemporary LDS life, some of which echo the Scriptures and some of which go beyond them.

1. The God-ordained unit of society is the family.
2. The family begins with the marriage of a man and a woman.
3. Males and females are created in the image of God.
4. Humans are the literal and beloved children of God.
5. Gender is eternal.
6. Humans chose to come to earth to obtain bodies.
7. Families constituted on earth can be preserved eternally.
8. Husbands and wives should have children.
9. Only husbands and wives should have children.
10. The creation of life is divine and should not be interfered with.
11. Parents are responsible to see their children raised in love and righteousness.
12. Children are entitled to be born to married parents and raised by them.
13. Fathers preside, provide, protect; mothers nurture children.
14. Though fulfilling different functions, parents cooperate as equal partners.
15. Failure in these matters will bring about calamities.

The Proclamation can be read in conflicting ways. It is a strong affirmation of family values when they are under pressure, but it also underscores Mormon belief in the family, not the individual, as "the basic unit of society." The downside of that principle is that it disregards adults outside of nuclear families. Feminists criticize the stress on paternal leadership, but patriarchy is muted. Males and females are mostly linked as equals—in marriage, as creations and children of God, as possessing eternal gender, as parents, and as faithful marital partners. The two are separated by divergent roles, not unequal status. Men have the outside leadership role; women raise the children. But again, they are "obligated" to help each other as "equal partners" in their mutually complementary roles. The only hint of hierarchy is the presence of the word "preside."

When asked why the Proclamation was issued, President Gordon B. Hinckley answered, because the family was under attack and the home was the place to address society's problems. Children learn what their parents teach them. Strengthening individual families improves the world.[6]

General authorities frequently warn against the dissolution of the family because it is the basis of civilization and national virtue. The authorities regret the working mother and the absent father. They urge that families, and particularly mothers, raise their own children rather than trusting the state, businesses, or schools to do the job. They also worry when women act like men. Elder Dallin H. Oaks, in a General Conference talk of October 1993, deplored the political, legal, and social pressures that confuse gender and homogenize the differences between men and women. "Our eternal perspective sets us against changes that alter those separate duties and privileges of men and women that are essential to accomplish the great plan of happiness." He condemned marital infidelity. "The expression of our procreative powers is pleasing to God, but He has commanded that this be confined within the relationship of marriage." Extramarital sex is sinful.[7] The Proclamation, then, projects a vision of a nation of loyal, happy, cooperative families.

Though highly conservative, the language of the Proclamation broadens the acceptable limits of the ideal LDS family. Within its parameters is the assumption that sometimes two incomes may be necessary and that creative solutions where partners "help one another" to raise and teach children may be needed. Church teachings formerly urged young people to marry early and not to postpone or limit their families. Birth control was then officially proscribed. Now it is not mentioned. The large LDS families of the past are shrinking along with others in the nation. Families are told to make their own decisions based on Jesus Christ's teachings.

THE REAL FAMILY

These attitudes are socialized into the young people of the Church, and the message is particularly strong at Brigham Young University, where marriage is viewed as important and even essential. The marriage stakes are high. What relationship is good enough to last an eternity? One must fall madly in love with a partner possessing all virtues. Is anyone good enough for the role?

Sometimes there is a happy ending. As one young wife and mother said, "I was always determined to marry in the temple. Growing up in the branch [with thin LDS membership] I saw a lot of part-member families, and I knew that I wanted to be married in the temple to someone who was active in the church. I still feel it would be better not to be married at all than to marry someone who is not active in the church. My life now is what was my dream: living in a nice home, in a suburb with a yard, having children, and having my husband go off to work at a day job."[8]

Not everyone can find the perfect mate, and the difficulties have led to blunting the romantic message. In a talk to BYU students, Bruce R. Chadwick, a sociologist, told listeners to forget the Cinderella syndrome— waiting for the prince. Instead, search for "someone you like, someone that is worthy, someone who inspires you to be a better person." Romance should be played down in favor of rational choice.[9]

In the Utah culture, the average age for a first marriage is twenty-one for women and twenty-three for men, four years younger than the national average. Women in Utah between twenty and twenty-four are 63 percent more likely to be married than others. This is a place where singles feel out of step. To match them up, the Church has activities—dances, athletic events, temple outings, church meetings in place of the usual clubs, bars, and the dating services many other singles resort to. In the face of all the pressure, young Latter-day Saints have to be patient. Though always looking for the perfect mate, they tell themselves that being single isn't the worst trial. One says, "If I can't be happily married then I'll be happily single. . . . I would like to be married, but I'd rather not be married than get married just to get married." The number of nuclear families in the nation is shrinking. The trend in America is toward more unmarried couples, more single parents with their children, and more singles. In the twenty-first century, fewer than a quarter of the population, 23.5 percent, according to the 2000 census, lived in nuclear groups compared to 45 percent in 1960. The Church's efforts to preserve traditional marital patterns run against broader trends toward more working women, later marriage, longer lives, and fewer children.[10]

The Church emphasizes quality family life. President David O. McKay, quoting J. E. McCulloch, said, "No other success can compensate for failure in the home." Family failure means failing the test of life. President Harold B. Lee said, "The most important of the Lord's work [you] will ever do will be the work you do within the walls of your own homes." The Church prepares manuals to teach communication and problem-solving skills.[11] "Preparation for Celestial Marriage" is a popular BYU class.

This eternal family emphasis influences the way Mormons live and relate. Knowing they were together for the long haul gave one young husband perspective. "Having a concept of being married for time and eternity affects my behavior toward my wife and children. It helps us not get excited over the problems that are trivial in comparison with eternity. It must be unnerving to go about all the arduous tasks of developing a relationship and feeling close to somebody just to know that it's all over once you die."[12]

To strengthen families, the Church encourages a weekly Family Home Evening, an institution in its own right. In support of this activity begun in 1915, wards schedule no Monday night activities. At these meetings, families coordinate their schedules, discuss problems, sing, study the Scriptures, play games, eat, plan service projects, go to a ball game, or anything else to strengthen family bonds. Family members rotate in planning, leading the music, teaching the lesson, and preparing treats. Manuals suggest activities and ways to improve family unity and harmony. Families swear by regular FHE's as a way to improve relationships. Similar programs are springing up in other churches and are occasionally recommended by government agencies.[13]

A regular Family Home Evening in suburban Pittsburgh is typical. The parents are a housewife with many interests and a doctor who serves as a counselor in the bishopric. The five children are four, seven, eight, ten, and twelve. The first evidence of FHE is eight-year-old Nadia's busyness in the kitchen; she is making chocolate chip cookies. At 8 o'clock, the mother begins to play the piano. Although the children are off in various corners cooking, reading, watching television, and playing games, they immediately assemble for this familiar and pleasant ritual. The mother segues into a well-known Primary song, "Love Is Spoken Here." Everyone knows this two-part song and sings it out lustily. Ten-year-old Luke opens with a prayer. The father teaches a lesson about family responsibility, saying that no one is alone in the world. When we do good things do we bring happiness to others? When we do bad things, do we hurt other people?

Then he asks the two visitors for stories from their lives. One says how he used to go on long bicycle rides, and when he would not get home for dinner, his mother was upset and worried. The other told how she had to change the cat's litter box. When she remembered to do it, everyone in the family was pleased. The children's father tells how he fell into the rushing water of a canal when he was young, and how he could not get out without help. The children ask questions about these stories as they eat the cookies.

Then everyone joins in a new game—Cranium Cadoo. Four teams are chosen, and each draws a card that requires acting or making pictures to be guessed by other players. The family members, who play many games, like this one. The meeting, which has taken an hour and a half, ends with a closing prayer and a few tears before bed.

President Hinckley, in 2002, asked families "in the strongest terms possible," to regard their Monday evenings as sacred commitments and urged school officials to curtail Monday night events. His remarks prompted a Salt Lake City backlash. People outside the Church felt that Hinckley, who is generally sensitive to interchurch tensions, had gone too far. Schools should not favor one group.

Besides Family Home Evening, the Church encourages family and individual Scripture study. Many families rise at 5 A.M. to read several chapters of the Book of Mormon before they go off separately to work and school. Families report reading through the four scriptural "standard works" several times over the years. Others start each school year with resolve and break down within a few weeks or months. Sometimes "ward families" assign readings and celebrate when goals are reached. Leaders also encourage family prayer, morning and evening. Families kneel together, grateful for past benefits and hopeful for future help. At testimony meetings, adults and children often say they are grateful for the family prayer and scripture reading that unify and strengthen their families.

Extended families meet regularly for dinner. They have family organizations and gather for family reunions. These reunions, extending interest in the family and genealogy over time, are very much part of the Mormon scene. Some reunions are huge annual events with four or five generations; others are small.

One family converged on the Oregon coast in 2002. Four generations descended from a married pair born in the early twentieth century were represented. Since the deaths of the founding couple, family members have met less often. They came together at a seaside resort curious about their cousins. Included were the three children of the original pair with spouses, children, and grandchildren who have driven and flown from distant places. Of the missing, one was on a Church mission, another in the military, another far away, and others had commitments. They talked and ate, visited historical sites, learned about ancestors, renewed friendships, and gave the children a chance to play together.

The oldest grandchild, at age twelve, hobnobbed with the adults. Others paired with cousins the same age. They played soccer and kickball on the field near the big, beach front lodge and played board games and watched television inside. Babies were traded back and forth.

Most large reunions run for a single day with people meeting at a park and bringing their own lunch. This reunion ran for four days to a week because people had come so far. Some events commemorated the family's past: a tour of old family houses, a history program with old pictures, and funny stories. The evening's climax was a video of the reunion to date. During the day, the group visited tidal pools. They toured an old fort, flew kites, and waded at the beach. At the end, they returned to family matters. Many reunions end with testimony meetings. This one had a nondenominational service because of members without Church commitments. A new baby received a grandfather's priesthood blessing. Each family presented a story, a song, or a speech; all were cheerfully applauded. Then came the goodbyes. The lodge emptied; the cars were driven away.

Of the fifty people attending this reunion, five were second-generation, fifteen of the third, and about twenty-five of the fourth. What did this evolving Mormon family look like? Most were white Anglo-Saxons, but there were variations. One second-generation blended family, with his three children and her daughter, also adopted three boys of mixed race. One of the Anglo sons married a Latina and later a Jew. One girl married a black, another a Catholic. Most of the family were identifiably Mormon; some were unchurched.

Lots of non-LDS families have family reunions, too. Are LDS families then really any different from other middle-American families? Statistical studies reveal four ways that Mormon marital patterns differ from the mainstream: Mormons (1) are more conservative about sexual behavior before marriage; (2) are more likely to marry, less likely to divorce; (3) have larger families; and (4) have families marked by more male authority and a traditional division of labor between husbands and wives. The Mormon families differ from others by small amounts.[14]

Mormons (1) are more conservative about sexual behavior before marriage. Young Church members are strongly and repeatedly admonished to refrain from sexual activity before marriage. Nationally, 80 percent of teens have had sexual relations by the time they reach twenty. Among the Mormons, the number is 50 to 60 percent, lower than the national average, but much higher than people would like it to be.[15]

The results of the National Study of Youth and Religion, a four-year telephone survey of 3,370 randomly selected young Americans ages thirteen to seventeen, combined with personal interviews of 267 more, showed that on most measured criteria, Mormon youth were the most engaged in practicing their faith. More than 80 percent of American teens believe in God, but their religious knowledge is "remarkably shallow." "The LDS Church asks a lot of its teenagers, and it would appear that, more often than not, they get it," concluded researcher Steve Vaisey. When belief and "social outcomes" are measured, "Mormon kids tend to be on top." Sociologists suggested that early morning seminary, the scriptural study program, might be the reason Mormons scored so well, "traversing the choppy waters of adolescence" by "avoiding risky behaviors, doing well in school and having a positive attitude about the future." In the study, LDS youth were 73 to 75 percent very similar to their parents' religious beliefs, compared to 30 to 50 percent for other religions. Fewer young Mormons engaged in sexual intercourse, smoked pot, drank alcohol, or watched x-rated or pornographic films. "LDS affiliation and practice tends to have a protective effect," says Bartkowski, a Mississippi State University sociology professor.[16]

Mormons (2) are more likely to marry, less likely to divorce. Information from the long form questionnaire of the 2000 Census yielded the expected conclusion that Utah and Idaho, with high Church populations, were the states with the highest marriage rates. The place of the least divorce is the densely Mormon town of Provo, Utah. On the other hand, the Census yielded the surprising information that Utah tops the national average for the percentage of women in the work force. Statewide, 61 percent of all women over sixteen were working in 2000 compared to 57.5 percent nationally. Low pay and large families were suggested as reasons. The number of residents who have never been married was the highest also, but that group representing 27.9 percent of the population may be less significant as the number includes those from age fifteen and up plus Utah's many students.[17] Mormons want to be married and are less willing to give up on their marriages than others.

Mormons (3) have larger families. Active LDS in the United States have one more child, on average, than other predominantly American groups of English and Scandinavian backgrounds. These trends rise and fall parallel to national trends, but the consequences of big families differ. An Ohio State University sociologist, Douglas Downey, compared family size, religion, and intellectual achievement. He concluded that children from large families are low achievers, except LDS youth. The higher achievement among big Mormon families, he speculated, may result from their directing a larger share of total resources to their children than other parents.[18]

This being so, large families cost more, and Utahns with their modest incomes have the highest tax burden in the West. Utah must educate 17.0 pre-school and 40.2 school age children for every 100 workers, compared to 11.3 pre-schoolers and 30.5 school children nationally. Utah's per-household tax burden is 8.3 percent of personal income, 1 percent higher than the average of western states. At the same time, Utah has more big houses than other places. The typical Utah house has six and a half rooms, and 28.3 percent of Utah homes have eight or more rooms, the nation's largest share of big houses. Utah has many large, flamboyant houses, reflecting the importance of home in Mormon ethos. They must have big houses for their ideal families and are often house-poor. People with smaller houses are also house-poor. The U.S. Department of Housing & Urban Development reports very high rates of foreclosure in Utah. In 2002, HUD foreclosed on 1,391 Utah homes insured by the Federal Housing Administration loan program, compared to 769 foreclosures in 2001 and 72 in 1997.[19]

Early marriage, large families, and big houses may partially account for Utah having the highest bankruptcy rate in the nation: one of every thirty-five households for the fiscal year ending in 2002. Financial fear may also at least partially account for the well-known vulnerability of Church members to scam artists. Always hopeful, members entrust their savings to investors who promise significant returns. Investigators note that most victims meet a fraudulent solicitor at a religious event.[20] Members try to make prudent financial decisions, but they also believe in miracles.

Will large families continue in the Church? One young mother spoke of wrestling with the issue.

As members of the church we feel that we need to multiply and replenish the earth. How far we're supposed to multiply is my question. I don't know how I could possibly manage to have five children, but I do. How many will I end up with? I don't feel terribly adequate as a mother. I feel like they're missing out on having a happier mother, but I'm always rushing around changing a diaper or nursing a baby or stopping a quarrel. Sometimes I wonder if God expects me to have baby after baby or does he expect us to use our free agency and our intelligence to decide for ourselves? We have read the church's statement on birth control so many times that it is dog-eared. When I pray about not having more children the answer is that it is up to my Heavenly Father. I don't feel that I can use birth control, but when I die is he going to say, 'You dummy'? If I have more, I guess I'll manage somehow. [21]

Mormon families (4) are marked by more male authority and a traditional division of labor between husbands and wives. A compilation of numbers from several national surveys during the past thirty years, mostly from the 1990s, compared Mormons to American families. Sociologist Tim Heaton, speaking at a session of FAIR, the Foundation for Apologetic Information and Research, came up with the following statistics. Mormon couples who attend church together are less likely to divorce than those who do not—about 20 percent compared to more than 50 percent for non-attenders. Mormon women are more likely to be happy when they find they are pregnant, and they are more likely to breast-feed their babies. The better educated an LDS woman is, the more likely she is to bear children; nationally, the reverse is true. The suicide rate among Utahns is higher than the national average, but lower among active Mormons. The use of anti-depressant Prozac is higher in Utah than the national average. Mormons consume more Jell-O, ice cream, marshmallows, and chocolate chips than others. He concluded that more religious people led a more family-oriented life and tended to be happier than others. [22] These descriptions put a colorful edge on Mormons as a group, but they are still just a little different than other Americans and are squarely within standard norms for the United States. Mormons like marriage and are a little more likely to marry earlier and to remain married than others.

Mormons, like other families in the United States, divorce, remain single, and bear children outside of marriage. And always, there are single people and single parents. A few single women build families on their own, adopting children or resorting to test-tube fathers, but the Church discourages these measures, saying children need two parents. Unmarried women who become pregnant are encouraged to marry the fathers or to put their babies up for adoption. LDS Family Services, a private, non-profit agency, provides support and resources for birth and adoptive parents. The message of the agency is that children born of unplanned pregnancies, particularly to teenage, unmarried mothers, will have better opportunities in the world when placed with stable families. Abortion is strongly discouraged. A website with a leading title, www.itsaboutlove.org, provides information. Unmarried mothers, they tell us, who give up their children generally go on to more education, better jobs, and are more likely to marry as well as less likely to repeat a later out-of-wedlock pregnancy.[23] A statement of the First Presidency, dated November 19, 2001, stated, "We affirm the sanctity of life and its importance in God's eternal plan. We honor adoption as a positive way to provide children the blessings of a family and commend the many single women and men who choose adoption for their newborn infants." The Church also favors the adoption of older children into existing families.[24] Adopted children are connected or "sealed" to their parents in the temples. Although fathers are considered essential, no one encourages widows or divorcees to give up their children.

The demands upon an LDS family can be seen by observing a bishop and his wife. These couples are expected to hew to high standards. The calling of bishop is akin to an additional full-time job; the wife is expected to pick up the family slack with fortitude and cheerfulness. An observer might wonder about their marital relationship when the men assume these heavy duties. Both partners feel pressure. The bishop's job is certainly demanding and difficult, but he receives the adulation of his flock. The strains show more in the bishops' wives who are expected to be model Mormons at all times while their husbands are absent and bogged down with seemingly insoluble problems. These women generally smile and keep their own counsel, but some spoke frankly for *Meridian Magazine,* an independent online LDS journal.

Jeannie Vincent said they had been warned that life would "radically change" on this "blessed, but arduous journey." There would be a "substantial amount of criticism and scrutiny." She had to spend seven or eight-hour Sundays at church with her children, waiting for her husband so they could drive the forty minutes home. She learned to pack a basket of food and books, the children learned to cope, and the family eventually bought another car. Looking back, she valued welcoming scores of people into their home for meals and longer stays. They felt enriched by the involvement.

Bishops' wives are enraged when their hard-working husbands are criticized. Ward members expect access to the bishop at all hours of the day and night. Needed household repairs are delayed. Bishops who announce that Monday will be Family Home Evening or who require appointments are often resented, even as they try to guard a little family time. Still the wives speak positively. "I have always felt that when he is serving the Lord he is really serving our family. . . . It has not been a sacrifice to have him serve, but a great gift to us." Another says, "My only advice is to rely daily on the Lord and to enjoy the calling for the SHORT time [generally about five years] it lasts!"[25]

Bishops' wives are not the only ones with problems. Every mother with a large brood has her Sunday woes. One young mother reported that her family was stricter about Sabbath observance than other LDS families. "The children don't play outside. I try to stay in a dress or at least a nice robe. If I wear pants, I'm more inclined to vacuum. The meetings are a marathon. I struggle with the kids through breakfast; we get out to the car but someone's forgotten something or David messes his diaper at the last minute. I sit in church, if I'm lucky, through the sacrament, go out to the car, nurse David long enough to leave him with his daddy while I teach Primary. Then I nurse David again during Relief Society. We have a roast or something in the oven for dinner. I put the little guys down for a nap, listen to the other kids squabble and complain about what they can't do. We either play [games] or read scriptures. We try to do what we're supposed to do, but it's tough."[26]

THE SHADOW FAMILY

Many hard realities work against Latter-day Saint family ideals. Out of the Church's own past, the controversial issue of polygamy continues to rise. Polygamy was practiced openly among Utah Mormons from 1847 until 1890 when it was disavowed and banned. The Church repudiates plural marriage (technically polygyny, a single man married to multiple women), and polygamists are excommunicated. But the heritage of "The Principle" lives on in shadow fundamentalist churches, organizations claiming to practice authentic Mormonism even as leaders of The Church of Jesus Christ of Latter-day Saints disavow their apostate practices.

Plural marriage allowed several powerful men to marry a number of women and raise large families. Brigham Young is said to have married fifty-six wives, many of whom he did not live with, and had fifty-seven children. Joseph Smith was "sealed" to about thirty women, although his only securely documented progeny is from his first marriage to his wife Emma. The huge Mormon clans that result from previous generations of polygamy still dominate Church leadership and life in Utah. Descendants are proud of their polygamous forebears.[27]

A study of marriage in the small town of Manti, Utah, indicates some of the generalities about polygamy in its earlier form. The largest number of plural marriages occurred in the 1850s, declining every decade after that. More than half of the women born before 1852 and first married in Utah were in polygamous marriages for some time in their lives, but the practice thinned out. Only one woman in ten marrying from 1870 to 1890 became a plural wife. Single women found marital partners easily as plural marriage created a scarcity of women. This scarcity served to improve women's position in Mormon society despite its patriarchal nature.[28]

A great deal of effort went into maintaining nineteenth-century polygamous households. Many families were at least placid until outside forces intervened. Some difficult episodes in Utah history resulted from the persecution of polygamists, when the men were arrested and imprisoned for cohabitation or disappeared into the hidden world of the "underground" while pregnant women were hounded off to bear nameless children. This persecution united the Mormon people against the government.

After great national pressure, the discontinuance of the practice came suddenly in 1890 when Church president Wilford Woodruff issued a document called the Manifesto. Critical sources say that polygamy was jettisoned to allow Utah to enter the Union. President Woodruff read the Manifesto to the apostles, telling them that this meant an end to further plural marriages and also an end to living in the plural marriages they had already entered into. Polygamy had been justified for fifty years of official Church practice, and when it suddenly stopped, many were upset and confused. A plural wife of Samuel Spaulding later wrote, "I was there in the tabernacle the day of the Manifesto, and I tell you it was an awful feeling. There Pres. Woodruff read the Manifesto that made me no longer a wife and might make me homeless. . . . But I voted for it because it was the only thing to do."[29]

A follow-up Manifesto was needed fourteen years later in 1904. And even then plural marriages continued among those who felt the proclamation was only a public exercise. Out of this trauma emerged a host of splinter groups refusing to comply. These "fundamentalists," as they are called, carry on despite the proclamations. They believe that plural marriage is a divine commandment and, although they believe most of the standard Mormon teachings, they think that the Utah Church has strayed from the divine path.[30]

The polygamists of Short Creek, Arizona, were raided by U.S. government officials in 1935, 1944, and 1953; polygamists were arrested, imprisoned, and prosecuted, producing extreme family disruption. But the raids failed to wipe out the practice and in fact backfired. The colony continued to double each decade. By 1992, 4,500 fundamentalists lived in the town renamed Colorado City/Hilldale. A religious, charitable trust called the United Effort Plan holds the land. Their cooperative life echoes the communal living of the Church in the nineteenth century.[31]

The outspoken patriarch of another group, the Apostolic United Brethren, living in Bluffdale, Utah, was polygamist Owen Allred. With eight wives, he raised twenty-three children and twenty-five stepchildren and counted 208 grandchildren. The family lived in four houses on a private road. Allred, urbane and sharp-witted, was excommunicated from the Church in 1942 when he married his second wife. In 2002, at age eighty-eight, he spoke to the *New York Times* to deny that he and his followers were wicked or crazy. "We believe in the original word handed down through the prophet Joseph Smith. I want to say that religion can't just change whenever you want it to. What kind of religion is that?" He estimated that 50,000 people live in polygamist families. (Michael Quinn estimated 21,000 in 1998.) His own group had about 5,000. "I'm a Mormon, that's what I was taught and I can't deny it to save my life."[32]

Allred deplored the child abuse and welfare fraud of some polygamists. His group required wives to be of consenting age and husbands to support their families. His family had a dairy farm, a cattle ranch, and a cabinetmaking factory. One wife admitted that, "When we were young, it was difficult and there were jealousies of course. But you grow older and you find your place in life. We all love each other, visit and spend time with our own families." Allred himself noted, "I hate to be hated. I think everybody does . . ., but I want to be myself and live the way I believe, the way the Lord told me to do. Now does that make me an evil person?"[33]

Anthropologist Janet Bennion reported on the women living in Allred's group. Fundamentalist women are often underestimated, she says, because they are considered prisoners of a male religion. Instead, she found women drawn to these groups after being marginalized in the mainstream church and larger society, deprived economically, socially, and emotionally. In fundamentalism, they found solidarity as they clung together for survival, supporting themselves, manipulating a male doctrine to fit a female reality. She found polygyny a viable alternative for women looking for alternative forms of sex, marriage, and family.[34]

Bennion found a grand paradox in patriarchal religious movements. Women were better suited to succeed in fundamentalism than men. The range of marital prospects for girls was wide as every man was eligible. The divorce rate was 35 percent. Women who joined the sect had striking upward social and economic mobility, and high-status women had more power than low-status men. Single, educated women who joined the sect in their thirties did the best. Men who joined the group for sexual reasons soon left it dissatisfied by sexual taboos during pregnancy, lactation, and menstruation and because of disharmony with the leaders. Younger sons were ignored, and some turned to drugs and alcohol. A small number of prestigious males controlled the distribution of wives and resources.[35]

The elite males of polygamy were not always as sensible as Owen Allred. Some were clearly delusional and violent. In the early 1970s, Ervil LeBarron executed rival polygamists in Mexico and Utah. LeBarron died in prison, but his followers continued the murders. In the late 1970s, after John Singer, who withdrew his children from public schools, was shot by law officers, his son blew up a building and led his clan to an armed stand-off with police. In the early 1980s, Dan and Ron Lafferty killed a sister-in-law and her daughter because she supported the decision of Ron's wife to leave him. In 2003, Brian David Mitchell, attempting to set up his own polygamous enclave, abducted and abused fourteen-year-old Elizabeth Smart.[36] All these cases involve patriarchy gone amok, revealing potential violence in absolutist systems. The fundamentalists would say that they are not typical.

Once married, fundamentalist women find it difficult to leave. At least 25 percent say they would drop out if they could take their children. Meanwhile, the women cooperate in informal friendship circles and household service projects. More than half also work for wages. These women are willing to share and scrounge and be formally dominated by elite polygamous men, sacrificing a comfortable mortality for what they hope is exaltation, acceptance, and admiration.[37]

Polygamous women have gone into print to defend their lifestyle. Three plural wives collected 100 testimonials of women who felt that revelation required them to live polygamy. They saw the Manifesto as ransom paid for statehood and as advice, not a binding revelation. They saw the Mormons moving from being persecuted to persecuting those who had not given up the principle.[38] They said they had freely chosen this life, entering the principle for true freedom and to get the highest blessings that God offered.[39] .

The younger women wrote romantically and spiritually of their marriages. "This principle puts my soul to the test as it divides my carnal, selfish nature from my spiritual nature and makes me choose between them every day," said one. The women choose their husbands and his new wives. "It isn't often that a woman is able to select the man of her choice and know that he is a good man, and still be able to keep her identity." Several would have preferred to be the first wife. One's story was a fairy tale with a prince and the two princesses living happily ever after.[40]

As Salt Lake City and Utah geared up for the Olympics in 2002, polygamist Tom Green visited television talk shows, becoming an embarrassment to the state. Green, who lived with his five wives and twenty-nine children in a group of trailers in the remote West Desert, was eventually arrested. He may well have been guilty of welfare fraud, but he was tried for bigamy. Although the state had not prosecuted polygamists for 100 years, Green was taken to court and sentenced to five years in prison for having multiple wives. A year later he was tried again for child rape because one of his wives became pregnant in 1986 at age thirteen. They had married in Mexico a few months before Utah's legal age. Green was sentenced to five more years to life for this crime. The wife, Linda Kunz Green, remained faithful and devoted.[41] Utah once protected polygamists against the national government, but she has come to rooting them out herself. Critics pointed out the irony that Green's prosecutor, David Leavitt, brother of the Utah governor, Michael Leavitt, later named as head of the U.S. Environmental Protective Agency, was proudly descended from polygamous stock.

CONCLUSION

Family was important to Mormons when they practiced and defended plural marriage in the nineteenth century. Family is important today when Church leaders defend the nuclear family and the divided roles of men and women. Church leaders solemnly declare what is desired in the Proclamation on the Family. But most agree that this is an ideal rather than a description of reality. Some Church members criticize the Proclamation for its stand against the current world morality and for leaving out single Church members. But even Mormons who cannot rise to ideal behavior defend the Proclamation as the way things should be. Like many LDS aspirations, this is a tough one, but one that many strive for and some may have achieved.

THE MISSIONARY EXPERIENCE AND THE INTERNATIONAL CHURCH

I'll Go Where You Want Me to Go, Dear Lord.

—*Hymns* (1985), *#270*

On a Sunday morning in July, people gather in an LDS chapel for the "farewell" of a young man soon to leave on a Mormon "mission." The Sacrament Meeting congregation includes his family, his grandparents, his mother's siblings and their children, uncles, aunts and cousins, and friends from other congregations, some from distant states. Like infant blessings, baptisms, weddings, and funerals, missionary farewells are family events.

Other priesthood holders are much in evidence in the service's standard rituals. The bishop asks the congregation to endorse the promotion of a twelve-year-old to be ordained a deacon and two sixteen-year-old young men to be priests. Three young priests, sixteen or seventeen years old, stand to break the bread while the congregation sings a hymn. Then the priests kneel and bless water and bread for the "sacrament." These ritual ordinances are handled by boys of junior high and high school age. Ten deacons and teachers, twelve and up, pass the bread and water trays to everyone in the room. They will all be missionaries in a few years.

When the handsome young elder, a year of college behind him, stands at the pulpit to speak, he discourses on faith, quoting Joseph Smith, the Bible, and the Book of Mormon. He works out the parameters of faith, sets up analogies, and distinguishes between our own accomplishments and those from heaven. Faith begins as a gift from God, but we should strive to increase what we have, nourishing the seed by practice.

Faith had led him to serve a mission. He had been taught to go, but he wanted assurance for himself. His BYU friends had received their assignments. His papers were in, but he had not received his "call," the letter telling him where to go and when. Despite his prayers, he had no confirmation that he should go at all. One sleepless night, as he read the Scriptures, paced the halls, and prayed, he felt peace. But he wanted more. He looked at a world map where other missionaries had marked their destinations and prayed to know where he would go. The feeling came that he would go to Russia. When the call came, it was to Samara, Russia, the assurance he had been seeking. He was elated to go to a challenging, distant place.

The elder's parents gave the two final talks. Although his mother had mixed feelings of pride in her son's commitment and sorrow at his departure, she had decided to be happy about this event for which she had prepared since his birth. Glad about her son's willingness to go, she thanked his teachers for their preparation. She also believed the things he would teach, that Heavenly Father hears our prayers and guides us.

The elder's father proudly identified his son's missionary potential: He had grown up in Europe and survived a French grammar school, becoming bilingual and cosmopolitan. He loved people and had a heart of gold. The father advised his son to seek the Spirit, to obey the rules, and to lose himself in the work. He should be humble enough that he could help change lives and establish righteousness. The father prayed that his son would be "led to the honest in heart," people willing to listen to him.

The closing song, "We Are All Enlisted," a Civil War-period borrowing from a Protestant hymnal, underscored the militant style of young men leaving families and friends to live among strangers in foreign countries. Their callowness compelled them to rely on God for strength and wisdom. No one doubted that the missionary would face rejections and severe trials. Again, the Church has entrusted its difficult and important work to inexperienced young men.

Two years later, the family again gathered to welcome this missionary home. The elder was taller and thinner, and he gave the perfect talk, beginning with his mission struggles. He related three discouraging incidents, such as the time when he and his companion were invited for a visit, only to be yelled at and thrown out. He then showed how each experience ended well. The landlady invited them to teach the gospel to her friends. The new ward took hold and grew. The cab driver was baptized. The elders felt that the Lord was using them to do His work. He believed that if he trusted the Lord and lived the gospel, he could act according to the

Lord's plans. He left for his mission believing the gospel was true; he returned knowing that it was. He had seen miracles. He felt that he had fallen short of being a good missionary, but he could still improve.

In 2002, soon after this event, the Church issued an edict to families to scale back their elaborate missionary farewells. In some wards, so many missionaries left each year that farewells monopolized the Sundays. From then on only the missionary himself could speak. Open houses and receptions were to be simplified or eliminated. Many families were relieved to be spared the competitive aspects. Others regretted the limitations.[1]

Soon after, the Church announced that it was "raising the bar" on missionary qualifications. Elder M. Russell Ballard said, "This isn't a time for spiritual weaklings. We cannot send you on a mission to be reactivated, reformed, or to receive a testimony." In the future, he said, "we need vibrant, thinking, passionate missionaries who know how to listen and respond to the whisperings of the Holy Spirit." Missionaries would have to keep themselves honest and pure, avoiding drugs, pornography, immoral conduct, and profane speech, not indulging now to repent later. They were to have a solid understanding and testimony of the gospel. Ballard asked bishops to recommend only young men and women who were "spiritually, physically, mentally and emotionally prepared" for the rigorous work. Those who did not make the cut could stay home and be local missionaries. The ruling pressured young men to reform their checkered lives. President Hinckley later noted that "Missionary work is not a rite of passage. . . . I am confident that raising the bar on eligibility will cause our young people, particularly our young men, to practice self-discipline, to live above the low standards of the world, to avoid transgression. . . . We will not knowingly send young men to reform them."[2] Prospective missionaries would have to shape up to clear this raised bar.

Each year more than 20,000 Latter-day Saints leave on missions to keep a labor force of about 45,000 to 50,000 missionaries in the field. About a third of the young male members in North America serve missions along with increasing numbers of young people from other countries. Missionaries strong in energy, exuberance, and enthusiasm set out for unknown places to knock on doors, talk to people in crowds, deliver lessons, and to give community service. They may baptize many people, maybe two or three, maybe none. They are lively and inquisitive, short in experience and even good sense. Elders Bardsley and Crismon, for instance, made the news when they climbed a fifty-foot water tower in Paterson, New Jersey, to photograph the city. Dressed in suits and ties, the pair scaled an eight-foot fence topped with barbed wire and were climbing the tower itself when spotted by the police. Fears that they were contaminating the city's water supply proved unfounded.[3]

The missionary program has traditionally been borne by young males and some females. Most young men leave at age nineteen; young women, about 18 percent of all missionaries, go later at age twenty-one. Until recently, a faithful Latter-day Saint woman from a strong Church family would never choose a mission before she had exhausted all romantic possibilities. But the Feminist Revolution imbued young women with a new sense of entitlement. Now young women plan for missions and are effective missionaries, creating a new ideal female model. They are actively in charge of their lives, interested in scriptural study and in lives of service.

Retirees also serve missions. They supervise missions or temples, work with public relations or genealogy libraries, teach classes, and serve in dozens of other positions. The Church calls them instead of hiring them. This work, like the service of young missionaries, is voluntary. There are now more positions for older missionaries than can be filled. In 2001, Elder Robert D. Hales of the Quorum of the Twelve, in an effort to sign up more senior missionaries, spoke to their concerns, addressing the "four F's:" "fear, family concerns, finances, and finding the right mission opportunity." He reassured potential missionaries that they already had valuable experience, that their missions would be just a few brief moments away from their own aging parents and new grandchildren. He promised that abundant blessings would follow financial sacrifice, and that the right mission opportunity would be found.[4]

When President Hinckley addressed the World Affairs Council in Los Angeles in 2002, he spoke on volunteer service, which he called the "genius of the Church." He spoke particularly of the 5,300 retired men and women then serving as LDS missionaries around the world. According to Hinckley, full-time, voluntary missionary service invigorated them. "They go where they are called. They serve where they are needed. Friendships are being established, skills are being shared, opportunities are being opened." There are educators, doctors, business executives as well as ordinary good people. He said proudly that he knew of no other organization that so harnessed the abilities, the capacities, and the willingness of the retired men and women in an organized program of service around the world.[5]

Take Nigel and Avalon Wappett as examples. The Wappetts had planned to go on a mission after his retirement, but a call from the

Church's president in 2001 sent them sooner. They left home in Alaska to supervise the Phoenix Arizona Mission, as mission names are punctuated, one of 338 missions scattered through 171 countries, where they directed some 200 missionaries. Nigel, a busy obstetrician, put his practice on a three-year hold. Wappet said of himself, "We're ordinary people. Our lives have been motivated by our faith. . . . That's been the central aspect of our lives and I hope our children's." A call from the prophet meant that he automatically said "yes" and worked out the details later.[6]

President Hinckley has said that missionary activity is "inherent in our basic philosophy. The Gospel has been restored by divine revelation and we must carry it to men . . . . We disseminate the Gospel to the world to further establish the principles set down by the Lord Jesus Christ . . . . We work under a program where we expect every member to be qualified to teach the doctrine."[7] Although the LDS Church in modern times has become much more concerned with its image and public relations, it has not wavered from this original commitment to growth through proselyting. New generations of Mormons are inculcated into this system of religious service. Each group of returned missionaries revitalizes the pool of leaders.

Missionaries are prepared from childhood. They are enlisted by bishops who judge them qualified for the rigors of mission life. They received letters from the Church president with dates to report to the Missionary Training Center in Provo, Utah, many to learn another language. This is a turning point for Mormon youth. The two years will try their souls. They will eschew worldly attractions, or should, cut off from movies and magazines, cars, and girls. They will live in cheap digs, like the indigenous peoples they visit. They can't dance, romance, or listen to popular music. They will be rejected, dismissed, and insulted. They will work for ten to fourteen hours a day, trying to share their convictions. They will learn of new cultures and come to love real people. They may offend and disgust the people they try to teach. They may make lifetime friends. They may convert themselves to The Church of Jesus Christ of Latter-day Saints even if they don't convert anyone else. Many will come home as adults.

The telling moment of receiving this call, which may change a missionary's life forever, is anxiously awaited and greeted with a variety of emotions. Missionaries can be sent anywhere, their stated preferences ignored. Not everyone is immediately thrilled with his call. One missionary, after two years of study at Harvard College, was called to the New

England States where the headquarters was located in Cambridge, Massachusetts, Harvard's home. Another, who dreamed of studying art in Vienna in his brief free time, was disappointed to go to New Jersey. Both regretted the lost opportunity to learn a language. A missionary called to Oakland, California to learn Tongan wondered about the benefits of his new language. Still most are quickly, if not always happily, reconciled to their mission locations.

In the last century, before going out, missionary farm boys were taught basic table manners and given a few shots to protect them from illness. In 1961, when visa problems delayed departure, the Church instituted language training, and two years later, the Language Training Mission was organized so missionaries could have several weeks of language study. Spanish was the first foreign language instituted, soon joined by German, French, and Italian. The Scandinavian languages and Dutch were taught at Ricks College, now BYU-Idaho. The Asian and Pacific languages were taught at the Church College of Hawaii, now BYU-Hawaii. By 1968, missionaries studied sixteen different languages at these colleges. The new languages are shaky, and missionaries have been known to confuse similar words, leading them to say in Finland, "We are American missionaries and we go around killing people," or in Japan, "Do you know the meaning of carrots?" In Hmong, some elders have said, "When we are resurrected, we will receive a body with new chicken skin."[8] These malapropisms have become part of the folklore.

In 1978, the Missionary Training Center near Brigham Young University consolidated language training at a new $15 million campus. The "MTC" has handsome buildings, lush greenery, and the military efficiency of early hours and dedicated study. About 600 young men and women arrive each week. In 1997, 27,000 missionaries went through the MTC. They spend up to two months learning the rudiments of the forty-five languages now taught there, studying the Scriptures, drilling on missionary techniques, and disciplining themselves in this culture of hard work. A telling joke asks the difference between the MTC and a nearby prison. The answer: You can call home from the prison.

As the Church grew internationally, fourteen new training centers were established in South America, Europe, Asia, and the Pacific. The first was begun in São Paulo, Brazil, in 1977. In 2002 the first fifty-four missionaries entered the training center in Africa, in Ghana. Young people serve missions all over the world without coming to the United States.[9]

These centers reflect the vision of President Spencer Kimball who, in 1974, with his eye on wide-world expansion, proclaimed that the gospel should be preached to a wider geographical area and in greater density, declaring that "every [worthy] young man should fill a mission." He urged each country to provide a missionary force of people who knew local customs, and language. He hoped for enough well-trained, young people to carry on the work if the doors were closed against Americans. President Kimball called for worthiness, doctrinal knowledge, personal testimony, and saved money.[10]

Missionaries are supported by themselves and families, not by the Church. The earliest missionaries traveled "without purse or scrip" (meaning no metal or paper money), New Testament style, finding meals and accommodations as they could. But today missionaries save their money; their families make sacrifices, work second jobs, and go into debt. Donations from affluent Church members put other missionaries "in the field."

Missionaries work six days a week, including Sunday, and write home, do the wash, and clean house on the seventh. They use telephones, but only for their church work, calling home only on Christmas and Mother's Day. Missionaries are allowed to e-mail once a week from libraries or public facilities—not from Church members' homes.[11]

Missionaries today are taught what to preach. In 1844 Hyrum Smith, Joseph Smith's brother, exhorted departing elders to "Preach the first principles of the Gospel . . . to make them plainly understood . . . , so that you meet scarcely any honest man who will not obey them. . . . [give] sufficient reason to prove all things, and you can convert every honest man in the world."

Gradually leaders created curricular materials, publishing the first Church-wide set of lessons, the *Systematic Program for Teaching the Gospel* in 1952. The lessons are fine-tuned from time to time. A program adopted in 1961 had six discussions to be memorized perfectly. The *Uniform System for Teaching Families,* adopted in 1973, advised missionaries to memorize the discussions and then use their own words, providing teaching techniques. "Keep in mind how you want the family to feel," the manual instructs. "Do not force them to say what you want them to say—TEACH THEM—help them feel good about the gospel. . . . Seek to understand their real reservations."[12]

The lessons adopted in 1985 suggest that missionaries master principles, not memorize lessons, asking open-ended questions so people can share their feelings. Missionaries should prepare people to "feel the Spirit." Missionaries are sent out, in the words of Mormon Scripture, to "preach [the] gospel by the Spirit, even the Comforter which was sent forth to teach the truth."[13] They are to teach simply and let the Lord do the converting.

In 2003, the new plan focused on memorizing key scriptures, depending on the missionary, to determine what each person or family needed. This plan moved customized teaching from "structure-based" to "principle-based." *Preach My Gospel*, a missionary manual released in 2005, stressed goal setting and planning, adding emphasis on "using time wisely, finding people to teach, improving teaching skills, [and] helping people make and keep commitments."[14]

Missionaries travel in pairs after the New Testament model where Jesus sent forth missionaries "two and two." As a returned missionary noted, "You are constantly with someone else and this someone is not of your choosing. In some cases, he is definitely not of your choosing." These companions "eat, work, study, and pray together; they sleep in the same room." They cannot part, even for a walk or a shopping trip. "From day one, my companions were like another part of my body, although at times I thought that amputation might be in order." Mission presidents pair new missionaries with more experienced "senior" companions for several months until a "transfer day." A senior companion, like an older sibling, explains things, particularly in a foreign-language mission. With the mission president and wife functioning as surrogate parents and the other missionaries as additional siblings, the group is another family, with all its warmth and stress.[15]

A missionary divided the elders into "those that do and those that don't." Motivation levels differ, and sometimes one pulls while the other feels dragged. One elder recalled, "We were at each other's throats in our minds, but outwardly didn't show hostility. It turned out to be a total waste of a month. . . . I vowed after that transfer to try to be more accepting." Missionaries learn teamwork. "I learned when to put my two bits in and when to just listen." Ideally, missionaries transcend differences in personality to serve productive missions.[16]

The complex culture of missionary life extends to girlfriends left behind. Thousands of young women wait for their missionaries—or, they don't. Some create shrines with pictures, countdown calendars, gifts, and candles to remind them of that distant special someone. Brigham Young

University has 6,000 nineteen and twenty-year-old women compared to the 300 men of the same age not out on missions. The missionaries write their girlfriends weekly, usually with faith-promoting tales rather than sentimental love letters. Missionaries dread the "Dear John" letters by which girls end the relationships. Hayward Alto, who studied girls waiting for missionaries, concluded that 90 percent of the girls eventually give up on their men. Of the 10 percent who wait, 7 percent resume the relationship to break it off later. Only 3 percent of couples where the girl waited actually go to the altar together.[17]

In the field, missionary folklore shapes the culture. William Wilson and John B. Harris have collected more than 3,500 narratives that initiate the elders into the system. They also serve as an escape valve, letting missionaries live vicariously through bold, brash stories. Another purpose, according to Wilson, is that these stories tell the missionaries that God and Satan are intimately involved in their lives. In these outrageous, but simplistic, accounts, the wicked are punished and the righteous rewarded.[18]

One story illustrates the seriousness of God's priesthood. "Two missionaries were messing around, and they decided to confer the priesthood on a dog which they saw on the street. Before they could complete the ordinance, a bolt of lightning came and struck the dog and the two elders, and it zapped them."[19] The moral: Don't mess with sacred matters.

Another folk narrative speaks to the special protection that missionaries feel and call on.

> [This] guy was on a mission in one of the wilder type towns like New York. And they had a lot of gangs and stuff, and they were in a bad part of town, and they were in teaching a family, and when they came out there was a gang waiting to beat up these missionaries. And the missionaries got really scared and ran to the car and got in it. And they started to start the car, and it wouldn't start, and they tried to start the car [again], and it wouldn't start. Meanwhile, the guys with the chains and the knives are starting to get closer and closer to the car, so they get really scared. And the one guy says, 'Well, let's have a prayer.' So they said a prayer and turned on the ignition, and sure enough, the car started up and they took off, and they got about five or ten miles away or so—anyway they decided to find why the car wouldn't start. And they got out and they opened the hood, and there's no battery.[20]

Moral: Prayer makes anything possible.

Observers are unnerved by missionaries, so different from regular nineteen-year-olds. The missionary corps and the Church itself strike them as exhibiting dangerous indoctrination and thought control. Social scientists Gordon and Gary Shepherd describe the military mindset of missionary religions. Preparing for a mission requires sacrifices to supply the troops, mobilizing the society's resources and personnel. Individual interests are subordinated to a transcendent cause. Solidarity requires stereotyping the virtues and objectives of one's own noble society against an enemy. Individual dissent is stifled, discipline and orthodoxy encouraged, information is controlled, and communication is primarily exhortatory. People are expected to suppress misgivings and express support for the established policies. Successful missionary religions, such as The Church of Jesus Christ of Latter-day Saints sustain a crusade mentality. [21]

This crusade mentality is magnified in missionary training where the troops are disciplined, interviewed, evaluated, and indoctrinated. In order to recruit more than 20,000 new missionaries each year, the Church is permanently mobilized. The Church must generate and sustain a strong collective commitment to the "sacred cause of expanding God's Kingdom on earth from one generation to the next." The Shepherds think that it is less remarkable that the Church loses some of its youth every generation, as does every religion, than "the extent to which the LDS Church succeeds in capturing and holding young people's loyalties in a pluralistic environment." Missionary service is the Church's single most important practice for maintaining the continuity of the society, especially for young males. Children are trained with "anticipatory socialization," leading toward the experience of separation, transition, and experience as well as hardship and deprivation; missions have their own vocabulary, mythology, and behavior. A returned missionary is reincorporated with new rights and responsibilities. "The missionary cause of the LDS Church simultaneously inspires and channels the idealism of its youth while deflecting youthful alienation and rebellion away from the religious strictures of Mormon society."[22]

Young women get less encouragement to serve missions. "Women should not feel obligated or be urged unduly to serve full-time missions," said the 1999 *General Handbook of Instructions*. Female missionaries are supervised by the males and, lacking priesthood, are unable to baptize the converts they teach. Although serving a mission may reinforce the acceptance of a male priesthood hierarchy, female missionaries, often possessing more religious zeal than the men, are liberated by their demanding duties, developing new skills and confidence and finding a new sisterhood. Young women, less threatening than a pair of strange males, are often more effective proselytizers than the elders. In 1997, when Church President Gordon B. Hinckley told young women that they were not obligated to serve missions, he admitted that the sisters are more often invited into homes than elders.[23] Many marry fellow missionaries, becoming their older and more equal wives.

Although most missionaries perform effectively and complete assignments, some become disillusioned and demoralized. Less enthusiastic elders may read anti-Mormon literature. Others have accidents or get sick. About 2 percent come home early. Most of those who return early for physical reasons return to finish their assignments. About a fifth of those with mental health concerns go back to the mission field, and many of them come home again without completing their assignments. Church leaders provide health counseling for early returnees and their families. About 10 percent of those who complete their missions are later disaffected.[24]

Young missionaries seem a strange breed to newspaper reporters who follow them around and interview them. Helen Ubinas of the *Hartford* (CT) *Courant* spent a day with the elders. She said they worked hard and maintained a good attitude through plenty of rejection. They told her of their homesickness, the rules they live under, and their budgets of $147 a month; when out of cash, they survive on macaroni and cheese, called "yellow death." Ubinas notes their happiness when a door opens and people listen. "It's awesome. Just awesome." Ubinas concludes that they are "young men of God" but also young men.[25]

Genevieve Roja, of San Jose, California, spent a day with two of the lady missionaries, Sister Hatley, twenty-two, a BYU mechanical engineering student from Copper Creek, Alaska, soon to go home, and her "green" companion, Sister Ashton, a nursing student from Salt Lake City. Roja was "flabbergasted by their dedication, their ability to persist even when stubborn, godless mules kicked the door in their face." She was surprised they could walk twenty miles a day in dress shoes. They are stared at and rejected. Roja was impressed by their maturity.[26]

Diane Lewis visited Derek Waldron, twenty, of Costa Mesa, California, and Sean Cowley, nineteen, from Medford, Oregon, Spanish-speaking missionaries in Garden City, Kansas. They are up at 6:30 every morning to study. At 9:30 A.M. they begin to knock on doors, talk to people in the streets, and hold appointments. They keep this up until 9:30 P.M. Waldron says, "It all comes with being a missionary. I can and will give it my best and do everything I've been asked to do." He thought it was "awesome to see the families before and after they find out about Jesus. People's lives change." Neither Waldron nor Cowley knew Spanish before. "You study your language and how to teach in the MTC," Waldron said. "Then you get to the field, and that's where you really learn." Cowley said, "Sure, sometimes you miss your girlfriend or your mom, but this is the goal I set for myself."[27]

Mike Hayman returned from a mission in Colombia to Grand Island, Nebraska, with only the suit on his back; he had given away everything else. He advised missionaries to learn from the culture and live with the people. He coped with 110-degree days and a dangerous political climate. One day he visited a family to find their house destroyed by a mud slide. "I just sat with them and cried." He found the people humble and generous, always offering him food and drinks. "It's when I realized they couldn't afford to give me anything but did anyway that I was really amazed by the Colombians." Mike thought he had had "a life-saving experience, I had witnessed a lot of odd and great things, and it was just wonderful."[28]

Kate Silver of Las Vegas followed Elders Hampton from North Carolina and Davis from Florida around for a day. They knocked on doors, but were sent away. They later visited a member family where they are great favorites of the children. They often came by to read scriptures and play board games. They adjusted their message to their audience, and after much prodding, they morphed into "lyrical gangstas," unveiling a rap they call "Mormons in the House." Hampton beat boxes while Davis rapped.

Hey, yo, would you stop and listen/
I wanna drop a beat to you about my mission/
We got this book we call the bomb/ [BoM]
The Book of Mormon that is it, this is not a con/
We got Lehigh, (sic) a prophet, he left Jerusalem/
He asked his friends and family if they would like to come/
They said, "Yeah, sure! I come along with you/
To hear the word of God, He can tell us what to do."

The beaming kids clap along. These elders, "with their slight Southern drawls, quick smiles and down-home politeness," have baptized eight people in three months. They note that only one of every 100 residents invites them in and only one of every 1,000 is baptized.[29]

One young man joined the church for his high school girlfriend. She would not marry him unless he went on a mission, so he worked and saved money for a year, arriving in his first mission area the day his girlfriend married someone else in the Salt Lake Temple. He came back a different person. "That mission was the whole foundation of my life. Even when times have been bad, I've known that the church is true, that the gospel's true. All the things that happen are insignificant if you know that the gospel's true. The missionary who baptized me probably knew I was doing it for the girl. I wish I could tell him that I went on a mission and that fifty more people joined the church and two or three of them went on missions, that now I have two children, and about all the positions I've held. I'll bet he'd be shocked."[30]

One woman refused to pay any attention to the missionaries her husband had invited in. "But I got curious. They started coming for meals and the first thing I knew we were all scheduled to be baptized. . . . I liked the good, clean living. I liked the missionaries. I thought, 'This is the way I'd like my boys and girls to be.' They were all enthusiastic about it. They've all stayed good members except one daughter who has turned Catholic. That's not a bad record."[31]

A serious conflict of interests marks the initiation of new members into the Church. Missionaries want to baptize as many people as they can before being transferred to another area or heading home, leaving congregations to integrate converts. The converts may have been insufficiently introduced to the rigors of Latter-day Saint life; they may be under the spell of a particularly charismatic missionary. If baptismal decisions were up to ward members, they might wait for stronger signs of conversion. Church leaders agree that retention is a serious problem. To meet this challenge, the Church has brought local missionary work, which had been under stake direction, under ward direction to encourage member involvement. Baptizing new members and socializing them have been brought together.[32]

Mormons say that their missionaries do not convert people. Only God could "get a religion so radically unique, with a history so young and tempestuous to work . . . attracting everyone from Adventists to Zoroastrians."[33]

THE INTERNATIONAL CHURCH

International growth has come from missionary labors. In the early days, missionaries traveled through the United States and then England and Scandinavia. During the twentieth century, Mormons already in the United States began to leave Utah and the Mountain West to travel west and east for education and work, crossing the mountains to California and Oregon, and then establishing outposts in Washington, D.C., Boston, New York, and elsewhere. After World War II, far more Mormons left Utah than gathered there. They took Zion with them, reproducing in city wards a similitude of the close-knit LDS communities. Wards organized dances, speech contests, three-act plays, and choral performances. Comprehensive Church cultural programs of athletics and arts filled members' time. The aim was to recreate the Mormon villages.

As growth has moved from new areas within the United States to Latin America, Africa, and the Philippines, however, the Church abandoned this labor-intensive establishment. Leaders have consolidated meetings and emphasized programs that travel easily to other nations. The process of streamlining and coordinating is termed by Church leaders "correlation."

In April 1979, concerned with the plethora of Church-published materials, leaders in Salt Lake City demonstrated that just a single copy of every handbook printed would fill two trucks. President Kimball described this as "a perilous problem [that] must be solved." Leaders were urged to reduce, streamline, and simplify. Fewer, widely translated publications resulted. The big conferences of the past, which served to coach members for Church positions, were replaced with simpler, comprehensive materials, published in sixth-grade language.[34]

A result of this "correlation" plan is the codification of Church doctrine into a simple and positive message. Complexities, evolutions, and questions have been smoothed out. Church programs and teachings have been trimmed down for world use. To maintain uniformity worldwide, financial differences between units have been leveled. Donations collected in the wards all go into the central Church where they are rationed out, diverting funds from the strong to the weak. Elaborate recreational and cultural activities have been slashed and the focus shifted to missionary and service activities.

For many years, The Church of Jesus Christ of Latter-day Saints was clearly a North American institution. Although there has always been a strong emphasis on international missions, in 1955 only 12 percent of the Church membership and only one stake and one temple were outside the United States and Canada.

By 1978, the Church was expanding worldwide in almost every dimension. International membership had doubled to 25 percent. A fifth of the stakes and temples were outside the United States and Canada. About one third of the copies of the Book of Mormon sold and distributed were not in English. More than one of ten full-time missionaries came from outside the United States. General conference, the semi-annual Church-wide meeting, went from being broadcast to nine western states to being available in all fifty states as well as Latin America, Australia, the Philippines, and parts of Africa, Europe, and Asia. In 1999 with satellite transmission in place, audio and video copies went out worldwide in forty-three languages. With the Internet, the general conference is available to anyone anywhere.[35]

In 1999, the international Church surpassed the United States and Canada. Fifty-one editions of the Book of Mormon plus Braille editions and selections in forty more languages were available. The translations indicate an explosion of international converts. If the trends continue, sometime in the 2020s, half the missionaries will come from outside North America. Lagging behind these changes was the low percentage of international General Authorities—10 percent by the end of 1999.[36]

In the last half-century, Spanish-speaking nations have experienced the greatest growth. Settlements in Mexico began in the 1880s as Utah Mormons went south to escape prosecution for polygamy. Some descendants still live there in those towns. By the 1970s, missionaries were called from Mexico. By the 1980s, Mexican membership was second only to the United States. The first Mexican temple was dedicated in 1983. Development in Central and South America followed. The Church became established in Peru (1959), Bolivia (1963), Ecuador (1964), and Colombia and Venezuela (1966), even as activity in Brazil began. By 2002, thirty temples were operating in Latin America. In 1998, the Church in Latin America numbered over 3,500,000 members, 38 percent of the Church population and three quarters of the non-U.S. membership. Of the twenty countries with the largest LDS populations, thirteen are in Latin America.[37]

The revelation that opened the priesthood to males of African descent, to be discussed in chapter six dramatically changed the face of the Church. Before 1978, when the revelation was announced, the Church's only African mission was in Johannesburg, a largely white community. Even there, a quota on foreign church missionaries kept numbers small. Although missionaries had been discouraged from teaching black people before the revelation, thousands of Africans joined anyway. They waited up to twenty years for baptism, during which time they were publicly attacked for their Mormon beliefs. Joseph W. B. Johnson, in Ghana, said that once, "a crowd came and shouted at us. They said we were anti-Christs, and adding to the Bible. . . . A group of people came and passed out anti-Mormon literature and we were booted out. . . . There was a paper in Ghana which had pictures of our prophets and they wrote filthy statements about them with the intent to sway us from the Church. However, we were undaunted, we knew they were telling us false things."[38]

The first LDS missionaries arrived in Nigeria in 1978 immediately after the revelation that preceded granting the priesthood to all worthy males. Within twenty years, membership was over 37,000. Temples were announced in Ghana and Nigeria fewer than thirty years after missionary work began there. By 2000, more than 17,000 members were counted in sixty West African congregations. Unlike other places, West Africa has a high percentage—more than 50 percent—of baptized members who attend church meetings. Still, the Church, with annual membership growth of 3.84 percent, is often compared to the Seventh-day Adventists with 230,000 members and the Jehovah's Witnesses with 65,000. Those groups grow 7 to 11 percent a year.[39]

How many of those the Church considers members identify themselves as members? "Mormon" was included as a category on the Mexican Census for the first time in 2000. About 205,000 people claimed membership on the census compared to just under 850,000 on Church records. The LDS designation went on the census in Chile in 2002 with similar results. Although the Church claimed 520,202 individuals on her rolls, only 19.94 percent or 104,735 people identified themselves as LDS. These numbers suggest different levels of commitment. *The Encyclopedia of Mormonism* has noted that attendance at sacrament meeting varies substantially. Attendance in Asia and Latin America is about 25 percent.[40]

In the United States as a whole, only 59 percent of baptized males receive the Melchizedek Priesthood, reserved for men who have proven their faithfulness for a year or more. In the South Pacific, the figure drops to 35 percent, in Great Britain, 29 percent. In Mexico, the figure is 19 percent suggesting high inactivity. Many are baptized, fewer are retained. President Hinckley has admonished the missionaries to make sure that conversion is real and life-changing. Only those who will become solid Church members should be baptized.[41] In the twenty-first century, the emphasis is on retention.

The international Church has continuing growing pains. The problems of dealing with local bureaucracies at home to build chapels and temples are multiplied abroad. Long legal and technical delays and expenses sometimes exceed construction time and building costs. The Church built a large meetinghouse in Ufa, Bashkortostan, Russia, at a cost of over $2 million dollars, obtaining all necessary legal permissions. Months later the building was still unoccupied because an adjacent property was under construction. An official spokesman warned that "this should not be construed as oppression of believers by the local authorities." Mormons are not singled out. An Adventist building in Turkmenistan, legally constructed in the early 1990s, was bulldozed to rubble in 1999 with three days notice. Building chapels and temples in the U.S. is difficult; building them abroad is much harder.[42]

Critics have warned that the future success of the international Church depends upon Mormonism's capacity to adapt to other cultures. Mormonism comprises a distinct way of life, but world religions must adapt to the diverse ways of world cultures. As colonialism and Western culture fall under attack from a variety of directions, the Mormon message stands at a crossroads. Can the Church adapt to other parts of the world? Will Mormonism produce ethnic forms transcending indigenous culture, or will it produce little Utah enclaves? Will a global Church reproduce American wards? Church growth has always been uneven suggesting the complexity of a single strategy.[43]

Mexican Church member Eliseo Escalante Hernandez sees the Church as native to each place. "One has nothing to do with the other," he says. "You can't link political things with religious things." Another leader agrees: "Our concepts are neither Mexican nor American; they are universal. We respect the sovereignty of each country and uphold its laws."[44]

Others, however, see complications arising from Church interaction with international cultures. David Knowlton, an anthropologist living in Latin America, observed the tensions of the American church, noting that Chile, with high Latin American LDS membership also has a high incidence of Mormon chapel bombings. He reported local suspicion of this "new religion," beginning with the "massive invasion" of young, blond Americans who quickly constructed "lavish" new buildings. Natives feared exploitation.

Knowlton saw LDS expansion in Latin America as part of a larger conflict between the established Catholics and growing non-Catholic groups involved with socioeconomic development. In this widespread politicization of religion in the area, Mormons, considered conservative, have been used politically by governments to undercut the rebels challenging their authority. Also notable is that local LDS leaders are often employed by the Church. Members, dependent on the jobs, create a local professional clergy, giving the leaders more incentive to hold on to power than in the central Church. These characteristics create an organization freighted with more than religious aims.[45]

Mark L. Grover, a BYU scholar, gives another interpretation of the Church situation in Latin America. He suggested that the explosive growth in the 1980s, now purposefully slowed down, resulted from the movement of millions of people to the cities where they lost touch with family and their traditional Catholic Church, and from the replacement of several military dictatorships with democracies between 1983 and 1988. The growth outstripped the Church's ability to train leaders and retain converts. He quoted President Hinckley as saying, "The days are past, . . . when we will baptize hundreds of thousands of people in Chile [who] drift away from the church." Hinckley was almost "driven to tears over the terrible losses we have suffered in this nation." After his visit, baptisms dropped from 900 to ninety a month. Latin American membership is still expected to be more than half of the LDS Church by 2020.[46]

Vast changes have been made in some areas, but as historian Jan Shipps points out, the process of assimilation is far from complete. "Notwithstanding the rosy picture of a world filled with Mormons which is being projected by the *Church News* and the official *Ensign,* the power of the LDS gospel to sustain communities of Saints throughout the world without requiring them to adopt peculiarly American attitudes and stereotyped life styles has not yet been fully proven."[47]

Directions, interpretations, and methods are likely to change. The Church now seeks to relate to other nations through technical help and humanitarian aid, a burgeoning part of its program. But missionary work will doubtless remain dominant. Missionaries will continue to travel the world to engage listeners, and the Church will seek to open channels, through diplomatic and humanitarian initiatives, to put its young men and women on the ground. This effort will continue, so Mormons believe, block by block, elder by elder, sister by sister until Christ comes again or the work is done, whichever situation comes first.

TEMPLES AND GENEALOGY

We'll sing and we'll shout with the armies of heaven,
Hosanna, hosanna to God and the Lamb!

—*W. W. Phelps, Hymns* (1985), #2

Traffic in suburban Boston was snarled. Barriers blocked access to roads. Guides at the intersections directed cars to a huge parking lot near the Alewife subway station where drivers parked and boarded special buses to be shuttled a mile up a hill and back again. By the end of the day, eighty busloads had carried nearly 17,000 people to the structure crowning the summit. Crowds of "temple-worthy" Mormons had gathered from the northeastern United States to enter the stately new granite building on a hilltop in Belmont, Massachusetts. What was going on? The Mormons were dedicating their Boston Temple.

Four dedicatory sessions, ninety minutes each, were scheduled. Of the huge crowd, only 3,400 members held tickets for the 850 chairs set up in the temple. Others went to a nearby LDS chapel where television monitors showed the live ceremony. Each scheduled group entered the temple as the previous group exited. As the lines moved toward the door, each person was shod in little plastic overshoes to protect the carpets. The rented folding chairs had been similarly shod in little crocheted footlets held on with threaded elastic.[1]

The session itself, similar to other church meetings, included opening and closing prayers, several anthems from a well-prepared volunteer choir from Maine, and talks.[2] What set the session apart from regular Sunday meetings was the location itself, a dedicatory prayer, and the "Hosanna Shout." The dedicatory prayers, much alike from temple to temple, refer to the building's future uses, but a portion of President Gordon B. Hinckley's dedicatory prayer for the Boston Massachusetts Temple reflected the contentious process of getting town approval. The final issue, the height of the steeple, had still not been settled by dedication time, and the building was dedicated without a steeple. The temple looked a little stumpy, as if it had been struck by lightning and lost its upper reaches. The prayer, in part, said:

> We are assembled to dedicate this Thy holy house. . . . We extend our gratitude to all who have labored so faithfully and diligently, often in the face of serious opposition, to bring to pass the miracle of the completion of this temple. . . .

> We pray that Thou wilt bless it with the presence of Thy Holy Spirit. May it ever be sacred unto Thy people. May even those not of our faith look upon it as a hallowed structure, and do so with respect. . . . We pray that those who have been bitterly opposed may experience a change of feeling. . . .

> The building has no steeple. We dedicate it as being complete, but pray that the way may be opened for the placement of a steeple with the crowning figure of Moroni, Thine ancient prophet.

> We pray that Thy people in this temple district may make themselves worthy of every blessing to be found here. May they come, pure in heart and clean in hand, to the House of the Lord with gratitude in their hearts for the marvelous blessings to be gained here. May they be endowed with power from on high and be granted a knowledge of things sacred and divine. May the covenants which they make be binding upon them. Keep them always in the way they should walk. May they sense the wonders of the blessings of eternity to be gained here and here alone.[3]

After the prayer, President Boyd K. Packer, of the Council of the Twelve Apostles, led the congregation in the Hosanna Shout, used at the dedication of the Kirtland Temple on March 27, 1836, when the congregation shouted "hosanna, hosanna, hosanna to God and the Lamb" three times sealing it with "amen," "amen," and "amen." The waving of white handkerchiefs began with the Salt Lake temple dedication in 1893. President Packer said this action was in similitude of waving palm fronds during the Biblical Feast of the Tabernacles. After the shout, the choir sang "The Spirit of God like a Fire is Burning," composed by W. W. Phelps for the dedication of the Kirtland Temple and the antiphonal "Hosanna Anthem," added to the hymn for the dedication of the Salt Lake Temple.

Mormons are exhilarated by these dedications. They praise the beautiful buildings, the stirring talks, and the music. In the dedicatory services of LDS temples across the world, Mormons feel "reverential awe, a sense of oneness [with] God." They see temples as an enduring material symbol of God's relationship to His people. Temples connect Mormons with the Old Testament and underscore LDS' claims to restoring ancient religion. In temples, a covenant people occupy sacred space and time and transcend daily life, symbolically encountering divine powers. President Howard W. Hunter, speaking in 1994, urged members to make the temple the center of their membership. He told families to emphasize their temple work. "Secure and honor your priesthood and temple covenants; encourage your family to do the same."[4]

Joseph Smith, who translated his visionary impulses into finite structures, planned and built his first temple from 1833 to 1836 in the frontier crossroads community of Kirtland, Ohio. His vision far exceeded his resources. For three years the people devoted their means, time, and energies to building a temple used only briefly before the Saints were forced to leave. Smith planned temples in Independence and Far West, Missouri, but could not even begin construction before the Mormons were forced out. Smith's final temple rose in Nauvoo, Illinois. In each case, the temple was to center a planned city, ordering a theocratic community. In the Doctrine and Covenants a temple is described as "a house of prayer, a house of fasting, a house of faith, a house of learning, a house of glory, a house of order, a house of God."[5]

The outside walls of the Nauvoo Temple, dedicated in 1846, were only partially completed when Joseph and Hyrum Smith were killed in 1844. Knowing that they would have to leave Nauvoo and the temple, the people worked harder to complete it. By December 1845, the rooms were ready for temple ceremonies. During the next eight weeks, 5,500 members participated, day and night, before leaving for the West. They built the temple, used it briefly, and abandoned it, leaving Nauvoo beginning on February 4, 1846.

Once in the Salt Lake Valley, Brigham Young, following Joseph Smith's example, planned Salt Lake City on a grid pattern centered on a temple. Four days after arriving in 1847, he marked the temple site. He did not live to see the structure completed, so massive was the undertaking. The Salt Lake Temple was dedicated in 1893, forty years after construction began.[6]

The expansion of the Church is apparent in the placement of temples. By 1900, the Church had built temples in six cities: Kirtland (1836, now owned by the Community of Christ), Nauvoo (1846, rebuilt and dedicated in 2002), Salt Lake City (1893), and three smaller Utah temples along the line of LDS settlement in St. George (1877), Logan (1884), and Manti (1888). By 1950, the Church had expanded temple-building into Hawaii, Canada, Arizona, and Idaho. By 1975, temples had risen in Switzerland, New Zealand, and England, as well as the densely Mormon regions of Ogden and Provo, Utah. Three imposing temples dominated city views in Los Angeles and Oakland, California, and Washington, D.C.

Temple worship has accelerated in the last thirty years. In 1975, the Church had sixteen temples; by 2000, when the Boston Temple was dedicated, the Church had 100. The additional seventy-four temples were constructed in medium-sized U.S. cities such as Dallas, Las Vegas, San Diego, Baton Rouge, Albuquerque, and Anchorage, and in countries such as Brazil, Japan, Chile, Australia, Taiwan, Germany, South Africa, Korea, Peru, Spain, Ecuador, and the Philippines. In the 1980s, a temple was built in Freiberg, East Germany, "behind the Iron Curtain." In 2005, 119 temples were in service. Another ten had been announced or were under construction in places such as Helsinki, Kiev, Panama City, and Sacramento.[7] Rather than growing away from this early and unique worship, leaders have intensified the practice.

International Church growth has modified this temple culture. When plans for a temple in Switzerland were announced in 1953, President David O. McKay asked Gordon B. Hinckley to find a way the temple could serve many languages and nationalities with a small group of workers. The leaders decided to film the rituals. They turned a three-story room on top of the Salt Lake Temple into a movie studio, and after an intense year, an English-language film was completed. They then reproduced the film with translated scripts and new actors into French, German, Dutch, Finnish, Swedish, Danish, and Norwegian. Additional films have since been produced.[8]

President Gordon B. Hinckley had another idea that changed temple culture. In 1973, he proposed smaller, less expensive temples to be built in more places. The filmed liturgy required fewer rooms. The laundry and the cafeteria could be left out. A smaller size suited conditions in diverse locations. Initially, the smaller temples were too small. Three years after its 1998 dedication, the first small temple in Monticello, Utah, was remodeled and almost doubled, the 6,800 square foot building enlarged to 11,000 feet. Most small temples now have about 12,500 square feet of floor space.[9]

THE USES OF TEMPLES

Temples are not used for Sunday worship; members meet on Sunday at thousands of chapels. The ceremonies at temples contrast dramatically to the noisy, public Sunday School and Sacrament meetings. Temple services are serene and hushed. To enter a temple, members must have been baptized and confirmed and must be privately interviewed in searching discussions by two levels of ecclesiastical authority every two years. Successful applicants receive signed, card-sized certificates, known as "recommends," which they show at the temple door.

President Gordon B. Hinckley, in a June 2001 talk to the Saints in San Antonio, Texas, described the temple interview content. Mormons should believe that God, Jesus Christ, and the Holy Ghost live; that Jesus Christ is the Savior and the Redeemer of the world; and that the true gospel has been restored to the earth through Joseph Smith. They should sustain the leadership of the Church and observe the law of chastity. They should maintain a good spirit at home, keep distant from apostate groups, obey commandments, and attend meetings. They should pay honest tithes, and live the Word of Wisdom. As they may need to repent to be found "worthy" of attendance, they should resolve past sins; in the end, they themselves judge whether they are worthy of a "temple recommend." "I hope, I pray, I plead with you, every one of you," Hinckley concluded, "Resolve this very day, that you will live worthy to go to the House of the Lord."[10]

Each temple is supervised by a married couple called to be temple "president" and temple "matron," and two counselors and their wives, all unpaid. They administer temple business jointly, supervising a large staff of volunteer workers who work daily or weekly shifts. Temples are beautifully kept buildings, constructed from costly materials. Many command distant views with their gleaming whiteness and otherworldly architecture. Some resemble bastions or have central spires. Some are in the prairie style; two are round. Although they are thronged with people, there is no dust and dirt, no disorder. People move away from the outside world, alone together. Windows are frosted or draped against the busy streets outside. Daily life seems to recede.

Temples have no great cathedral halls but are divided into a number of specific ceremonial rooms for marriages, baptisms, and instructional sessions. Through these ordinances, members believe that all of Heavenly Father's children, the living and the dead, can hear and accept the gospel of Jesus Christ and be united for eternity. The "Plan of Salvation," a long vision of the meaning of life with its symbolic rebirth, is played out before them. Although individuals are welcome, the subject of temple work is really the dynastic family and the strengthening of its links back in time and forward into the future.

The first time a person enters the temple he or she "goes through the temple for his own endowment." On subsequent visits to the temple, he or she assumes the name of someone already dead, serving as a proxy for that person. Missionaries go through the temple before their departure for the field. Brides come with their families or fiancés to "receive their own endowments." Couples marry "for time and all eternity." Ceremonies are attended by temple-worthy family and close friends. On other happy occasions, legally adopted children or those not "born under the covenant" are "sealed" to endowed parents. The elderly and families, often appearing in groups during reunions, attend the temple as proxies for deceased family members. Teenagers are introduced to the temple on field trips to do "baptisms for the dead," the first of the proxy ordinances. One thirteen-year-old girl described that experience. "It was neat to see the temple rise above the road and to think we were lucky enough to go into that beautiful place. . . . After we saw it, we sang 'I Love to See the Temple' over and over until we arrived. . . . We changed into white jumpsuits and watched each other be baptized for the dead. It was all quiet, and I felt kind of nervous, but happy that I could do it. It was very uplifting. I hope I will always be worthy to visit the House of Our Lord."[11]

The most heavily attended temple activity is the "endowment" session. The temple sessions begin every half-hour or so depending on temple use and overlap, so there is much busy coming and going as people arrive and leave throughout the day. Sessions may begin as early as 5:30 A.M. before work hours and continue until 10 P.M. Those traveling to the temple come prepared to spend two or three hours to "do a session." Some spend the day doing additional sessions. Adult temple patrons present their recommends and change into temple clothing in dressing rooms. This clothing can usually be rented in the temple at a modest cost, but many patrons enter carrying small suitcases with their own long white dresses or shirts and pants. The uniform whiteness of these garments suggests equality, purity, and separation from worldly fashion. Inside a temple during sessions one would find many people dressed in white, silent or speaking in hushed tones, and standing quietly or moving purposefully from place to place. The general impression is a folk-art view of heaven with many kind-faced, wingless, slightly rumpled angels.

The endowment dramatizes the Mormon view of creation. The individual who is "receiving his endowment" is guided along, taught, and tested. The endowment service resembles in some respects the rituals of the Masons, though the overall pattern is different. Masons claim that their ceremonies are rooted in Solomon's temple; the Mormon endowment is organized around biblical events, the Creation and Fall of Adam and Eve. Mormons honor their covenants with God by wearing special undergarments reminiscent of the "coats of skins" Adam and Eve wore as they left the Garden. Genesis 3:21 KJV. Like Masons, Latter-day Saints generally decline to discuss temple ceremonies on the grounds that the ordinances are sacred. They object to claims that their ceremonies are "secret," contending that they are available to all who prepare themselves through baptism and Church service. The ceremonies are discussed freely within the temple itself, but people who have revealed details of the ceremonies to the media have had their recommends revoked. The endowment has been pirated and published on several occasions, but members limit discussion to protect the temple's sacred space. Over the years since the endowment's introduction in Nauvoo, the ceremonies have changed. Some Masonic elements have been toned down and the ceremony shortened.

When they attend the Salt Lake Temple, members speak of doing a "live" session. They symbolically move from one stage of life to another by physically moving from room to room where extensive murals create the background. Temple workers take roles in scenes illustrating lessons pertaining to the stages of life. In newer temples, patrons are shown the film recreating these scenes in a single room. The film covers the same material as the live session. Here the patrons move forward virtually rather than literally, some listening to other languages through headphones.

Mormons invest Adam and Eve's "fall," a key element of the endowment, with a particular meaning. Although Eve is disobedient in partaking of the forbidden fruit, she makes the right choice. She eats the fruit, understanding that only then can she know good from evil as God does. "Were it not for our transgression," Eve says to Adam, "we never should have seed, and never should have known good and evil, and the joy of our redemption."[12]

Carnality is not involved in this high-minded version of original sin—the fortunate fall. Producing families is the main purpose of earthly life. God brings spirit children to the world to obtain bodies, teach them correct principles, and bring them back to heaven after death. In LDS belief, temple ordinances grant "the power of godliness" to living people.[13]

In the temples, women officiate in priesthood ordinances. Women's work is essential to the endowment ceremonies. Not everyone, however, is satisfied with the role of women in the temple, which reflects the counsel of Paul in the New Testament, that the "husband is the head of the wife, even as Christ is the head of the church." Ephesians 5:23 KJB. Critics say the teaching is outdated and demeaning to women. In 1990, when Church leaders softened some of the gendered language of the ceremony, the event attracted press attention. One woman "greeted the changes with a great deal of joy," noting that "some portions of the temple ceremony have been painful to some women." Another woman said, "I still have concerns that haven't been addressed, but I personally find the temple endowment ceremony empowering of me as a woman, more so than demeaning."[14]

Faithful Mormons find temple blessings worth large investments in time and effort. Some save money for years, sometimes their whole lives, to attend the temple. Stories of sacrifice to attend the temple become part of family lore. In 1946, when temples were still distant for many Mormons, three cousins, Grissom, Thurman, and Rodolph Harper of Albertson, North Carolina, bought an old city bus to transport their families and a few friends, thirty-one in all, to Salt Lake City for temple sessions. The Harper boys fitted the bus with luggage racks and a big wooden water keg and set off on state roads before the interstates were built. Going up the mountains, the bus was the slowest thing on the road. Some got out and walked. Some got out and pushed. Some broke out with chicken pox. All slept on the bus to the clinking sound of repairs. After the bus arrived in Salt Lake, the families were sealed in the temple. Five days later with a new bus engine, they started home. The Harpers saw themselves as plains-crossing pioneers, and their epic journey illustrates the importance of these rituals to members.[15]

TEMPLES AND COMMUNITIES

For the most part, Mormons build their temples in predominately non-Mormon communities, and the Mormon presence can create tension. The Church prefers affluent residential areas where crime is low and land will hold its value. Unfortunately, these are also places where homeowners are sensitive about their neighborhoods, and not eager for a large white-steepled church structure, dramatically lit at night, visited by many but closed to the public at large, to be erected nearby. Zoning ordinances, land use commissions, negotiating committees, lawyers, and courts have all been invoked to stop the building of LDS temples or to scale them down. Leaders are always engaged in multiple negotiations.

The Church has given up on some projects. A temple in suburban Nashville, Tennessee, was abandoned when the neighbors objected to potential traffic problems and nighttime lighting. The mayor thought the temple threatened the suburban estate character of the area. The Church sold the site to a Southern Baptist congregation and built a smaller temple in nearby Franklin, Tennessee. By contrast, a planned temple for Redlands, California, even with a 130-foot spire that will soar above a mostly two-story city, sailed through. Churches there are exempt from height requirements. Traffic does not loom as an issue, because, as a city councilman said, "someday we will probably widen Wabash Avenue."[16]

It took five years to obtain permission to build the 70,000 square-foot Boston temple on its seven-acre plot above Route 2, one of the spoke-like highways pointing toward Boston's hub. The finished product was smaller than originally planned. An early architectural rendering called for a large structure with six steeples like the Salt Lake City temple. In carrying their case to the U.S. Supreme Court, the neighbors challenged the Dover Amendment, a fifty-year-old Massachusetts state law allowing large religious buildings in residential neighborhoods. Neighbors charged that the zoning exemptions violated the U.S. Constitution's First Amendment ban on established religion because it gave "enormous power and privilege to religious individuals and institutions to determine the characteristics of neighborhoods." They claimed that the temple would light the neighborhood at night, produce steady streams of unwanted visitors, and make nearby homes unmarketable. The Supreme Court sustained the findings of the First Circuit Court of Appeals, however, and turned down the challenge without comment. In a later ruling, a state judge banned the construction of a high steeple, and the dedication occurred while the ruling was being appealed.[17]

The dispute ended in May 2001 when the Supreme Judicial Court of Massachusetts ruled the steeple essential to the religious mission of a Mormon temple, though the neighbors considered it an eyesore. The dispute hinged on whether the steeple was critical to the temple's work, and the Supreme Judicial Court overturned the appeals court judge who had distinguished the religiosity of the different parts of the building. Chief Justice Margaret Marshall, in a seventeen-page opinion, ruled that as the structure as a whole would be used for religious purposes, "the steeple is an essential part of the religious mission of the temple because the Mormons believe it is." This ruling effectively ended the case, and the steeple was soon in place.[18] The Church bought the houses of some neighbors unhappy with the outcome.

No litigation resulted from the Church's 1999 announcement to rebuild the Nauvoo Temple, though there were some local grumbles. The original structure, Joseph Smith's last temple from the early 1840s, was constructed at a time of violence and abandoned. By the 1850s, the temple had been leveled by fire and tornado and the limestone remains carried away. The reconstruction on the same high bluff overlooking the Mississippi River followed the original architectural drawings that surfaced in 1948. The original building cost about $1 million; the next time around, this large and elegantly crafted edifice, cost about $30 million. Craftsmen replicated the thirty human-faced sunstones, as well as moonstones and starstones, on limestone pilasters. The artisans also carved twelve limestone oxen to support the baptismal font, a feature of every temple replicating an Old Testament pattern.[19]

As the completion neared, another event attracted attention. Rocky and Helen Hulse began a nearby ministry to the Mormons. Rocky, a former Mormon, and his wife Helen, sounded the alarm because the Nauvoo temple, dedicated June 27, 2002, might well draw people away from other churches. Hulse wanted to educate and warn people about Mormonism. He considered the temple "an insult to Christianity." Six hundred people attended the Hulses' first presentation at a Danville, Iowa, church. For their second presentation, they ran a full-page ad in a local paper. "It is sad that we will have to work so hard to educate people about the beliefs of Mormonism," said Rocky Hulse. "Every Christian denomination and every other religion works at making its beliefs known." But the Hulses and other nearby pastors saw conspiracy. The "Mormon church does not want people to know what they really believe." Hulse continued, "The Mormons aren't bad people, they are just deceived people."[20]

Only about 250 Mormons live in the Nauvoo vicinity, but 350,000 attended the open house. Some locals welcomed the financial windfall visitors brought, but others saw menace rather than grandeur in the building, fearing that the Mormons would dominate the area's economy, culture, and politics as they did many years ago. The expected surge in real estate prices, driven by new Mormon settlers, mostly retirees, caused some residents to leave. LDS Church spokespeople asked for tolerance, promising to be good neighbors. "We would support them in the ways they worship, and we ask that they do the same for us."[21]

GENEALOGY

Despite local friction, temples continue to rise. Brigham Young predicted that during the milennium thousands of temples would dot the earth. They are a critical part of the Church's huge genealogical enterprise. In the past, Church members, eager to find family names for vicarious ordinances traveled to foreign countries to pour over parish registers, old Bibles, cemetery stones, and censuses, searching for connecting ancestors. Genealogists still search for such missing leaves, but in another of the ways that technology has influenced traditional activities, genealogical records are now gathered wholesale. Microfilm, databases, computers, and copiers are employed to link families for eternity.

Teams of professional genealogists visit depositories of vital statistics worldwide to film records. These films are processed, and in the "name extraction" program, volunteer workers scour them for family connections, recording names and dates of marriages and births. These names are alphabetized and indexed on the massive Ancestral File database containing 35.6 million names with family relationships. The International Genealogical Index (IGI) database contains about 750 million individual names. These indices are available online, displaying about 10,000 search results per minute. They refer to microfilmed records, which can be sent for and perused. The names, dates, and relationships are submitted to the temples, and names are given out to temple patrons who perform vicarious temple work for the deceased people.[22]

Mormons justify this work with Paul's statement to the Corinthians in the Bible. "Else what shall they do which are baptized for the dead, if the dead rise not at all? Why are they then baptized for the dead?" Leaders point to Peter's mention of spirits who hear the gospel in the afterlife. "For this cause was the gospel preached also to them that are dead, that they might be judged according to men in the flesh, but live according to God in the spirit." Mormonism's own Scripture amplifies these teachings. Joseph F. Smith, Joseph Smith's nephew and the sixth President of the Church, recorded a vision he received in 1918 (now Doctrine and Covenants section 138) while meditating on Peter's account of Christ's visit "unto the spirits in prison." He noted that "faithful elders" preached the gospel of repentance and redemption "among those who are in darkness and under the bondage of sin in the great world of the spirits of the dead." Those who repented were "washed clean" and rewarded "according to their works." Smith saw leaders "laying the foundations of the great latter-day work, including the building of the temples and the performance of ordinances therein for the redemption of the dead." This work, "the redemption of the dead, and the sealing of the children to their parents" creates "welding links" between all members of the human family.[23] These verses justify the vast genealogical work.

Latter-day Saints take intangible, spiritual ideas and ground them in the specific physical world. Once the commitment to do genealogical work for those no longer living accelerated in the early 20th century, Church members performed endowments for millions of people, teaching that the ceremony is necessary to redeem the deceased from "spirit prison." Although according to church teaching the ceremonies are not binding on any who choose to ignore them, living descendants of people enrolled on Church records have objected. In 1995, Jews were aghast to discover that 400,000 Holocaust victims had been baptized and endowed by enthusiastic Mormons. The Jews demanded that the names be removed, and the Church agreed to do so. Seven years later, the Jews charged that there were still at least 20,000 Jewish names on the list and demanded removal. Jewish leaders called the baptismal practice well-meaning, but "arrogant and insensitive." All the ill feeling notwithstanding, at a "warm and satisfactory" meeting in 2005 between Mormons and Jews, the groups came to an amicable resolution, planning a joint oversight committee to monitor the Church's lists. Holocaust victims have been deleted from the lists, and additional names will be removed when brought to the Church's attention. Both sides agreed that finding and removing the names of all deceased Jews in the 400 million-name list would be impossible. A three-million–name Yad Vashem database will not be mined or posted on Mormon databases. Mormons are to submit only the names of their ancestors.[24]

Jews are not the only group threatened. Peter Love, a Maori who manages the affairs of Maori tribes and a Mormon himself, opposed the microfilming of 100 years of New Zealand vital records, which would lead to the baptism of his deceased ancestral people into the Church. The Russian Inter-Religious Council described as "deliberate abuse" the Mormon practice of enrolling deceased people in their church. Leader Roman Silantyev called the practice "abuse of the memory of the deceased." Incidents such as these may foreshadow more difficulty in gathering records and performing posthumous ordinances.[25]

Despite the objections, the Mormon desire to link family members has resulted in the large Salt Lake City repositories, which benefit everyone interested in genealogy. The genealogical library, founded in 1894, gathers data for members performing temple work for their ancestors and everyone else wishing to reconstruct their family trees. The current Family History Library, built in 1985, the world's largest genealogical library staffed by 230 paid workers and hundreds of volunteers, is open free to the public. Each year some 750,000 people visit the library, where more than two billion names are recorded on 2.2 million rolls of microfilm, 740,000 microfiche, 300,000 books, and 4,500 periodicals. Each month, about 5,000 rolls of microfilm and 700 books are added. Two hundred cameras in forty-four countries busily snap millions of images a year. To protect the filmed records from nuclear disaster, the originals are housed in a massive stone vault drilled out of a canyon near Salt Lake. The financial and psychic devotion to this operation underscores its importance to the Church.

Besides this central library in Salt Lake City, the Church maintains 5,000 family history centers operating in seventy-five countries and territories. Staffed by volunteers and visited by more than five million patrons annually, these satellite libraries are set up in Church meeting houses around the world to make the Salt Lake collection accessible. In eastern U.S. locations more than 90 percent of the visitors who order copies of more than 100,000 rolls of microfilm monthly are not Mormons. Small fees for postage and copying are charged. The site at www.familysearch.org, launched in 1999, has had billions of hits. Continuing uploads have brought the online names to more than a billion.[26]

The family history department uses its resources, records, and volunteers to turn out specialty CDs of specific records. This work builds better relations with the public than baptizing their ancestors unaware. In 2001, the department released the records of the Freedman's Bank, a Washington, D.C.-

based bank chartered in 1865 to help recently freed slaves. An estimated 70,000 customers opened and closed accounts with deposits totaling more than $57 million during the bank's nine years of operation. Seeing the potential for the genealogy of black families, Marie Taylor, a Church employee, organized the material into usable shape and enlisted volunteers to extract the 480,000 names, link them as families, and index them. The project took eleven years. Among the volunteers were 550 prisoners at the Utah State Prison. This invaluable resource for the genealogical work of African Americans was issued as a user-friendly database on a CD for $6.50.[27] Within a month of release, 30,000 copies of the CD had been requested, mostly by African Americans. One recipient said, "The black community has an insatiable thirst for family history, and [the Church] has given us the well to satisfy that thirst." Prison inmates who worked on the project felt a special empathy for the freed slaves and were surprised by their emotions while extracting information of fathers sold away from their families, mothers who were traded, and others who were shot. At an introductory luncheon, members of the black community applauded spontaneously and at great length for the prison inmates who assisted.[28]

In a similar project, 12,000 Church volunteers spent much of eight years extracting the names of immigrants, business passengers, and tourists who arrived at Ellis Island from 1892 through 1924. During some 5.6 million hours, Church volunteers transcribed twenty-four million individual records from 3,685 rolls of microfilm. Descendants of Ellis Island immigrants locate ancestors by searching for them by name on computers at the Ellis Island Museum or online at www.ellisislandrecords.org. The website reported getting 27,000 hits *per second* on the first day, or an estimated eight million hits in total. If a person can type in the actual name of a passenger, and suggestions are given for alternate spellings, he will be able to determine dates of departure and arrival, a description of the ship, the nationality, age, occupation, home, and American contact person of each listed immigrant.[29]

In a third project, Church members have digitized the 1880 United States Census, the first published, and put it online. This database covers thirty-eight states and eight territories and represents seventeen years and eleven and a half million hours of work by LDS extractors. Fifty-five million records are included, searchable by name, date, state, occupation, race, gender, household or neighborhood. "Wild card" searches find people despite handwriting and spelling variations. The Census, a valuable tool for historical and genealogical researchers, is rendered usable. Soon after the site database opened, visitors pored over the material at about three million hits an hour.[30] As Richard and Joan Ostling noted in their book, *Mormon America,* "Never in the history of organized religion has a doctrinal tenet produced such an elaborate and expensive archival effort."[31]

CONCLUSION

The building of temples illustrates the way Latter-day Saints couple spiritual, abstract concepts with practical, bricks-and-mortar solutions. The concrete aspects of construction contrast with the heavily symbolic purposes of temples: to create holy ground where humans meet God and link all generations for the eternities. Temples bring together the modern church with the Hebraic church of the Old Testament. Because temples have been important since the earliest days, temple ceremonies preserve and promote the church's own past as well. Mystical spaces, cloistered rituals, and cosmic thinking linked to a grand program to bind everyone who ever lived into families bring out the transcendent and practical sides of Mormon culture. Others wonder, doubt, and criticize, but the Mormons show no signs of slackening their temple programs.

RACE, ETHNICITY, AND CLASS

All of our brethren who are worthy may receive the priesthood.
—*LDS First Presidency,* 1978

When Vincente, a hotel concierge, met the missionaries, he wanted to know more about the Church. "The first time we taught him was a glorious experience," a missionary said. "He knew the church was true." He came to church every week. Then they had to tell him that people of African lineage needed special permission to be baptized.[1]

No issue has troubled Mormons more in the second half of the twentieth century than race. Until 1978, the Church withheld its priesthood from men of black African ancestry, long beyond the time when African Americans won national civil rights victories. Although African Americans were not denied Church membership, they were denied priesthood, a policy increasingly difficult to justify in the turbulent 1960s. Before then, the policy had drawn little attention. In 1957, Catholic sociologist Thomas O'Dea's extensive study of the Church did not mention the denial among the "strains and conflicts." But thereafter commentators considered the limitation of the priesthood as the Church's primary problem, a racist doctrine out of place in a democratic society.[2]

How did this exclusionary policy come into being? The Book of Mormon supports universal equality. One reads there that the Lord invites all the children of men "to come unto him and partake of his goodness; and he denieth none that come unto him, black and white, bond and free, male and female; and he remembereth the heathen; and all are alike unto God, both Jew and Gentile."[3] The book speaks of people "cursed" with a "black" skin, but that was a temporary, reversible curse. Skin color changed with righteous living. The origin of Negro priesthood exclusion seems to be rooted in history, not doctrine.

The Church was founded in 1830, a time of growing strife over slavery. Racial issues emerged after the Saints moved to Missouri, a slave state. An 1833 editorial in the LDS paper *The Evening and Morning Star*, warned the Saints against bringing free blacks to the state, to avoid the wrath of local slaveholders. Missourians misunderstood this editorial as an invitation for free blacks to settle. Explanations unavailing, violent conflicts soon erupted, dividing Mormons from their neighbors.[4]

Although this first clash may have been a misunderstanding, continued friction led to a Church statement on slavery in April 1836. At the height of anti-abolitionist sentiments when anti-slavery petitions were being stifled in Congress under the "gag rule," an editorial in the Church newspaper declared that it is "unlawful and unjust, and dangerous to the peace" for anyone to interfere with "human beings . . . held in servitude." The Saints were not to deal with "bond—servants, neither preach the gospel to, nor baptize them contrary to the will and wish of their masters, nor to meddle with or influence them in the least to cause them to be dissatisfied with their situations in this life, thereby jeopardizing the lives of men." That strong statement, possibly the product of momentary anti-abolitionist sentiments, was reversed a few years later. Church attitudes returned to a forthright anti-slavery position. Joseph Smith ran for U.S. president in 1844 on a platform calling for "national equalization"—setting slaves free, educating them, and giving them civil rights. Although he may have shared the common idea that blacks were descended from Ham and so subject to the curse of Cain, he said nothing about the priesthood and ordained some blacks to priesthood offices.[5]

The priesthood policy took a new turn under Smith's successor Brigham Young. In 1852, Young, operating under the Compromise of 1850, legalized both black and Indian slavery in an attempt to acquire Utah statehood. In a strikingly plain statement, Young said, "Any man having one drop of the seed of [Cain] . . . in him cannot hold the priesthood and if no other Prophet ever spake it before I will say it now in the name of Jesus Christ I know it is true and others know it." Absorbing the racist literature of his time, Young spoke of the biological inadequacies of blacks. Though freed from slavery during the Civil War, former slaves were not granted LDS priesthood.[6]

Over time, Church members worked out doctrinal explanations for exclusion. One justification originated in the papyrus rolls that Joseph Smith bought in 1835 and translated as the Book of Abraham. A passage links ancient Egypt's government to the cursed Ham through Pharaoh, Ham's grandson. Pharaoh, the passage says, was "of that lineage by which he could not have the right of Priesthood." Abraham 1:25, 27, Pearl of Great Price 1981. Because Smith had identified blacks as Ham's descendants, subsequent leaders went the next step to withhold the priesthood from black Africans. Although the Reorganized Church in the Midwest embraced black members, the Utah Mormons, with few blacks among them, clung to separatism, held in place by earlier Church rulings.[7]

Another explanation looked beyond mortality. With no scriptural basis, some Mormons justified exclusion by interpreting the pre-mortal war in heaven. In this battle between the spirits, the Lord's faithful vanquished Satan's legions, who were denied human bodies. Blacks were said to be those who did not fight against Satan in the pre-mortal conflict. As fence sitters, they received a lesser earthly stature. In the twentieth century, Apostle Joseph Fielding Smith elaborated the doctrine: "Transgression in the first estate," that is, in the pre-mortal spirit world, "deprives him in this second estate," that is, in mortal existence. Smith's book *The Way to Perfection*, published in 1931, contained the most extensive treatment of priesthood denial. Smith summarized past Church policies, providing a theoretical foundation. His "pre-existence hypothesis" held that "those who did not stand valiantly" came to earth life with restrictions. "The negro race, for instance, have been placed under restrictions because of their attitude in the world of spirits, few will doubt. It cannot be looked upon as just that they should be deprived of the power of the Priesthood without it being a punishment for some act, or acts, performed before they were born." Organizing the scanty evidence from the Pearl of Great Price and the teachings of Joseph Smith, Apostle Smith concluded, "But we all know it was due to [Joseph Smith's] teachings that the negro today is barred from the Priesthood."[8] This "preexistence hypothesis" was frequently presented from 1931 until 1949.

The Civil Rights Movement in the United States heightened awareness of the contradictions in the Church's policy. In 1964, in response to questions, Joseph Fielding Smith justified withholding priesthood by referring to rights he claimed black members already had. His mimeographed sheet argued that negroes should be given complete equality with all other citizens in respect to legal rights, education, and employment; the Church would defend these privileges, he said. Nevertheless, "it is not the authorities of the Church who have placed a restriction on [the Negro] regarding the holding of the Priesthood. It was not the Prophet Joseph Smith nor Brigham Young. It was the Lord! If a Negro desires to join the Church we will give him all the encouragement that we can, but we cannot promise him that he will receive the Priesthood."[9] Outside of that, he said, blacks should enjoy all rights of membership with no hint of segregation. Mormons were condemned during the Civil Rights era because of this explanation. The national news derided the priesthood policy. Brigham Young University athletes were threatened and endured tomato throwing, bomb scares, and heckling; athletic games were cancelled and boycotted. As one rival black athlete said in 1968, "You've got to understand how we feel. Those Mormons say we're the mark of Cain and that we can't go to heaven because we're black. Man, I just don't want to associate with those people in any way." *Sports Illustrated* noted in 1970 that a BYU basketball team did not know whether to expect "a man-to-man defense, a zone, or a grenade." By the early 1970s, the former rationalization was dropped, and no justification whatsoever was offered.[10]

The policy caused pain for all and especially black members. In 1942, some Relief Society sisters in Washington, D.C., objected to sitting beside "two colored sisters who are apparently faithful members of the Church." The ward appealed to the First Presidency who advised: "We feel sure that if the colored sisters were discretely approached, they would be happy to sit at one side in the rear or somewhere where they would not wound the sensibilities of the complaining sisters." Katherine Warran, a black woman, looked up the Church in the telephone directory and began to attend. "I investigated the church for about three years. They were prejudiced in that church. They didn't want any blacks. There weren't any blacks there. Yet I felt good when I would go. I kept going, even though nobody said anything to me."[11]

Darius Gray, a black man who joined the church in 1964, found out the night before his baptism that he could not hold the priesthood. "I had a testimony of the gospel, but I was also a proud, black man." He was set to call off the event, but instead, "took it to God that night" and received "a succinct answer" that this was to be his faith. He joined a church with an exclusive priesthood policy, right in the middle of the Civil Rights Movement. Gray believes that blacks are descended from the biblical Ham and traces his line back to Melchizedek, for whom the higher priesthood is named. As Gray says, "I'm not saying that Melchizedek was black, but I am saying he was hanging with the brothers."[12]

Many white members were pained by the practice of withholding the priesthood. A Stanford University student, converted to the Church, said, "The hardest thing for me in joining the church was the blacks and the priesthood. I'd been raised to be very much devoted to the idea the black people were as good as anybody. Here was this church that practiced institutional racism. Here I was joining this church. I knew it was the right thing to do and I wanted to do it, but it was hard."[13] Some Mormons openly apostatized. Some became closet apostates. Many, embarrassed by the situation, felt the exclusionary practice was indefensible, but continued to be active in the Church. Others spoke out. English professor Eugene England, a branch president in Minnesota, in the 1970s, said that explaining priesthood denial to his parishioners was "in its way, the heaviest cross I have to bear." England pointed to the difficulties for whites as well as blacks. "When God asks us, as we believe He does, not to give blacks of African descent the priesthood at this time, He asks us to sacrifice not only our political and social ideals and the understanding and good will of our colleagues and friends, but seems to ask us to sacrifice the very essence of His own teachings—the divine potential of all His children, the higher ethical vision of possible exaltation for all people, concepts that are among the most attractive and vital features of our faith." England suggested that racist white members must repent to change the policy.[14]

Another thoughtful response came from Arthur Henry King, a learned white convert to Mormonism in 1966 who had worked for the British government in Africa. His "difficulty" with priesthood denial required intense reflection. "I realized when I came to terms with myself that I had knowledge from my own experience that showed that the Church's teaching in this respect was not wrong: the blacks were not ready to come in and the Church membership was not ready to have them in. At the same time, I thought, and I realized that other people in the Church also thought, that this did not absolve us from a deep and profound social responsibility to that race. God had not cursed them, but humankind had cursed them; for a curse is not an arbitrary thing—it is a kind of acknowledgment of what is. And the nightmare of the blacks has been the most terrible of the human nightmares."[15]

Priesthood denial points up the difficulties, as well as the advantages, of a church open to revelation. Practices can be changed in the twinkling of an eye by a brief fiat from the current prophet. The disadvantage is that the fiat must be received. In this case, despite the denial, there were promises of full blessings at some time. Brigham Young said that blacks would get the priesthood in this life. Hugh B. Brown, a General Authority, said in 1969, that blacks would eventually be given priesthood "in the not too distant future."[16]

Near the end of the 1970s, the Church seemed a fortress defending itself against national disfavor. Leaders explained that only a revelation could change the policy. Experienced observers believed that the Church policy would never change under attack. As the Civil Rights Movement peaked and diminished, the Church stood firm. But as missionaries preached the gospel to a wider world population, the practice of barring anyone with Negro blood from the priesthood raised problems of definition. Brazil was a particularly difficult place to determine ancestry as slavery was legal until 1888, and more than three million African slaves had been brought in as workers. Interracial marriage was widespread, segregation illegal, and prejudice unacceptable. Church leaders attempted to screen prospective converts to eliminate mixed-blood members, inconsistently administering awkward policies. When a Brazilian temple was announced in 1975, the Church was on a collision course. Some of the most faithful and best-educated members in Brazil, people who contributed money to build the temple and send others on missions, could not hold the priesthood.[17]

On June 9, 1978, Church President Spencer W. Kimball announced a revelation reversing the policy and extending the priesthood to all worthy males, including those of African descent. The full text of the letter to all priesthood officers of the Church worldwide follows:

Dear Brethren:
As we have witnessed the expansion of the work of the Lord over the earth, we have been grateful that people of many nations have responded to the message of the restored gospel, and have joined the Church in ever increasing numbers. This, in turn, has inspired us with a desire to extend to every worthy member of the Church all of the privileges and blessings which the gospel affords.

Aware of the promises made by the prophets and presidents of the Church who have preceded us that at some time, in God's eternal plan, all of our brethren who are worthy may receive the priesthood, and witnessing the faithfulness of those from whom the priesthood has been withheld, we have pleaded long and earnestly in behalf of these, our faithful brethren, spending many hours in the Upper Room of the Temple supplicating the Lord for divine guidance.

He has heard our prayers, and by revelation has confirmed that the long-promised day has come when every faithful, worthy man in the Church may receive the holy priesthood, with power to exercise its divine authority, and enjoy with his loved ones every blessing that flows therefrom, including the blessings of the temple. Accordingly, all worthy male members of the Church may be ordained to the priesthood without regard for race or color. Priesthood leaders are instructed to follow the policy of carefully interviewing all candidates for ordination to either the Aaronic or the Melchizedek Priesthood to insure that they meet the established standards for worthiness.

We declare with soberness that the Lord has now made known his will for the blessing of all his children throughout the earth who will hearken to the voice of his authorized servants, and prepare themselves to receive every blessing of the gospel.

The declaration was signed by President Spencer W. Kimball and the First Presidency.[18]

Gilmore Chappell, a black American working in Holland, had been a member for six months when he heard the news. Chappell, overcome, went out to sit in his car, laughing and crying. "Then I went back into priesthood [meeting] and they welcomed me in with open arms." Mary Frances Sturlaugson, who joined the Church while attending college, was living in Provo. A former bishop told her that her people had been given the priesthood. She walked outside, "crying like a happy kid at Christmas-time." Horns were honking. She stopped for a red light and a car pulled up. The driver asked if she had heard the news. As she half mumbled and half nodded a disbelieving yes, he whooped and blew his horn. At her apartment, her roommates ran to meet her, jumping up and down screaming with joy. Each said a prayer, "sobs punctuating every one." Within a month, she had submitted her paperwork for a mission.[19]

Leonard Arrington, Church Historian at the time, pieced together an account of how the revelation came. In 1976, two years prior to the announcement, President Kimball had begun to pray, fast, and supplicate God to rescind the exclusion of blacks from the priesthood. Kimball intensified his efforts in April 1978, going every day to a special room in the temple. On June 1, according to Arrington's account, Kimball invited the First Presidency and the Quorum of the Twelve to stay beyond their regular meeting. Those present shared a profound spiritual experience and the mutual awareness that a new doctrine had been revealed to them.[20]

Kimball's queries, said Arrington, pointed to three tensions between doctrine and practice. First, the traditional notion that the gospel be preached to every nation and people was prevented by the exclusion. Second, the scriptural emphasis on the worth of all souls made the exclusionary practice seem unjustified. Statements supporting equal opportunities seemed incongruous with the denial. Third, Church members understood that someday the priesthood would be available to all worthy males. When would those promises be fulfilled?[21] The new revelation brought teachings and practice into line. Because the change came by revelation, it was quick and absolute. Like the fifteenth amendment to the U.S. Constitution granting black men the franchise, this document gave no concessions to women.

Armand Mauss noted that the revelation changed only a policy and did not address any doctrine. Not surprisingly, the policy was reversed well after the Civil Rights Movement had waned. Public pressure had subsided, and people had given up on the Mormons ever entering the modern world.[22]

One fruit of the revelation was the LDS congregation on 129th Street in New York's Harlem. A large sign on the small building proclaimed "The Church of JESUS CHRIST of Latter-day Saints." In 2001, the congregation numbered about sixty, with members from Puerto Rico, the Caribbean, African nations, Harlem residents, and some Caucasian Mormons from the western United States. The numbers doubled in four years, straining the facilities. The Church dedicated a much larger building around the corner on Lenox Avenue in 2005.

Harlem members joined for various reasons. Agnes Martinez was attracted by the "families are forever" motto on television. She enjoyed the temple and was sorry to "come back to what we really live in."[23] Gloria Lynch, a social worker born in Harlem, was baptized after a lifelong search for the "right faith." She had grown up Catholic and practiced Islam and Christian Science before becoming a Mormon. Ralph Acosta admitted that he was attracted to a lady who came by and invited him to come to the Church. He became a strong member.[24]

Are the black members assimilated into the Church? The reports are mixed. Delphrine Garcia Young, a hospital worker and counselor in a bishopric, says they are. "I have been truly well-accepted by white Latter-day Saints. When you are around a white Latter-day Saint, it is just like going around with your brothers and sisters." Elijah Royster joined the Church while serving a military tour in Hawaii. A Mormon friend invited him to church. "We sat through the sacrament service. The chapel was full, so we had to sit in the [back]. . . . I noticed with the children back there there was a lot of noise. We were really trying very hard to listen to the speakers. There was a negative mood there. Then I noticed how all of the Saints were so friendly and kind and shaking our hands. Having been in life the way that I had, immediately I recognized that it was genuine; it wasn't a put-on; it wasn't something phony. That had a great bearing on my feelings and my thoughts about the Church."[25]

Barbara Ann Pixton was in the military, lonely and thousands of miles away from her family. The first time she went to church she was "overwhelmed by the love, especially being black. We walked in, we sat down in the back, . . . After the meeting, the majority of the sisters got up, came in the back, introduced themselves to me, and shook my hand. They were very warm. I thought to myself, 'I want to learn more.'"[26]

Some have more nuanced comments. Bobby Darby of North Carolina noted that "We were accepted pretty good, better than we would have expected. We see in some people that they really do not like being around us; but out of a love of Christ, they do it anyway. We can respect that, too. A lot of things that I do, I do not like doing; but if the Lord says it is the right way to do it, then we just do it and just expect the best."[27]

There are signs of greater openness and inclusion. In 2002, Rob Foster, a twenty-five-year-old black man from North Carolina who joined the Church when he was fourteen, was elected student body president at Brigham Young University, where just 0.7 percent of the student body is black. While young, Foster chose sports, religion, and education, whereas other relatives opted for drugs and crime. After a year playing basketball at Ricks College (BYU–Idaho), Foster served a mission in California. Foster sees little racial tension at the school but encourages campus groups to work together toward a "Zion community"—Mormon talk for a cooperative, utopian community.[28]

Darius Gray led an organization of black members and others called Genesis, founded in 1971. They began meeting under the direction of the general authorities to "meet the needs" of black members. All-black branches have given African American members the chance to fill responsible positions they might not hold in large wards. Although assimilation is not complete, no one denies a black man or a twelve-year-old-boy the priesthood when standards are met. One black leader has retired as a General Authority, and several black area leaders have since been added to the Quorums of the Seventy.[29]

On the twenty-fifth anniversary of the "priesthood revelation," Darius Gray said that the Church had been changed from a "small, parochial institution into an international church." He spoke for broader cultural inclusion. "We need to not only bring people in, but share in what they have to offer." As an example, Gladys Knight, the Grammy Award-winning singer who had previously regretted that LDS hymns were not very exciting (they could "use a little zip."), brought her gospel choir, Saints Unified Voices, from Las Vegas to Salt Lake City to perform gospel versions of LDS hymns. The "toe-tapping, hand-clapping, bench-thumping music praising Jesus Christ" presented a new version of the hymns. Knight thanked the leaders for their encouragement and "urged the audience to widen their embrace of the cultures, music and customs of all people."[30]

More than a quarter of a century after the change, tensions remain. Some members regret that the Church has not apologized for the past. An apology would imply that past prophets were mistaken, a possibility the official Church is reluctant to acknowledge. Lacking this renunciation, the old explanations for priesthood exclusion persist in LDS folklore and sometimes turn up in publications. Darron Smith, in *Black and Mormon,* a book he co-edited with Newell Bringhurst, regrets that the Church "refuses to acknowledge and undo its racist past, and until it does that, members continue to suffer psychological damage from it."[31] The racist past still haunts the Mormon present.

NATIVE AMERICANS

The Church's relationship with Native Americans suffers from a different set of tensions. Mormons believe the Book of Mormon contains a history of the Indians, linking them to ancient Israel and foretelling their destiny. They are chosen people and will be instrumental in building a New Jerusalem. But the Book of Mormon position is ambiguous: Indians are descendants of the book's rebellious Lamanites. In some periods, over the book's long history, the Lamanites are heroes; more often they are hostile to the book's narrators. Nevertheless, the book promises that they "shall blossom as the rose."[32] As early as 1830, missionaries taught Indians about this heritage in New York, Ohio, and Missouri.

The affinity with Indians led to immediate problems. In Missouri, just as the Mormons were considered too soft on free blacks, so they were feared to be in league with Native Americans. The Church was charged with "Indian tampering," or stirring sedition. When the Mormons were driven from Missouri in 1838, the committee took care that they not go toward Indian Territory for fear they would join the Indians and come back to attack the white frontier settlements. Both accusations—that Mormons held illicit communication with Indians and were opposed to slavery—frightened the Missourians.[33]

Arriving in large numbers in the Great Salt Lake Valley, Mormons attempted to live peacefully with the Indians. Brigham Young advocated kindness and generosity, hoping to assimilate them into mainstream Church culture despite disparate lifestyles. Some joined the Church, others were adopted into LDS families, but most lived distant from LDS communities. Attempts at peaceful coexistence proved elusive.

In the 1940s, the Church created missions to the Native Americans to teach farming and religion. Some Indian children, at their parents' request, were placed in LDS families in white communities to go to school. Mormons served as foster families for the children, paying for transportation, room and board, and clothing. The children, beginning at about age eight, lived at home in the summer, returning to the foster family through high school.

Starting with three students in 1947, the program peaked in 1970 when nearly 5,000 students left reservations to study at white schools and live in LDS homes. More than 70,000 young people participated in the Indian Student Placement Services (ISPS) program. Although parents emphatically stated that they had applied for the program, critics charged that the program fragmented Indian families, weakened cultural pluralism, and caused psychological damage by shuttling children between white and Indian worlds. Accusations that the LDS Church pushed children into the program prompted the U.S. government in 1977 to commission a study.

The study determined that 34 percent of the students remained in the program through high school; 66 percent dropped out for homesickness, requests to return, or incompatibility; yet 82 percent of the group completed high school, twice the number of a control group. After the experience, participants were more likely to work comfortably in better jobs. The main goal of the ISPS, promoting the educational attainment of Indian participants, was achieved. But as reservation schools improved, the ISPS receded in size and importance. In 1990, only 500 students participated.[34]

One outgrowth of the program had an unfortunate ending. A Native American, George P. Lee, a full-blooded Navajo and an early graduate of the ISPS, was made a General Authority in 1975, the first Native American to achieve this position. After ten years of service, Lee publicly criticized the Church for neglecting its mission to the Lamanites. He was excommunicated in 1989.[35]

What is life like for Native Americans in the Church today? Like Ron Singer, a Navajo who spent years in the ISPS, they live in a dual culture. Singer balances Mormonism with Navajo traditions and religion: "After I joined the LDS Church, it was kind of hard to juggle the two religions. . . . My grandparents still live the old traditional ways. I had to learn to respect that. When I got ready to go on my mission, I sat down with my step dad, and we talked. . . . All of a sudden my eyes just opened. It all fit in. My mission really helped me because that brought more of the Navajo religion into it. . . . My testimony was strengthened."[36]

Shirley Equerra Moore, half Native American and half Latina, regretted that "most non-Indians think that Lamanites maybe aren't as bright, and therefore, couldn't possibly have a testimony." Non-Indians, she thought, equate intelligence and spirituality. She didn't think a person should be surprised when a Lamanite was a Church leader. "I am a brown person, and yes, brown people are capable of doing these things."[37]

Ken Sekaquaptewa, with a Hopi father and a Chinese mother, also had problems with cultural differences. He thought Indians and Chinese people were both disadvantaged because they show little emotion. Singer, Moore, and Sekaquaptewa all talked about a leadership style and behavior based on an Anglo model that constricted less gregarious cultural groups. Donna Fifita, a Sioux married to a Tongan, felt required to confront the stereotype of shy, lazy, and backward people. After moving to Utah, she felt "really uncomfortable in my regular ward. . . . I wanted to prove to Heavenly Father and to [ward members] that I wasn't like an Indian that would be inactive, an alcoholic, or whatever stereotypes they had. . . . I would bear my testimony boldly to them in sacrament meeting. I would tell them how I knew this Church was true."[38]

These comments reveal the persistence of stereotypes about Native Americans along with the efforts to overcome them. Perceptions of the LDS treatment of Indians as racist have led to a softening of the Lamanite characterization. The mixed message of the chosen people also being the cursed people has shifted the good/evil dichotomy toward the encompassing "children of Lehi" to include the good Nephites. To escape some of the negative connotations, a popular BYU performing group once called the Lamanite Generation is now the Living Legends.[39]

Whether the Native Americans should assimilate into predominately white LDS wards or remain separate is a question played out in the choice of which wards to attend. When Shirley Moore saw prejudice in the English-speaking ward, she began attending activities in the Native American Branch. "There were almost all Lamanites there except for the leaders, because, of course, the Indians couldn't be leaders. What did they know? I'm being sarcastic." After Shirley married, she moved to the Native American Branch. Things went well with her husband as branch president. However, when the family moved away, the branch dissolved. She sadly said, "I know that some of those people won't feel good about going to the [Anglo] ward. But you can't always sit back and say, 'I'm just a poor Indian and people will look down on me,' although I certainly have had those feelings." She spoke of Sister Redhouse, a "typical Navajo woman." "People could learn from Sister Redhouse, but I don't know that she'd ever go to [the Anglo] Ward."[40] Tensions between Native Americans and whites in the Church are yet to be resolved.

SPANISH-SPEAKING MEMBERS

Hispanics introduce a third cultural tension into the Church. In recent years there has been major growth in South and Central America. In 1975, only a few Church members who spoke Spanish as their first language could be found in Utah. Within a few years, there were more than twenty Spanish-speaking congregations along Utah's Wasatch Front. Spanish-speaking Hispanics, many also English-speaking, have become the Church's preeminent sub-culture. In 2002, when the Church numbered about eleven million members worldwide, South America counted two and a half million members, Mexico about 900,000, and Central America about 472,000.[41] Migrations from these areas have led to Spanish-speaking wards within many stake boundaries.

James W. Lucas, writing on "Mormons in New York City," described how overall Church membership there increased from 6,500 in 1990 to 17,000 in 1998 during the years of heightened Hispanic migration. By the end of 1998, twenty-one of the forty-six LDS congregations in the city spoke Spanish. The Mormon Latinos in Manhattan and the Bronx are mostly Dominicans; in Brooklyn, most come from Mexico. Many joined the Church in their own countries and so have leadership experience. (Most black members come from the West Indies, some from Africa.) About 20 percent of the ethnic converts in New York City are illegal immigrants, which will test the Mormon belief that Church membership facilitates upward economic mobility.[42]

White members, mostly from the western United States, may comprise only 10 to 15 percent of all LDS New Yorkers, but with their experience and education, they dominate the high leadership positions, a fact some Latinos resent. The two groups also have different personal styles. To Hispanic members with their openness and food-related socials and a preference for visiting before and after meetings, Anglo Americans seem too business-like, even rude, leaving right after meetings. Joaquin Arcia of Nicaragua calls his branch his family. "We all speak as friends, with love. We try to serve one another when there is the need to serve someone." When Spanish speakers go to English-speaking wards, they complain that Anglos won't speak to them or sit by them. Samuel Victor Miera said he was "ignored." Stella Maria Abraham Vallota of Argentina described members who "were doing all the nonverbal behaviors . . . like raising their voices, opening up their eyes, and acting as if 'are you understanding what I'm saying?'" She complained that whites considered her foreign even though she was a well-informed American citizen.[43]

Should ethnic Mormons attend racially segregated branches or wards? In 1992, there were at least 405 non-English-language wards and branches in the United States, more than half speaking Spanish. By 1997, the number had grown to at least 533, and two thirds were Spanish-speaking. Many bilingual young people attend with their families to retain their ethnic identities. Anoulone Viphonsanarath, a Laotian who joined the Church in northern Virginia, felt that the ethnic branches provided a necessary transition after conversion, but dealing with the cultural diversity of Southeast Asians was difficult. "We have Cambodians, Laotians, and Vietnamese together. . . . Our languages are totally different. . . . It is not a big barrier. I don't think the problem is so big that it would stop people from going to church." A completely Cambodian ward was organized in Long Beach, California, in 2005.[44]

How this ethnic segregation is to be dealt with remains a question. New ethnic congregations are organized as others are dissolved. Language difference is divisive. English and Spanish speakers smile and co-exist, reluctant to attempt conversations. Yet in five to ten years, this ethnic diversity will characterize every LDS area, even the Utah heartland. The 2000 Census found about 9 percent of the Utah population was Latino and posited that this was an undercount. Mormons in Utah have difficulty realizing how Latinized the state has become. Jorge Iber, who studied the Spanish speakers in northern Utah, found that by the 1990s, the missionary effort had led to the migration of thousands of Spanish speakers into the state, mostly from Mexico, many of them not Mormons. The migrating Mormons, however, had the advantage of instantly connecting with the most powerful institution and network in the state.[45]

To acknowledge the change in ethnic composition, the Church staged a completely Spanish-speaking Christmas devotional in Salt Lake City in 2002. This first-ever event was so popular, with 13,000 in attendance, that it was moved from the Tabernacle to the much larger Conference Center. General authorities spoke, and a 500-voice, Hispanic choir sang. Ignacio Garcia, a professor at Brigham Young University, thought the event was "fantastic" and "long due coming." He welcomed the recognition that Hispanic Latter-day Saints are a "significant, growing population that isn't going away." Mike Martinez, a local attorney who wrote for the *Deseret News,* noted, "It's not about 'tolerance' any more, it's about 'acceptance.'" Chilean Ricardo Carvajal was delighted. "Whenever you see a thousand Hispanics," he said, "you know there are 10,000 more that would love to be there. We could have packed the place. But you know us," he joked. "We tend to arrive a little late to things—so late, sometimes, that we don't arrive at all." The speakers, including high Church officials, told personal stories and spoke Spanish, though some did not know the language. "I felt proud," said Carvajal. "I felt important. And I felt happy for those who will follow me. I can speak English, but I love to speak Spanish. And it was wonderful to hear the apostles speak Spanish. Next time, we might even hear some native Spanish speakers who are becoming our leaders in the church." Additional all-Spanish programs have been held since. "Luz de las Naciones," a celebration of Latino culture, was presented before 16,250 people in the LDS Conference Center in 2004.[46]

Throughout the history of the Church, missionaries have gone out to preach the gospel. Sometimes the lineage identity of new converts has limited their opportunities in contrast to the Church's universalistic aims. But as Armand Mauss explains in his book, *All Abraham's Children*, as "the racialist framework ceased to be useful and began to encumber rather than facilitate the worldwide growth of Mormonism, it was gradually abandoned." The old teachings have never been officially repudiated; they just fell into disuse. By the end of the twentieth century, "early Mormon universalism once again dominated official discourse."[47]

CLASS

Since the beginning, the Church has attracted socially and financially disadvantaged converts. Early Latter-day Saint converts were drawn from poor farmers and factory workers. Today converts come predominantly from the lower-middle and working classes. In developing countries, Mormons are typically peasant families displaced to cities. With its promise of stability and transcendence, Mormonism appeals to poor and unsettled people who want to improve their lives. And the Church does help them; families that stay with the Church tend to rise. Habits of thrift, sacrifice, and diligence have helped members to enter the middle class.

The influx of converts means that in many congregations poor people mix with prosperous members. The rich are often very generous, but the tension between rich and poor is still a problem. In the scriptural ideal, the pure in heart live together harmoniously, all contributing their talents and labor for the good of all. In the Book of Mormon, the Church after Christ's visit to America held all things in common. In the city of Enoch, an example to the early Church, "The Lord called his people Zion, because they were of one heart and one mind, and dwelt in righteousness; and there was no poor among them."[48] This utopian vision has been scripturally and practically presented to Mormons since early times, but attempts to live the "United Order," under which goods were equalized or held in common, have always failed. They may live the United Order someday. For now, they practice generous capitalism.

Some Mormons have condemned capitalism and its attendant materialism as ungodly. Hugh Nibley, a learned LDS scholar of the ancient world who took strong positions against worldliness and war, thought private property stood in the way of a perfect society. "Zion has [always] been pitted against Babylon, and the name of the game has always been money—'power and gain.'"[49] The capitalists, he asserted, are not building up the Kingdom of God but only themselves. He noted that the Scriptures accept only one reason for seeking wealth: to help the poor. He saw the law of the marketplace marking an "expansive, acquisitive, brittle, untrustworthy, predatory society."[50]

Others Mormons are more positive about capitalism. Unabashed by the early ideals, some LDS leaders and Brigham Young University professors defend it as the way to succeed personally and improve the world.[51] They praise the elements of the market system: freedom of choice and action, private ownership of property, incentives for investment, and productive effort. Historically no other system has promoted prosperity like capitalism, and the success of the Saints in business has enabled them to support a welfare system that aids the poor.[52] Many smart young Mormons go to graduate school in business and work hard to succeed in corporate or entrepreneurial worlds. Utah has its share of millionaires and billionaires, many of whom pay a full 10 percent of their income to the Church.

In practice, the conflict works itself out in congregations where poor, uneducated converts will sometimes mingle with established business and professional people. Congregations are organized geographically, and rich and poor mix in communities where Church membership is thin. In cities such as New York, Chicago, and Boston, people of all classes worship together, but in densely populated Mormon areas in Utah and California, neighborhood segregation leads to Church segregation, perpetuating race and class division. Citizens living in large and expensive homes on the East Bench of Salt Lake City may never meet poor minorities. This means that the educated and affluent can easily abandon the inner city and attend church only with people like themselves.

An experimental program, the Salt Lake Inner-City Project, attempts to break down that pattern by assigning middle-class Latter-day Saints to impoverished wards in the center of the city. These service missionaries meet with families to provide friendship and advice, referring medical, dental, and financial problems to on-call experts. This program, begun in 1996, grew rapidly. In 2003, more than 500 missionaries were helping out in ninety-three inner-city wards. They work in the wards for an average of two years, often preferring them to their own neighborhoods.

Outside of Utah, rich and poor are more likely to congregate to worship. In areas lightly populated with Mormons many neighborhoods are needed to constitute a ward. Local leaders will often gerrymander the boundaries to achieve a mix so that experienced leadership is available to help the newly converted. Middle-class neighborhoods yield Mormons who can run organizations, teach classes, and make the local organization work. These experienced leaders teach less experienced members Church traditions. Although each congregation has a character of its own, this wide spectrum of incomes, education, and Church experience is the standard pattern.

This mix is harder to achieve in rapidly growing Church populations in Latin America, Africa, and the Philippines where the poor, uneducated, and inexperienced predominate. A scattering of Latter-day Saint expatriates helps out, and are indeed vital, but their numbers are too small to keep congregations going. The need for native leadership and the hope to help new converts get ahead has led to a program to aid upward social mobility in developing countries. President Gordon B. Hinckley introduced the Perpetual Education Fund (PEF) at April Conference in 2001, noting the similarity to the nineteenth-century Perpetual Emigrating Fund, which loaned transportation costs to Mormon immigrants. President Hinckley spoke of the dilemma of faithful members who serve missions and return home to unemployment and poverty. They had been brother missionaries with comparatively wealthy Anglos, wearing shirts and ties every day, and sleeping in neat apartments. After their missions, the Anglos returned home to college and prosperity, whereas their brothers from developing countries went back to crowded slums.

To break the cycle of poverty, Hinckley proposed Church educational loans at minimal (3 percent) interest. The loans, which come from member donations, mainly North Americans, pay for training programs in auto mechanics, banking, computer programming, hotel administration, and similar practical vocations. Funds go directly to schools as tuition. "We must do all we can to help [our people] to lift themselves, to establish their lives upon a foundation of self-reliance that can come of training. Education is the key to opportunity." The PEF, administered through the Church Educational System or CES, with no overhead costs, was immediately successful. The first year, contributions came from 250,000 people.[53]

Returning from a mission without skills, Rodolfo Uribe of Mexico, an early graduate of an experimental version of the program, studied welding at a Church-owned high school in Mexico City and later at Ricks College, now BYU–Idaho. He became an instructor himself. "I didn't have a good job and I didn't know how to do anything." Now, he says, "many companies want to pay me to work for them, but I stay with this program because I feel the hand of the Lord." Other early attendees have moved into management or started businesses.[54]

In eighteen months, the PEF loaned about $700 each to 5,360 students, mostly returned missionaries, planning expansion to 100,000 annually within ten years. The average student is twenty-six years old and will need two and a half years of training; 40 percent of the recipients are women. Elder John K. Carmack, who runs the program, says students follow the agenda of mission, temple, and education for a brighter future.[55]

The process of converting people at the bottom of the financial ladder continues, and Church resources help them. The money to build chapels and temples comes from the United States, as does the money for mission support. Now developing countries have the PEF to help poor converts improve their status. As children acquire more education, they improve the prospects for future generations. This commitment to helping the poor is ground into the Mormon ethos from the old Zion principle. Mormons have been accused of perpetuating class distinctions through their zealous involvement with capitalism, but in partial response, the PEF transfers wealth from the beneficiaries of capitalism to populations still trying to get a foot on the ladder.

The days when The Church of Jesus Christ of Latter-day Saints was primarily made up of white, English-speaking U.S. citizens have ended. The typical Mormon of the twenty-first century is tan or dark-skinned, urban poor or working class from a Latino background. He or she will not speak English.[56] Such people introduce into the Church the most divisive social issues of our time—race, ethnicity, and class. Like every other church and social group, Mormons have suffered from and coped with these tensions. Some of the tensions have been magnified by peculiar Mormon doctrines and practices. Yet breaches have been healed too. The race issue is less tense than it used to be. The class issue is addressed on many fronts. Another generation will likely resolve current ethnic tensions, even as new groups arrive and new tensions develop.

GENDER AND SEXUAL ORIENTATION

Women are useful, not only to sweep houses, wash dishes, make beds and raise babies.

—*Brigham Young*, 1869

The Church's leadership at almost every level is male. Most meetings are run by men in dark suits. Mormon men are actively engaged in church work in every congregation. As men are recruited, encouraged, refined, groomed, tried and tested, they become strong leaders. Men are essential. During years with heavy family and business obligations, men serve the Church.

The Church produces strong, capable women also, who like men serve despite heavy family, school, and work obligations. Usually outnumbering the active males in a congregation, women are considered their equals in spirituality, intellect, efficiency, human relations, and hard work. Mormons know that their all-volunteer congregations would collapse without this participation. Yet men hold priesthood, while women do not.

In the folklore that explains the disparity, some say the priesthood is necessary to make the men equal to women. Others say the priesthood should be a men-only club because if women were in charge, the men would retreat. Without serious duties, the men would stay home and watch football. Eileen Gibbons Kump, in a collection of her short stories, imagined premortal women having the choice of "sayso or sense." They took the sense and pretended to be obedient, leaving the sayso to the men.[1]

One convert said: "I've never seen such active, liberated women as in the church. I've never been to any other church where women spoke equally with the men. I think it is good that the men have a separate priesthood and the women aren't permitted to participate in it. That must sound strange because I am a feminist. . . . Look how the women run Relief Society. Can you imagine if they ran the church? The men would be totally out of a job."[2]

Socialization maintains the division. One young woman described her childhood: "I accepted authoritarianism when I was growing up. The husband was the undisputed and unquestioned leader of the home. The woman's role was to support and take counsel. My father was probably on the liberal end of the spectrum. . . . He respected my mother's talents and abilities and always supported what she wanted to do. I didn't, though, ever need anymore justification for doing something than that my dad wanted it that way."[3]

For the past quarter century, the gender roles have been debated in the Church. Are men and women equal in what seems to be a patriarchal institution? Do women want and should they have the priesthood? Is the mother's job valued? Should women avoid careers outside the home? The answers are clear to some but contradictory to others.

The issue goes back to the post-World War II years when Mormons led the return to American domesticity and suburbia. After a decade or so, the Church continued to stand by its conservative ideas as the nation moved toward a liberal counter-culture in the 1960s. In fact, in the Church's organizational structure, women's leadership roles were brought more firmly under the priesthood. Mormon women, who follow but lag behind national trends, faced a divided culture. In the 1950s they had exemplified the ideal American woman; by the1970s, some felt left behind. Many relished their traditional roles; a feminist minority felt ostracized.

This minority looked to Mormonism's past for models. Nineteenth-century Mormon women got the franchise in 1870, long before U.S. women did in 1920. Women's advocates Susan B. Anthony and Elizabeth Cady Stanton visited Utah on their western trips. Utah women's suffrage lasted only until 1887, when federal legislation disenfranchised all Church members and all females, but later Mormons used this short progressive experiment as evidence of male liberality. As further evidence, nineteenth-century male leaders encouraged Mormon women to seek education, and Utah had a high percentage of early female doctors. Mormon women often worked for pay, encouraged by Brigham Young, who said, "We believe that women are useful, not only to sweep houses, wash dishes, make beds and raise babies, but they should stand behind the counter, study law or physic, [medicine] or become good bookkeepers and be able to do the business in any counting house, and all this to enlarge their sphere of usefulness for the benefit of society at large. In following these things they but answer the design of their creation."[4]

Progressive LDS women were disappointed by the contracted role male leaders installed for them in the 1970s and 80s. Women have been busy with large families and congregational duties. They may not have noticed that their voices had been absent at the higher levels. But the institutional changes have increased priesthood powers and decreased women's responsibilities. Women have lost visibility and are scarcely involved in areas where they had been prominent: welfare, leadership training, publishing, and policy setting. Whereas LDS women had once assumed responsibility for running women's, children's, and cultural activities, they found themselves with less autonomy, just as American women pressed for greater influence.

A vocal minority staunchly believes that Joseph Smith did give women the priesthood or intended to. Upon founding the Relief Society in 1842, he said, "I now turn the key to you in the name of God and [the Relief Society] shall rejoice and knowledge and intelligence shall flow down from this time." Keys symbolize authority in the Church. But did he mean turn the key over to you or turn it in your direction? Whatever plans Joseph Smith may have had for women have been obscured by his untimely death, subsequent policies, and ambiguous documents. The phrase "I now turn the key to you" in the original minutes was edited to read in the 1850s, "I now turn the key in your behalf." In 1958, Joseph Fielding Smith, head of the Twelve Apostles, explained, "While the sisters have not been given the priesthood, it has not been conferred upon them, that does not mean the Lord has not given unto them authority," distinguishing between authority and priesthood.[5]

Some accommodations to the changed role of women have been made in recent years including an annual women's meeting and female speakers at General Conference. The Church teaches that gender roles are separate but equal, and that woman's place is in the home. Probably the majority of married Mormon women are content in the home. Those without husbands or children feel deprived and would be happy to fill the roles of mother and wife if they could. Others feel patronized by rhetoric equating priesthood with motherhood, asymmetrically leaving out "fatherhood" and "not scriptural."[6] Most LDS women tend to be good-natured and pragmatic: they work on the things they can change and forget the rest.

Lori G. Beaman, a Canadian sociologist, interviewed twenty-eight LDS women and categorized their strategies for negotiating relationships in the family, church, and society in three styles: the submissive Mormons, the moderates, and the Mormon feminists. Most LDS women, said Beaman, considered the priesthood a service-oriented calling, requiring heavy labor with few rewards. Only feminists saw the priesthood in terms of power. Moderates saw priesthood as strengthening man's weak nature. Submissive Mormons celebrated the male priesthood, equating it with their motherhood. Each group interpreted the teachings in accord with their own relationships to the Church.[7]

A picture of the ideal LDS woman can be found in descriptions of general authorities' wives. Tributes to one recently deceased woman characterized her as "a faithful, gentle friend who shared her rich love, testimony and talent with folks of all stations, a regal and refined woman who never forgot her farm girl good sense." She would be remembered for her "selflessness, patience and kindness and for her love of family, the Church and music." When she died in 2005, a mother of ten, grandmother of more than fifty, and great-grandmother of many more, she was remembered for the "wonderful, loving spirit about her." She enjoyed reading, "watching old movies," and had a knack for quilting, cooking, and sewing. She had made countless prom dresses and ballet costumes. This is the warm, loving, and supportive model that LDS women aspire to.[8]

Women who attempt to gain more voice in Church matters have focused on two issues: the ordination of women to the priesthood and the worship of "Mother in Heaven," the female consort of God who has had no earthly incarnation. The first would require a reshaping of the priesthood and family roles, and sharing a burden many do not want. A professional woman, a member of thirty years, said that she never wanted the priesthood. She had found ample opportunities to help others. She did note, however, that she sometimes wished priesthood leaders were "more mature, secure, humble and more sensitive to the feelings and challenges of and input from women." Still, women should "cease perceiving [themselves] as oppressed by men and begin to [act] WITH them."[9]

Most activist women look for self-expression in nonconfrontational ways that stop short of demanding priesthood. Lisa Butterworth, an Idaho mother of three children under the age of four, felt she could not talk in church meetings about history or feminism. "I wasn't interested in bashing the church; I wanted to find something that could be faithful, liberal and feminist." She created an online blog, FeministMormonHousewives.blogspot.com where she and like-minded women could discuss the daily challenges of mothering young children and the frustration they felt with the "limited roles women have in The Church."[10]

Feminist Lori Winder Stromberg took a more militant position on the priesthood when she noted that "feminists are constantly seen as being power hungry. . . . Perhaps I am power hungry, but my question is: Why aren't you, too? If by power hungry you mean wanting women to have a voice in the church, then yes, I am power hungry."[11]

When President Hinckley was asked in 1998 about women getting the priesthood, he said another revelation, which he did not anticipate, would be required. "The women of the Church are not complaining about it. They have their own organization, a very strong organization, four million plus members. I don't know of another women's organization in the world which does so much for women as this Church has. They're happy. . . . I don't hear any complaints about it." He repeated the same view in 2000. "The women have their place . . . they have a voice in determining policy and doing many things in the church. I haven't found any complaint among our women. I'm sure there are a few, a handful somewhere who may be disaffected."[12] Significant change is unlikely.

Attention to the second issue, Mother in Heaven, would make women more visible, advocates of the doctrine say, and add a familial aspect to the Church. The shadowy Mormon Mother in Heaven, is known only from Eliza R. Snow's poem, "O My Father," written in the early 1840s. Her quotation is "In the heav'ns are parents single? / No, the thought makes reason stare! / Truth is reason; truth eternal / Tells me I've a mother there" (Hymns 292). Snow, the preeminent LDS poet of the nineteenth century, later said the doctrine came from Joseph Smith, though he made no record of it. The idea is well accepted by inference and analogies to earth life: If there is a father, there must be a mother. Mother in Heaven's lack of definition allowed Her to be created according to individual desires. President Spencer W. Kimball characterized Her in 1978 as "the ultimate in maternal modesty" and "restrained queenly elegance." According to this interpretation, She has been shielded to protect Her privacy.[13]

From 1980 on, feminist LDS women fastened on this doctrine. Essays were published and prayers were offered. Official disapproval soon followed, labeling praying to Mother in Heaven "inappropriate" and the "beginnings of apostasy." No scriptural record showed Jesus praying to anyone but His Father in Heaven. Priesthood leaders were firmly urged to correct this usage "without equivocation."[14] Leaders may have feared a cult of the Mother in Heaven or the skirting of patriarchal structure. Perhaps they disliked the feminist source of the practice.

Speaking in 2002, Elder Cree-L Kofford laid out the roles of men and women in a pointed talk at BYU–Idaho. According to Kofford, Satan is the author of the design that makes women dissatisfied with home life:

> In an effort to draw all of God's children from the paths of righteousness, Satan has used deception from the beginning. His tools to destroy men have included pornography, alcohol, tobacco, dishonesty, greed and power. That plan, however, was only "marginally successful" because Satan had one fatal flaw in his plan: he forgot about the power of womanhood.

> Throughout that period, as men were bombarded with all that Lucifer's arsenal held, the vast majority of womanhood remained as faithful daughters of God. They were, by their nature, pure, clean, uplifting, strengthening and building. Where men would falter, women would encourage. Where men would doubt, women would believe. And in the process of this relationship, women inspired men to be able to withstand the entreaties of Lucifer, and thus his efforts brought only marginal return. . . .

> At some point, a careful plan was devised that would cause women to be dissatisfied with womanhood of old and seek to substitute it with womanhood as defined by Lucifer and his forces.

> In Place of modesty came immodesty. In place of superior standards came mediocre standards. In place of lifting and building all of mankind came becoming like mankind. Wifehood and motherhood became phrases to describe duties not honors. Devotion to home and family was replaced by the desire for status and power. A job, an office and a title replaced the nurturing of children, the encouragement of husband, and the honor of motherhood.[15]

"Modern" women, according to Kofford, had clearly lost their way.

Women feel they are sometimes given contradictory lessons. James E. Faust, then an Apostle, advised young women in 1986, "You should work very hard to prepare for your future by gaining marketable skills. . . . The struggle to improve the place of women in society has been a noble cause and I sincerely hope the day will come when women with equal skills will be fully equal with men in the marketplace." But just six months later, in a satellite broadcast address later published, Church President Ezra Taft Benson proposed another view. "Contrary to conventional wisdom, a mother's calling is in the home, not in the marketplace. . . . It was never intended by the Lord that married women should compete with men in employment. . . . Too many mothers work away from home to furnish sweaters and music lessons and trips and fun for their children. . . . Wives, come home from the typewriter, the laundry, the nursing; come home from the factory, the café."[16]

This talk by the Lord's prophet struck consternation into the hearts of many Mormon women. A majority of LDS mothers, as a survey taken at the time found, were then working, using their salaries for sweaters and music lessons as well as rent and food. The large families, low wages, and high aspirations of many homemakers took them into the marketplace. They were also motivated by a quest for significance and a desire to use their talents beyond their homes. What were they to do when the Church president spoke against working outside the home?

A pair of sociologists interested in reactions to Benson's talk studied a sample of 3,000 Utah women between the ages of twenty and sixty and found that about half of the LDS mothers, or 47 percent, accepted the prophetic instruction as binding despite economic stress. Another 6 percent accepted the message although they were angry, guilty, depressed, and resentful. Thirty-seven percent accepted the counsel with qualifications such as financial need. Six percent felt that they were in harmony if they worked while their children were at school. Only 3 percent rejected the message entirely, considering it unrealistic and out-of-date. Faithful women complained of a mixed message from the Church. Told to stay home, they saw career women honored whereas homemakers were overlooked. They resented newspaper articles praising professional women, ignoring stay-at-home mothers. Women struggle to comply with the instructions.[17] Some conservatives, for instance, engage in childcare, paper routes, and cottage industry to make money without officially working. Others begin work later in their lives or claim they would rather be home.

This research suggests that the majority of Church women are devoted, obedient, and uncritical. A minority of Mormon women want more. When President Hinckley said in 2000 that he had not "found any complaint among our women," several women fired off rebuttals. A letter to the editor of the *Boston Globe* from Courtney Black, an LDS woman from Seattle, and Maxine Hanks, the writer of *Women and Authority: Reemerging Mormon Feminism*, a book leading to her excommunication, argued that LDS women were not content. The writers complained, "If we disagree, we reap trouble; if we relent, we lose our voice." Women could conform or leave, intimidated into compliance. They "bear great responsibility for the success of our community without power to define our responsibility or ensure its success." In the past, writers have noted, our grandmothers gave blessings, created policy, led women's programs, and published women's views. Later on, women who disagreed with men's decisions were "ignored or dismissed, marginalized or ostracized." "Men do not speak for Mormon women, we speak for ourselves."[18]

Their letter caused dismay. Criticism of the prophet is not popular. Even feminists declined to be represented by Black and Hanks. One widely circulated e-mail from Elizabeth Harmer Dionne called the Church a feminist organization where "Mormon women find emotional support and personal and spiritual growth. . . . The Relief Society . . . provides a network through which we learn from, socialize with, and serve one another." Dionne, in a characteristic female strategy, reached beyond the patriarchal structure to a relationship with the Deity. The Church offered the redeeming power of Christ and was indispensable. Dionne nevertheless acknowledged merit in the Black/Hanks argument. More active female roles would "certainly ease any perceptions of unfairness in the LDS church policy" when "undeniably good men nevertheless misunderstand the needs and desires of women."[19]

Defining suitable women's lives has led to political involvement. In the 1970s, the feminist movement collided with the Church's emphasis on motherhood. The collision played out nationally with official opposition to the proposed Equal Rights Amendment to legalize gender equality. Church conservatives saw the amendment as threatening traditional roles. The idea, however, was nationally popular, and both houses of Congress passed the amendment in 1972 and sent it to the states. Thirty-three, of the needed thirty-eight states, quickly ratified the amendment.

Conservative groups in and out of the Church feared the ERA would destroy the family. The inflammatory rhetoric threatened free sex, birth control, abortion, and daycare centers. Some argued the ERA would allow the government to combat sexism in churches. The *Salt Lake Tribune*, the non-Mormon newspaper, feared the ERA might nullify women's protective legislation. The Church took no early stand.

Barbara B. Smith, general president of the Relief Society, was called into the Church's Special Affairs office soon after assuming her responsibilities in 1974. The leaders told her that it was appropriate for her to oppose the ERA if she felt so inclined. Committee members had gathered information on how best to defeat the ERA and suggested a direction. Her much publicized speech in December 1974 at the University of Utah suggested that the ERA was not the way to improve women's position. The amendment was too broad, too vague, too threatening. In January 1975, the "Church News" section of the *Deseret News* published an unsigned editorial opposing the ERA. State legislators interpreted the editorial as an official stand, whereas the Church stressed that members had "free agency" to decide for themselves. In 1975, pro-ratification Utah legislators switched sides to defeat the ERA fifty-four to twenty-one. When, in 1976, thirty-four states had ratified, and only four more were needed for passage, the Church began work against the ERA. Idaho rescinded ratification after a strong speech by an LDS leader.

In June 1977, grass-roots Church members were mobilized at the International Women's Year meeting. An IWY meeting was organized in every state, and in Utah, each congregational Relief Society recruited ten women to attend the conference. Some delegates were told to vote according to their conscience; others were specifically instructed to oppose the ERA. Organizers, expecting 3,000 women to attend, were nonplussed by 13,000. The Utah delegates shouted at others and voted down all national proposals. Some faithful Mormon women felt humiliated and betrayed by this behavior and defected, and the Church took some severe media hits. Barbara Smith later said that the Relief Society had been used by the far right.

Some LDS women organized Mormons in support of the ERA. The Virginia group was particularly strong and became increasingly confrontational. Their audacious highpoint was hiring a plane to fly a banner over the location of General Conference, the semi-annual, Church-wide meeting in Salt Lake City. "Mother in Heaven Supports the ERA," read the banner, declaring two feminist issues. The outspoken leader Sonia Johnson polarized her listeners. In one speech she said, "The very violence with which the brethren attacked an amendment which would give women human status in the Constitution abruptly opened the eyes of thousands of us to the true source of our danger and our anger."

Johnson was summoned to a disciplinary hearing in November 1979 and excommunicated for "evil speaking of the Lord's anointed." She was told that her attacks against the Church and its leaders had damaged such programs as temple attendance, the welfare program, family home evening, genealogy, and especially missionary work.

Are Mormonism and feminism at odds? Many Mormons think so. Others, who consider themselves both good Mormons and good feminists, do not. In one survey, more than half of Church members supported the content of the Equal Rights Amendment, when that content was not identified for them as the ERA, even after the First Presidency statements.[20]

In 1982, the ERA was defeated. Mormon activity had been instrumental, though not decisive, in the campaign. The controversy showed the determination of the Church to act on issues deemed threatening, mobilizing members to spend time, energy, and money. Mormon women were actively involved in politics, many for the first time. They wrote letters, organized, and demonstrated. The hierarchy successfully planned and directed a vast campaign across the nation, lobbying effectively. But some believing Mormons were dismayed by what seemed subterfuge and misrepresentation, hidden aims and actions.[21] By fighting against the ERA, the Church seemed to be reversing its pro-feminist, nineteenth-century style.

In 1975, early in the process, Elouise Bell, an English professor at Brigham Young University and a moderate, had urged the benefits of feminism.

> Let it not be said that BYU or the Latter-day Saint people stood on the sidelines while great and needed social reforms were taking place in the twentieth century. . . . To all those in the BYU community, I extend the challenge to examine the issues of feminism, to make decisions about them individually on the basis of reason and the light of truth within you, to welcome a new day when women can hold on to all that is traditionally fine and right and God-given and God-ordained and to encompass as well new alternatives, new options, greater fulfillment of potential, and an ever-increasing responsibility and desire and willingness to do our share in building the kingdom of God.[22]

Just four years later in 1979, a group of feminist Mormon women claiming to represent a "sizeable minority" of LDS women wrote to Spencer W. Kimball, then president of the Church, in a different tone.

> Dear President Kimball:
> Suddenly many devoted Mormon women are being treated like apostates. . . . We desperately need to know whether, after serious consider-

ation, soul-searching, and prayer, you . . . find us unworthy, a minority open to attack, and ultimately expendable. . . . If not, can the word get out that Mormon feminists are not to be subjected to intimidation, rejection for Church assignments, loss of employment, and psychological excommunication? . . . We are women who love the Lord, the gospel, and the Church; we have served, tithed, and raised righteous children in Zion. We plead for the opportunity to continue to do so.[23]

Mormon feminism has not been stamped out, but it has certainly receded since its high point in the 1980s. Groups have continued to meet outside of Church networks. They have gathered for discussion and activity. Some have met monthly, and several well-established groups have met annually for weekend retreats or revivals.

For comparison, there is the huge, official Relief Society, a sprawling women's organization with a chapter in each congregation. In pioneer times the Relief Society women met in their own buildings, heavily involved in large economic efforts like grain saving, silk manufacture, and home industry. Through the 1950s the groups met on weekdays to study homemaking skills, history, and literature. The women quilted, preserved food, and nursed the sick. Each woman, serving as a "visiting teacher," met monthly with a few other women assigned to them, keeping tabs on their spiritual and economic welfare.

Although visiting teaching remains a central Relief Society program, most of the larger activities have ceased. Since 1980, Relief Society has been an hour-long Sunday meeting with prayers, songs, and a short lesson. A monthly, evening, "enrichment" meeting teaches some homemaking skills, but the focus is now on the doctrinal message taught during worship services. A visit to one of these Relief Societies shows the organization in action. This New York City Relief Society meets at 9 A.M., the first third of the block of Sunday church meetings. Attendance is thin at first, but by 9:15 the room is full. The Relief Society president, a vibrant young mother of three, teaches a lesson on visiting teaching. Most sisters there "visit and teach" several women, some who attend church, others who don't, and has women who visit and teach her. The Relief Society aims to visit every member monthly but usually falls short. The president praises the good work being done, avoiding statistics. She admits that many sisters are tired of visiting teaching. She knows some of her listeners don't visit at all, that some visit as a matter of duty, and that few are enthusiastic. She used to be bored by the program herself. She urges the sisters to pray for direction and help because "charity never faileth."

In a short testimony meeting following the lesson, a woman carrying a toddler tells of her conversion to visiting teaching. Early on, she was not interested. Later, because of the friendship it supplied, she would die without it. Visiting teaching allows for mutual intimacy. A young single woman in another congregation said, "I see the members in a different light—at home with their families. Sometimes at church we want everyone to see how good we are. I like to see the other side, the side that's vulnerable. It strengthens me. We'll be talking about the [visiting teaching] message and all of a sudden we'll get onto other things. It helps me see I'm not the only one who has to go through things. The strong bond between the women in Relief Society comes from visiting teaching."[24]

Church-wide Relief Society leaders try to give a positive message to everyone. The general presidency [in 2005 Bonnie Parkin, Kathleen Hughes, and Anne Pingree] preach the creation of a "global sisterhood" among their four million members. They want LDS women to "stop being judged for working or staying at home, being single, divorced or childless." They want women to feel "valued and supported and bolstered" in life, not alienated and alone. The covenants of LDS women give them the strength of an "eternal perspective."[25]

These leaders urge the women to serve. "Here am I; send me," is one of their mottos. As Anne Pingree noted in a talk, "We can alter the face of the earth one family and one home at a time through charity, our small and simple acts of pure love." Bonnie Parkin has talked about self-reliance and welfare, noting that these principles mean having enough to share with others.[26]

Relief Society does not speak to everyone. A young single woman reported, "Most things in the church are geared toward families. People give talks about families and family home evening. That's why Relief Society and I never clicked. The lessons would be on health habits for your children or disciplining your children. I don't think there's too much emphasis on families, but they could put a little more on individuals. I'm not in the mainstream. When you're single you have to accept that in our church you're going to hear a lot about families."[27]

Single women felt greater inclusion after Sheri Dew, an unmarried author and publisher, joined the general presidency of the Relief Society in the 1990s. Dew's charismatic talks rallied singles as never before. She showed how a successful career woman, self-supporting and devoted to the Church, although questioning her single state and thwarted motherhood in public speeches, could make the standard categories work for her. She regarded all women, she said, even those without children, as mothers. "Motherhood is more than bearing children, it is the essence of who we are as women." "The Lord's timetable for each of us does not negate our nature. Some of us, then, must simply find other ways to mother."[28]

Without autonomy, women would seem to have little power in this religion. But what does it mean to be powerful in religion? Leadership seems important, but many religions, certainly most in the Judeo-Christian tradition, have stressed the humble vineyard worker as the powerful position. The greatest of all is the servant of all, as Jesus says in the gospels. Some are unconvinced. "I'm content to be at home with my family," a woman muses. "I would be even if I didn't have a family because I enjoy having the freedom that a job would take away from me, but sometimes I come away from Relief Society wondering how valuable I am, really. I wonder what will I have when my kids leave? What have I done with what my Heavenly Father has given me?"[29]

Other women are surer of their plans, aided by encouragement from Church periodicals that now recognize women who pursue serious out-of-the-home careers. Jessica T. Healy Ellsworth, featured in the *Church News*, dreamed of becoming a doctor. Married in 1975, she began college when her youngest child entered junior high and medical school when he turned eighteen. She served her medical residency at age forty-seven, finding it less demanding than being the mother of three. She did not regret the delay, having avoided the guilty struggle between medicine and motherhood. Her husband sold his business to move to medical school with her. "She supported me when I was going to school," he said. Mrs. Ellsworth explained that mothers, used to losing sleep, had many good years left. "If I could do it over again I would do it exactly the same way." Careers are acceptable—after meeting family responsibilities.[30]

Some couples, unwilling to postpone the wife's career, cooperate to help each other achieve professional goals. They go to school together, support each other, postpone having children, and share childcare so that both will have professional opportunities. Kathy Campbell, the mother of three, takes turns with her husband going to school, but she must still do her work. "By the time I run all the errands, fix dinner, play with the kids, and put them in bed, it's 10:30 and my husband's asleep. That's when I start studying for my classes." Young wives, used to balancing multiple activities, can often meet the conflicting demands of work, school, and family life.[31]

Probably all of these women would agree with Marjorie Pay Hinckley, the straight-talking wife of President Gordon B. Hinckley for sixty-six years, in her assertion that nothing was needed more than strong homes and families. She noted that her role in life had been a supportive one but felt no need to apologize. "I have known the frustrations of being a wife and a mother, but I have also known the joys." Her husband had always given her "space to fly. He never insisted that I do anything his way; it wouldn't have done him any good." She said that happy marriages came from getting used to each other, and she was finally used to her husband, and went on to say, "The other day as I watched him walk across the room I thought again of what an adorable little old man he has grown up to be."[32]

Despite the absence of the priesthood and only small roles in the general Church leadership, despite the encouragement to get education for home rather than career, despite little encouragement to go on missions and enter the professions—Mormon women are strong and effective, great achievers in education, professional life, and Church work. The ideal role of an LDS woman, judging from instruction given young women, is broadening. Each year a special meeting for women aged twelve to eighteen is conducted by adult women leaders and televised around the world. In the 2001 meeting, President Hinckley encouraged his listeners to "become the woman of whom you dream." "You are creatures of divinity, for you are daughters of the Almighty. . . . Magnificent is your future, if you will take control of it." He encouraged the girls to "find purpose in your life. Choose the things you would like to do and educate yourselves to be effective in their pursuit." The girls should be "qualified to serve society and make a significant contribution to the world." President Hinckley chose as a model a working woman. A skilled nurse he had met, a mother of three who "works as little or as much as she wishes," was the "kind of woman of whom you might dream, an educated, expert, loyal woman." Hinckley closed with a message of encouragement. "For you, the sky is the limit."[33]

SEXUAL ORIENTATION

As the Church was once considered to be racially prejudiced, so it is now considered to discriminate on the basis of sexual orientation. Church leaders have long stood against sexual relations between males and between females, asserting that those involved in same-gender relations harm spouses and children.

Historian D. Michael Quinn, the openly gay Mormon dissident, argues that same-sex relationships were tolerated in the early twentieth-century. Later leaders took a stronger stand. President David O. McKay considered homosexuality a "filthy and unnatural habit." In 1968, the *General Handbook of Instructions* added "homo-sexual acts" to other sins for which a person could be excommunicated. In 1976, the word was changed to "homosexuality." As with the Christian Right generally, strong negative reactions by LDS members have continued.[34]

Church leaders distinguish between homosexual feelings and homosexual activity. People may be helpless against the first, but they cannot act on their desires and remain in good standing.

> Our hearts reach out to those who struggle with feelings of affinity for the same gender. We remember you before the Lord, we sympathize with you, we regard you as our brothers and sisters. However, we cannot condone immoral practices on your part any more than we can condone immoral practices on the part of others. To be morally clean, a person must refrain from adultery and fornication, from homosexual or lesbian relations, and from every other unholy, unnatural, or impure practice.[35]

The justification for the pro-family (rather than anti-gay) activism is provided by the 1995 document, "The Family: A Proclamation to the World," which asserts the divine nature of the patriarchal, nuclear family and speaks implicitly against homosexuality. The Church has opposed recognition of same-sex marriage in several states, soliciting financial contributions and member labor, sharing the success of Nebraska's Initiative 416 against such unions. In 2003, eleven states recognized same-sex marriages; thirty-four states had so-called "Defense of Marriage" laws, but Nebraska's law alone banned any legal protections, health insurance, and other benefits for same-sex couples. This most extreme anti-gay law was challenged in federal court by the American Civil Liberties Union and struck down by a federal judge.[36] Meanwhile, the Supreme Court struck down Texas's anti-sodomy law.

U.S. senator Gordon Smith (R-Oregon), a Latter-day Saint, supports gay and lesbian political organizations. Although he does not agree with all the goals of the gay community, he wants fair treatment and protection against violence.[37] Senator Smith distinguishes between the civil rights of constituents and the policies of the Church.

The issue of homosexuality has struck close to home in conflicts within the Boy Scouts of America (BSA). The Church calls men to be scout leaders as Church service, and Mormons sponsor more than half of the national scout troops. In 1990, the BSA fired James Dale, a gay assistant scoutmaster from New Jersey. Dale appealed to the U.S. Supreme Court. The Court ruled in 2000, in a divided decision, that the BSA could exclude gay leaders. Public opinion divided over whether the organization should welcome all or exclude some.[38] Whereas the media and much of the public favored nondiscrimination, more conservative groups saw themselves preserving traditional lifestyles.

A year later, *Newsweek* magazine explored the issue, noting that Catholics and Mormons had together sponsored 750,000 scouts. Those churches had supported the Scout stand against homosexuality, although other churches opposed it; and the United Way, formerly a major supporter, had blocked and reversed gifts. Scout membership dropped 4 percent nationally. Some BSA executives, wishing to open membership to gay members and leaders, feared that the Mormons, with 400,000 scouts in Church troops, would fight the change, and if overruled, would bail out and start their own program. "The Mormons have all the cards," said one official.[39]

Mormon apologists object to gay Scout leaders because studies show that gays are more likely to abuse drugs and report a larger lifetime number of sexual partners. Apologists see boys' behavior as malleable, requiring leaders with healthful lifestyles. Camille Williams, the conservative columnist for online *Meridian Magazine*, said, "For gay activists to characterize those who disagree with them as ignorant, fearful, or prejudiced squelches public dialogue about public health issues and impoverishes moral reasoning on issues of central importance to individuals, families and organizations."[40]

Often unspoken in these debates is the fear that leaders, particularly homosexual leaders, will become abusers. The issues of homosexuality and pedophilia are intertwined, although most pedophiles are not homosexuals. Following in the wake of the abuse cases that rocked the Catholic Church are similar accusations and cases in Mormondom. As some respected Catholic priests have been accused of mistreating their young parishioners, so LDS priesthood and Boy Scout leaders have been accused of inappropriate behavior. Jeffrey Anderson, a Minnesota attorney who sued the Roman Catholic Church in sexual-abuse cases for twenty years, winning settlements of more than $60 million, surveyed green fields in Utah. "We're launching a major assault on the Mormon Church." He procured a $3 million settlement with the LDS Church in Oregon, charging that leaders knew of abuse they failed to report. In another Oregon case where the former scoutmaster was accused of six years of abuse, the attorney charged that the leader was acting as an employee or servant of both the Church and the Scouts, and both were liable. Several LDS scout leaders have pled guilty to similar charges. The Church has spoken out repeatedly against abuse and has pledged to "aggressively defend itself and its leaders."[41] As in the Catholic cases, the abuse is worse because it destroys public trust.

This disapproval of homosexuality, particularly same-sex marriage, could also be seen in the Church's support of California Proposition twenty-two, the Definition of Marriage Initiative known as the Knight Initiative for sponsor, State Senator William J. "Pete" Knight. The ballot measure prevented the recognition of same-sex marriages that might be performed in other states. Working within a coalition of conservative Christian churches, the LDS Church was involved in the election, which led to the endorsement of the measure by 61.4 percent of those voting. LDS leaders directed members to vote "Yes," to donate money, and to canvas voters door-to-door and by phone. During almost a year of activity, the involvement brought intense media scrutiny, some dissension in wards, and considerable pain to gay Mormons and their families.

The Church has been involved in similar efforts in Hawaii and Alaska where Church headquarters contributed more than one million dollars to bolster campaigns for successful "protection of marriage" ballot initiatives. In the California case, the members were encouraged to raise and donate the money and carry on the effort themselves. Letters were sent requesting specific amounts. Church involvement began in May 1999 with a letter signed by the North America West Area Presidency, which called on Church members in California to "do all you can by donating your means and time" to support the Knight Initiative. A later letter to the Church's Area Authority, identified as the request of the First Presidency, asked that "we assist in every proper way to assure passage of the Traditional Marriage Initiative." The Church has gone on to supporting the "Protection of Marriage" measures in Nevada and in Texas in 2003; 500 Church members showed up to support a bill banning same-sex unions. In 2004, Utahns voted to add a law banning same-sex marriage, already in force, to the state constitution. The Church had issued a statement backing such amendments.[42]

When the *San Francisco Examiner* investigated Church involvement in the issue in California, a Church spokesman said that although the message should be seen as "inspired and coming from the Lord," members had the "option" to oppose the measure. Some congregations were divided as active gay members, friends, and families charged the Church with exercising undue influence. Some thought that the fund-raising went "beyond the bounds" of appropriate church involvement.

Gays in the Church felt excluded. Stuart Matis, a thirty-two-year-old returned missionary, gay, and a believing member of the Church, called on BYU students to "re-assess their homophobic feelings. Seek to understand first before you make comments. We have the same needs as you. We desire to love and be loved. We desire to live our lives with happiness. We are not a threat to you or your families. We are your sons, daughters, brothers, sisters, neighbors, co-workers and friends, and most importantly, we are all children of God." Four days after this letter was published in the BYU *Universe*, Matis committed suicide on the steps of an LDS Church Stake Center. His former bishop, Robert A. Rees, noted at his funeral that although Matis had become "increasingly comfortable being truly and openly gay," he had difficulty feeling positive about himself "in the face of lifelong messages that told him such feelings were not only wrong, but that he was evil for having them."[43]

Few stories of Mormons with same-sex attraction end so bleakly. To support its contention that orientation is a choice rather than an inborn trait, the Church expends considerable energy and expense in a social services program with hundreds of full-time professionals trained in nationally accredited programs in social work, psychology, and marriage and family therapy. These professionals work with young Mormons who believe Church teachings even though private feelings lead them in other directions. They choose to undergo therapy to help them adjust to a heterosexual world. Not all who undergo therapy succeed, but apparently many do. Erin Eldridge, a Mormon woman who overcame her same-sex attraction, wrote *Born That Way?: A True Story of Overcoming Same-Sex Attraction, with Insights for Friends, Families, and Leaders*,[44] suggesting that others could do likewise. Like Eldridge, many Church members believe that same-sex attraction is a "confusion" to be overcome.

A vocal, liberal faction calls for a change in the Church's position, criticizing the public condemnation of homosexual acts. Others learn to work with the Church. At an AIDS retreat in Salt Lake City, organizer Dick Dotson said the Utah situation was like that of other places in the country. Dotson has a good working relationship with welfare officials who have provided food and clothing for the needy. The program gets all its eggs, butter, and milk from the Church and can even make emergency referrals, as bishops do. Several years ago, Dotson discussed AIDS and HIV with President Hinckley who offered the Church's help.[45]

There are some signs of greater tolerance for gays. A three-day Gay Pride event in Pocatello, Idaho, where Church membership is about 50 percent, was carried on with city cooperation. LDS leaders stayed out of the way, condoning the celebration and leaving controversy to other churches. Supporters noted that "Most people know someone who is gay." "Gays live in our communities. They have regular jobs, they have families, and they pay taxes." This stance in a small LDS community indicates a potential softening on this issue.

Many Church members would prefer to see some acknowledgement of same-sex unions, to see their brothers and sisters in committed long-term relationships rather than in promiscuous, temporary unions. Other members will want traditional boundaries enforced. The acceptance of same-sex marriages in Canada will put quiet pressure on the Church and the United States.

Aspects of sex and gender in all their variety form a crucial nexus in Latter-day Saint thinking. The official Church and millions of Church members are struggling to define gender roles in a rapidly changing world. Gay issues are hard for a slow-changing, basically conservative Church to respond to positively. The powerful image of a faithful family is behind these efforts. Mormons feel they are dealing with fundamental commandments in adhering to conservative standards. They wish to avoid hurting those caught in these crosscurrents, but the struggle inevitably introduces strains into Mormon life.

THE PUBLIC FACES OF MORMONISM

What a marvelous, wonderful thing it is, this church.

—*Gordon B. Hinckley*, 2002

In its first seventy years, the Church of Jesus Christ of Latter-day Saints largely looked inward. Missionaries traveled widely but made little effort to influence public opinion about the Mormons, even though negative views prevailed. Report after report implied that to join that outlaw sect was to turn one's back on civilization, propriety, and the law, and yet nineteenth-century Mormons made no systematic effort to combat the general disdain, concentrating instead on building up their own communities and strengthening their people.

Fleeing the United States for the desolate mountain valleys of Utah had not taken Mormonism out of the spotlight. Located along the overland trail, Utah was visited by curious reformers who wrote shocked exposés. In 1857, President James Buchanan, believing that the Mormon people were in rebellion, ordered troops to Utah from Fort Leavenworth, Kansas, to restore order. The Mormons prepared for war. They called home settlers from faraway outposts, sent their women and children into the mountains, and rather than lose their cities, prepared to torch them. They had to take a stand. California's Gold Rush had prevented further westward migration. It was Utah or nothing.

No shots were fired when the army arrived, but the Mormons lost control of their government with the imposition of a territorial governor and court. Images of Mormon insurrection colored eastern news accounts. Congress passed one punishing law after another beginning in 1862 with the Morrill Anti-Bigamy Act to destroy polygamy. President Lincoln did not enforce that act, and action was stalled for some years, but in 1882, the Edmunds Act disenfranchised all believers in polygamy, practicing or not. The Edmunds-Tucker Act of 1887 dissolved the Church's corporation, confiscated Church property, disinherited children of polygamous marriages, forbade LDS participation in government, and disenfranchised all women after twelve years of Utah female suffrage. More than 1,000 men went to prison for "unlawful cohabitation," and many others disappeared into the hiding places of the "underground." On appeal, the Supreme Court upheld the law. No despot could have more fully denied Utah civil rights than did the government. Over the years, six petitions for statehood were denied.

At this low point, LDS Church President Wilford Woodruff publicly foreswore the practice of polygamy, declaring his intention to submit to the laws forbidding plural marriage and urging others to do so. His document, the Manifesto, read at the Church's General Conference in 1890, stunned the congregation, who nonetheless raised their hands in unanimous approval. For fifty years the Church had preached, practiced, and protected this form of marriage. Suddenly it was stopped. The United States had disarmed, disenfranchised, and humbled the outlaws. In 1896, the nation granted statehood to the vast interior foreign enclave that became Utah.

Told from an eastern U.S. perspective, this story was the necessary and inevitable "winning of the West," the control and punishment of a sect threatening the values and morals of other North Americans. The trajectory is not unlike the treatment of Native Americans who were similarly driven west and warred with until no longer threatening. The experience of discrimination, persecution, and abridged civil rights underlies subsequent efforts of the Church to find a place for itself in American society. According to historian Mary Ellen Robertson, this history induced in Mormons a persecution complex. Sensitive to criticism and intolerant of critics, they see persecution as their test. Robertson calls this the "chosen people syndrome."[1]

Having been all but destroyed, the Mormons reconstructed their society after Utah's statehood, now on the basis of American patriotism and conventional morals. They became respectable, though largely remaining aloof from the larger society. In the early twentieth century, the Church made tentative forays into the greater world, achieving some success in government and education. Church leaders were generally respected, but were not often in the public eye outside of Mormondom. Visitors continued to visit Salt Lake City to probe for secrets, but when they published their findings, the Church ignored the damaging accounts.

This mainly isolationist stance lasted until the middle of the twentieth century when the Church, which had steadily grown in numbers, wealth, and influence, began to look outward, concerning itself with its public face. The Church organized a public relations office in Salt Lake City, and in the 1990s hired a New York public relations firm to shape the Church's public image. The Church began to send out news releases and respond to queries, trying to present a positive face to the public. The Tabernacle Choir, the semi-annual General Conference, the welfare and humanitarianism programs, and Mormon educational aspirations show Mormons at their best, countering less attractive images of a repressive Church with a clannish membership.

The huge Mormon Tabernacle Choir from Utah's primarily white, middle-class Mormon populace has been broadcasting inspirational music and hymns in the tabernacle since 1929 and is heard weekly on 2,000 radio, television, and cable stations worldwide. Along with a Christian commentary called "The Spoken Word," this music has become stay-at-home worship for thousands of listeners.

Membership in this body is hotly sought. To qualify, singers must pass through a series of strenuous auditions. Twice a year, half of the hundreds of applicants are invited to submit audition tapes. After a review of the tapes, fewer than half take a written exam. Half of those applicants go on to solo interviews and auditions. All must be worthy Latter-day Saints, between twenty-five and fifty-five, living within 100 miles of Salt Lake City. After twenty years or at age sixty, they must retire. The successful applicants, fifteen of the original large group, must be available for three rehearsals a week, performances, recordings, and trips. Choir members are not paid.[2]

The choir records, tours the country and the world, and sings at General Conference meetings in Salt Lake, another best-face occasion for the Church. The General Conference has outgrown the Salt Lake Tabernacle and moved to the 21,000-seat Conference Center, which fills completely at conferences in April and October. Mormons are addressed by their Church-wide leaders, the General Authorities, in five two-hour sessions—one for men only—in a worldwide virtual meeting. At this formal event, a large chorus sings; extensive and spectacular flowers grace the podium;

the dark-suited General Authorities are arrayed across the front of the hall flanked by a dozen women leaders in pastels.

All ward bishops and stake presidents used to come to Salt Lake City for conference, but now the meetings are televised, via satellite, to thousands of dimmed chapels. The Internet makes the messages increasingly accessible on members' computers in their own homes. Listeners take notes on general themes and on specific instructions and Church policy. At one conference, for example, they were told that new leaders had been called, that temple recommends would be valid for two years instead of one, and that Family Home Evening was newly encouraged. President Hinckley challenged his listeners "to rise to the divinity within you."[3]

The sessions are like large versions of ward sacrament meetings. But because members approve all the Quorum of the Twelve and First Presidency as "prophets, seers, and revelators," their talks carry greater weight than everyday sermons. The principle of continuing revelation means that the teachings of current leaders trump past teachings. The talks are not canonized as Scripture or included in the Doctrine and Covenants, but they stand above ordinary talks. Prepared in advance, vetted, and published in the Church magazine, they are frequently used as lesson material and as a source for Church members preparing sacrament-meeting talks.

Leaders also speak at stake conferences, when they visit to reorganize local leadership, and at special multi-stake events. In a typical instance, 25,000 Church members from the small Utah town of American Fork gathered in Brigham Young University's basketball stadium in Provo in 2002 to hear President Hinckley speak. Traffic was snarled for miles; people were lined up for seats. Crowds bunched in doorways and under hall speakers. President Hinckley's familiar message urged his listeners to believe in the teachings of the Church. Members should be grateful to pay their 10 percent tithing. "I look at other churches, struggling, even asking us for contributions to help them with their work," he said. He told the men to keep their priesthood sacred and stay away from "Internet sleaze." He urged his hearers to "believe in the divinity of this church. It isn't a burden serving the church. Why would it be a burden? Where would we be without it? What a marvelous, wonderful thing it is, this church."[4]

Similar meetings are held everywhere. In 2002, the Lartebiokoshi Stake of Ghana, held its tenth stake conference, extending this meeting style to Africa. The leaders, President Charles Sono-Koree and counselors

Emmanuel F. Sackey and Isaac Andoh-Kesson, spoke on issues familiar in American Fork. Given the theme of "Have Ye Spiritually Been Born of God?" the speakers warned that the philosophies of men could not replace the teachings of Jesus Christ.[5]

Listeners take conference messages seriously. Elder M. Russell Ballard's "Doctrine of Inclusion" encouraged Latter-day Saints to interact with people outside the Church, a theme increasingly heard in the last decade that acknowledges and tries to overcome the tendency toward clannishness. While loving each other, Church members are to be warm and friendly to strangers. The First Southern Baptist Church of Bountiful, Utah, benefitted from this attitude. The LDS neighbors pitched in to build a new chapel in 1999. The Relief Society brought lunch while the men framed, insulated, and roofed. Bill Cameron, chairman of the deacons for the Baptist group noted, "We were surprised to a certain extent to get LDS help. . . . [T]he neighbors have been very supportive, and we've really appreciated it." When a Baptist group purchased an old Mormon chapel in Oakland, California, they were invited to hold a fund-raiser in a larger Mormon building.[6]

Friendliness is more problematic when it comes to excommunicated Mormons. Disaffected Salt Lake Mormons complain of negative experiences after leaving the Church. Suzy Colver became "the neighborhood pariah." Her Mormon friends vanished, and she was no longer invited to volunteer at her kids' school. Another person was not allowed to say grace at Thanksgiving dinner. Excommunicated members often feel shunned and ostracized. Church promotion of inclusiveness has not yet been accepted by grass-roots members.[7] Theoretically as obligated to support former Mormons as anyone else, members feel awkward.

Mormons look better in the aid offered to the poor. Church leaders showed no interest in President George W. Bush's offer to channel government funds through religious organizations. The Church already distributes millions of dollars' worth of goods and services worldwide and wants to avoid dependence on the government. This tradition of mutual help goes back to pioneer days. In 1936 during the Great Depression, the Church organized an official welfare plan to create service opportunities, donate charitable goods, and find work for the unemployed. They aimed to establish industry, thrift, and self-respect, to do away with "the curse of idleness" and the "evils of a dole," and "to help the people to help themselves." Elaborate systems of welfare aid helped impoverished members with rent, employment, clothing, and food. When families are doing all they can and are still short, they can ask the bishop for temporary help. The bishop determines the needs and calls for goods or financial assistance in return for work.[8]

The welfare program is a natural extension of the Church's early cooperative ideal in a rural society. Farm-based production and volunteer labor underlie the system. In 1977, almost 150,000 acres of land were farmed. In 1985, the Church operated 199 farms, fifty-one canneries, about fifty grain storage facilities, and about eighty storehouses, large and small. Much of the manual labor is still assigned to wards and stakes whose leaders recruit volunteers to help with short-term tasks. By 1990, the Church was distributing commodities valued conservatively at $30 million a year. The system works because of the governing religious ideal. In 1986, Robert D. Hales, the presiding bishop of the Church, said, "The Welfare Plan builds a Zion people. . . . Zion is 'every man seeking the interest of his neighbor, and doing all things with an eye single to the glory of God'. . . . We need to understand that as much virtue can be gained in progressing toward Zion as in dwelling there. . . . The plan sanctifies both givers and receivers."[9]

Who gets helped and how well? The Church deals primarily with those capable of self-support whose income has been temporarily dis- rupted, usually helping for three or four months. The Church cannot replace long-term government assistance programs for the elderly and dis- abled. People need help while unemployed or ill, during family breakups, and while overcoming excessive debt. Under educated and large families, two-thirds of them male-headed, are typical on the welfare rolls. Formal welfare services are supplemented by informal Relief Society help— meals, house cleaning, and childcare. The program fills a gap for fewer than 5 percent of Mormons in the United States. Figures aren't given out, but counsel revealed in a legal dispute that in 1990 welfare services spent $4.6 million in Salt Lake City and in 1970 $17.7 million in Utah.[10] To sup- plement other resources, Fast Offerings, donations given monthly on fast day, go solely for poor relief.

Welfare Square, on seventeen acres in Salt Lake City, serves the local community with its bakery, cannery, dairy plant, granary, quality assur- ance lab, Deseret Industries retail store, and visitors' center. Deseret, a Book of Mormon word meaning "honey bee" Ether 2:3 Book of Mormon 1981, suggests that every worker bee does his or her part on behalf of the whole group. Volunteers, many on welfare themselves, donate 400,000 days of labor a year. Recipients contribute to the system while they receive help, doing tasks devised by the leaders. The beneficiaries gain self-reliance so that they can later help someone else. Around the world, the Church operates 109 bishops' storehouses with full shelves. Mormons help produce every item with the Deseret brand label—bread and milk, soap and shampoo, and canned goods. They plant the vegetables, pick them, can them, shelve them, and distribute them.[11]

The forty-seven Deseret Industries (DI) retail stores in seven western states are generally crowded. In these sprawling structures, half the space is used to sort and repair donated items. In the other half, inexpensive used and usable articles are displayed for purchase. Six thousand workers, 40 percent LDS, a quarter with some sort of disability, are trained to become employable and independent by working at DI. Immigrants from other countries find their first job there. Thrifty shoppers find a used highchair, a family room sofa, a piece of handwork, or a winter coat, all at very low prices. People are happy to give their castoffs to a place that uses them well; the inventory jumps off the shelves. Forty percent of the customers shop there weekly.[12]

The Humanitarian Resource Center of North America reaches out internationally to people of all faiths. As Dean Walker, a unit manager, says, "Our basic belief is that everyone is our brother and our sister. Wherever they are and whatever religion they are, if they are in need and we have the resources, we should help them." The HRC, housed in a 20,000-foot Church-sponsored warehouse, gathers and sends off donated items. The HRC provided emergency help to 123 major international disasters from 1986 to 2000 and distributed cash donations of $60 million plus material donations of $291 million in 147 countries. Tons of food, medical equipment, clothing, and educational supplies were sent out. They give food to soup kitchens, shelters, and food banks, as well as vouchers for Deseret Industries. The Church made a "significant contri-bution" to the Measles Initiative, a long-term vaccination project in Africa. In Houston, Texas, the church provided labor, jars, and lids at their peanut butter factory to the Houston Food Bank, which supplied the pea-nuts. Members sew quilts and clothing for distribution.[13]

Because of these programs, the Church has long been known as a group that takes care of its own. The Church traditionally opposes government assistance, although Utahns have certainly benefitted from government programs. The Church stresses individual preparation and cooperation. The opening up of its humanitarian programs to local non-Mormon groups and to people worldwide exemplifies the Church's widening focus in recent years.

After the terrorist attacks in 2001, programs preparing for disaster or unemployment were newly stressed. Members are urged to store a year's supply of food and clothing and perhaps fuel and funds. Mormons buy beans, sugar, powdered milk, wheat, and other non-perishable foodstuffs to be vacuum packed and stored at home; they store food in closets, under beds, and in the garage. They recommend a permanent backpack for each family member stocked with seventy-two hours worth of food, clothes, a blanket, cash, and copies of important documents for quick exit.

Moved by this counsel, an unusually zealous couple, Dennis and Faye Moore of Raleigh, North Carolina, built a 600 square-foot basement "pantry" to hold a year's supply of food for themselves and the families of their four nearby married children. They have four fifty-gallon drums of water, a canning machine, a manual grinder for their wheat, and food in cans, boxes, and barrels. They also have a vegetable garden, a well, and a generator; they are thinking of ways to store fuel. Members are told not to count on others to bail them out. They are to live within their means, get out of debt, and lay by goods for a rainy day, which has always come and will come again. Up-to-date suggestions are found on the Church website, www.providentliving.org.[14]

The Church gets public credit when the well-organized network kicks in for emergencies, quickly mobilizing supplies and volunteers. Members have come in numbers to sandbag Salt Lake City against flooding, to search for lost children, and to relay messages quickly. Congregations volunteer in community programs and begin their own. A successful program pairs college and high school students for tutoring at Stanford University. In the Boston Revere Second Ward, Bishop John Wright saw the students in his ward, many from immigrant families, floundering. He organized thirty struggling teenagers and thirty college-aged LDS tutors to work at "Books and Basketball." One Harvard graduate student remembered driving to Revere each week, picking up carloads of students. They set up tables and chairs in the Church's cultural hall and studied with the kids for an hour before breaking into a "frenzied game of basketball." Friendships resulted, mentoring occurred, and all had a good time.[15]

Influenced by their social gospel of hard work and self-reliance, individual Mormons privately organize programs when they see the need. These programs run parallel to Church needs but are not officially sponsored, in the Philippines, for instance, where unemployment is between 20 and 50 percent. In 1989, Milo F. Smith, a former mission president, teamed up with Warner P. Woodworth, a BYU professor of organizational behavior, to foster an entrepreneurial spirit. They organized graduate students to teach business skills and accumulated funds to make small business loans. Besides working in the Philippines, their foundation, Enterprise Mentors International, also raises and lends out money in Guatemala, Mexico, and El Salvador. In the first ten years, EMI held about 10,000 training seminars for 80,000 people, made 11,000 loans, and in 2000, served more than 6,000 families. Loan repayment runs at a success rate of about 95 percent. This program helps people, not all of them Church members, to get ahead.

In the Philippines, 69 percent of the almost 500,000 Church members live in poverty. Some cannot afford bus fare to meetings. Stephen W. Gibson, another entrepreneur, founded the Academy for Creating Enterprise to encourage self-employment. The Gibsons admit twenty-five students for an eight-week course to study business cases. Graduates might buy a stock of goods to sell or run a pre-school. Cipriano Bruce, of Cebu, worked from a home shop in a car upholstery and body repair business. He was assisted by his wife and two employees and averaged sixteen clients a month, grossing $1,350. To improve his business, he borrowed $1,500 to open a shop closer to the highway. In 2000, he increased his work force by two men and his gross sales by 59 percent. In Mindanao, Narciso Magno earned $75 a month selling oranges and fish. He applied to the Academy, noting that his little Church branch had 137 jobless members. He was soon earning $220 a month. He works five days, teaches business on Saturday, and does Church work on Sunday. "My dream is not to die in poverty, but to have poverty die in me."[16]

These sustainable programs help the poor help themselves. Warner Woodworth, at the heart of many programs, says Mormons cannot just pay tithing and expect the Church to take care of everyone. The bureaucracy moves slowly. Members must "take the initiative and engage in personal acts of righteousness." He organized Unitus, a non-profit umbrella group over many small operations. The group, with no official LDS connection, links donors and volunteers. Unitus encourages businessmen to open branches in third world countries and hire and train local workers. Woodworth says, "Like our ancestors, we are on a rescue mission. . . . The Saints around the world are suffering and we must help them." Twenty percent of the Philippine Mormons are land squatters; 60 percent have no running water. Ninety percent of Ugandan LDS members are unemployed. Forty percent of the LDS missionaries from Brazil cannot read the Scriptures.[17]

Mormon tithing and donations put Utah on top of the states for charitable contributions. According to the National Center for Charitable Statistics at the Urban Institute, Utahns donate 15 percent of their discretionary income to religious and non-profit causes, 4.9 percent of adjusted gross income. In Texas where 85 percent claim some religion, the citizens on average donate 1.9 percent of their income.[18]

BRIGHAM YOUNG UNIVERSITY

Education is another sector where the Church shines brightly most of the time. Believing in learning and getting ahead, the Church sponsors Brigham Young University in Provo, Utah, an hour south of Salt Lake City, as well as branches in Idaho and Hawaii. The Provo institution, with more than 29,000 students, is the largest privately owned religious university in the United States. The young people of the Church look to "the Y" for religion, a good and inexpensive education, and a potential spouse. Students sign rigorous honor and dress codes. For five straight years, Brigham Young University has been named the nation's top "stone-cold sober" school by *The Princeton Review*. The school also ranked first in the "most religious" and "lowest alcohol usage" categories. Student body president Rob Foster noted proudly, "We all came to BYU to live these standards."[19] Despite the codes, competition for admission has created such an academically able student body that many young Mormons cannot meet the requirements. To meet the need, the nearby Utah Valley State College, a public institution, has grown from a junior to a four-year college, providing a Provo-LDS educational experience with the same dense population of Mormon young people and well-organized student wards.

Although Brigham Young University, cupped in a small town in a mountain valley, might seem distant from the real world, 72 percent of the school's students speak a second language and the university teaches sixty languages, whereas Yale, which comes next, teaches twenty-five. Nowhere else are advanced courses offered in such languages as Tagalog, Vietnamese, and Bulgarian. A quarter of the BYU student body takes language courses each semester compared to a national average of 8 percent. More than half the students have lived outside the United States, mostly on missions, and more study abroad than from any other university, almost 2,000 in 2001. BYU students' language capability has attracted grants to teach Chinese and Arabic.[20]

Critics maintain that despite the beautiful campus, bright students, and well-trained faculty, academic freedom is in short supply. About a dozen faculty members were disciplined in the 1990s for researching topics potentially damaging to the Church, for feminist stands, and for speaking out on topics deemed heretical. In extreme cases, discipline takes the form of unrenewed contracts. Faculty may be interviewed and cautioned by their bishops, suggesting the blurred line between academic research and ecclesiastical obedience.

Academic freedom became a rallying cry in the 1990s. D. Michael Quinn, whose research on sensitive issues ranged widely, calls this an honesty issue, saying that those who "conceal or avoid presenting . . . evidence that contradicts the preferred view of the writer," commit fraud. The school has purged from the faculty most of those who caused the tensions. Meanwhile, a large majority of the faculty (85 percent) is happy at Brigham Young University.[21] The Mormons have gone a long distance toward creating a modern research university but they aim to teach LDS truth, not to undermine it. Defenders of the university point out that most schools have prevailing orthodoxies; and crossing the line of the acceptable results in difficulties anywhere.

HISTORICAL SPACES

As the BYU story suggests, even positive Church projects backfire. Mormons often undertake good will ventures and find they are upsetting someone. Church members have found themselves in trouble, for example, for reclaiming the lands of their heritage. Leaders have been buying important LDS historic sites events since 1905 when they acquired Joseph Smith's birthplace in Sharon, Vermont, and erected a monument there. In the 1960s, the Church began restoring a series of historical sites: buildings in Palmyra, New York, where the Smiths moved from Vermont; the Smith's farmland in nearby Manchester; Liberty Jail in Missouri where Joseph was incarcerated; and large portions of Nauvoo, Illinois. The Church has reconstructed the village of Kirtland, Ohio, where Smith and his wife lived from 1831 to 1838, restoring existing buildings and recreating others from archeological evidence. The Smiths lived above the Whitney store in Kirtland. A visitors' center has been installed to accompany the surviving Greek Revival temple long owned by the Reorganized Church, now the Community of Christ. To improve traffic patterns, the Church contributed funds to reroute two state highways. In 2005 the Church announced plans to rebuild Joseph and Emma Smith's home in Harmony, Pennsylvania, where the bulk of the Book of Mormon was translated.[22]

Restorations attract thousands of Mormons and other tourists to hear the Church's story, contributing to the local economies, but some arouse local opposition. The attempt to purchase Martin's Cove, Wyoming, caused a rumpus in Congress. Mormon pioneers in the Willie and Martin Handcart Companies, who began their trip late across the plains in 1856, struggled through snow for fifty miles to reach Martin's Cove, near present-day Casper. Before a Salt Lake rescue party arrived, 150 people perished, the result of poor planning and unseasonable weather. To commemorate these fabled pioneers, thousands visit the "sacred ground" annually. The incident has been worked into the Church's sacrificial mythology.

Although the state had ignored the land, the Church's attempt to buy 1,640 acres was opposed by state and national Wyoming legislators, perhaps fearing that other religious groups would want to purchase public lands too. The Church entered into a twenty-five-year lease with the Bureau of Land Management to care for and interpret the site, paying $16,000 annually to the BLM, and bought another ranch to serve as a gateway. Then the American Civil Liberties Union sued the BLM to revoke the lease, which allowed the LDS Church to create a "state sponsored sectarian religious enclave" on public land. Plaintiffs objected to the "pervasive, unavoidable and unremitting" Mormon presence. They objected to the controlling guides, who used the suffering of the pioneers "for proselytizing purposes." As in other places, the Church appeared to be a monopolizing institution, controlling public lands for propaganda purposes.[23]

If Martin's Cove brought bad publicity, another story is far worse. The Mountain Meadows Massacre occurred on September 11, 1857, ten years after the Saints arrived in the Utah territory. That year, the Arkansas emigrants of the Baker-Fancher party set out for California in thirty to forty wagons with hundreds of cattle. Their attempts to trade with local Mormons were rebuffed because rumors implicated them in the murders of Church leaders Joseph Smith and Parley P. Pratt. Expecting the invasion of the U.S. Army to regain control of territorial government, Mormons refused to sell their grain and objected when the Fancher cattle munched down their pastures. The Indians believed the Fancher party had poisoned their wells.[24] The Mormons remembered their previous persecutions, and with the army approaching, they feared they were being attacked again.

The Mormon settlers and Indians ambushed the wagon train moving near Cedar City, in Southern Utah. The emigrants circled their wagons, dug in, and fought. Five days later, the emigrants surrendered when the Mormons promised them safety if they disarmed. After the Fancher party gave up their guns, the LDS militiamen and the Paiute Indians set on them with guns and clubs and shot or beat to death some 120 men, women, and children, sparing only seventeen very young children. Two decades later, John D. Lee, considered a scapegoat by many, was executed for the massacre.[25]

That Mormons committed the brutal act is beyond question. They panicked as they awaited an invading army. What is still debated is the culpability of Brigham Young: Did he order the massacre? Was he responsible because of his inflated rhetoric against government and persecutors? Was this a premeditated act of vengeance? Young had certainly used strong language. He said, "We have borne enough of the oppression and hellish abuse, and we will not bear any more of it." But he and other leaders denied prior knowledge of the plans. The event is "the darkest chapter in Latter-day Saint history." An official army report written back in 1859 said that "for hellish atrocity, [this crime] has no parallel." One writer calls it "an act of religious fanaticism unparalleled by any other event in the country's history."[26]

Church leaders have dedicated a monument at the site and have tried to effect a reconciliation with the descendants of the murdered. But they stopped short of a complete apology. The event lives on. Novelists and historians revisit the massacre, sifting the remains, trying to implicate Young. Richard Turley, managing director of the Family and Church History Department of the Church, says, "Circumstance may explain [the acts of the local Mormons]; nothing can justify them."[27]

As the Church reclaims and retells its historical incidents, some members reenact them, replaying the western trek with covered wagons and oxen to experience the heroism of their pioneer past. In 1997, on the 150th anniversary of the great trek that took the first group of pioneers from

Nauvoo to the Salt Lake Valley, hundreds of descendants followed the 1,000-mile route with thirty horse-drawn wagons. They ate dried buffalo meat, apples, and beans, made lye soap, stuffed bed ticks with goose feathers, and prepared medicinal herbs. Some pulled two-wheeled handcarts, the pioneer economy vehicles. Many dressed as pioneers, cooked over fires, and walked the route, rising at 5 A.M. for three months to harness the horses. They recalled the Israelites' flight from Egypt. On arrival in the Salt Lake Valley, they felt they had reached the Promised Land. Replaying these historic treks has become very popular, so much so that the Bureau of Land Management now limits trail traffic to protect the land.[28]

To tell its story, the Church sponsors a variety of pageants based on the Scriptures or Church history with huge casts, brilliant costumes, and special effects. The senior pageant takes place in Palmyra, New York, at the Hill Cumorah, site of the golden plates. The pageant, an hour and a half of religious scenes performed on ten levels of the steep hill's face, celebrated its sixty-eighth anniversary in 2005. Staged over two weekends with a cast of 650 playing to an audience of about 9,000 each night, the show is full of effects, requiring 500,000 watts of electricity, "absolutely breathtaking and an experience for all ages," with special waterfalls, volcanoes, fireballs, and explosions. Similarly, the Mormon Miracle Pageant, "A Message of Peace," is played in Manti, Utah, a small temple town. Seven hundred participants perform for eight days to audiences that total 100,000. On a hillside stage larger than a football field, with the Manti Temple as backdrop, visitors watch scenes from Church history, climaxing with the local Mormon story. To celebrate Joseph Smith's 200th birthday in 2005, Nauvoo unveiled a new pageant.[29] All of this is very Mormon. Members play out their past to understand the lives of their ancestors. They also hope that their rocky, heroic history will engage the interest of others.

THE NATION AND THE WORLD

In Utah towns, celebrations often blend Mormon history with American patriotism. On a scorching July 4 in Provo, Utah, patriotism is in high evidence. Provo's "Freedom Festival" is a tribute to both Church and state. With the theme, "America Welcomes the World," the 2001 festival featured a week of baby competitions, speech and essay contests, historic tours, food and entertainment, golf tournament, carillon concert, art display, blood drive, race, parade, and fireworks. The early morning sky blossomed for two days with more than twenty hot air balloons, huffing and puffing their hot breath over town.

The large parade began with a group of town criers encouraging the crowd of 300,000 to rise and repeat the Pledge of Allegiance. As each group neared the end of the pledge, the next group stood to begin, making it the world's longest, rolling Pledge of Allegiance. People in chairs and on blankets along the tree-lined route watched the bands sweltering in winter uniforms, the helium-filled cartoon characters, and the town floats with pretty beauty queens in satin and tiaras, waving their white-gloved hands. Local Mormon stakes contributed floats and the most applauded entry in the parade was a crowd of white-shirted Mormon missionaries from the Missionary Training Center in Provo.

Small glimpses of distinctive Mormon culture surface in the parade. Family performing groups on big trucks might be expected, but the Clean-flicks float pledging to promote family entertainment by editing sex and violence from Hollywood films stands out. Company owner Ray Lines said "Some people think we shouldn't edit the movies we edit, but we live in the United States and we have the freedom to choose to edit or not." These R-rated movies, cleaned up to PG or PG-13, have developed a national market. Brigham Young University had quietly edited second run films at its Varsity Theater, but permission for the practice was denied, and the theater closed. Some say that altering videos violates federal copyright law; others note that films are cut for airline use.[30]

Mormons tucked away in small Utah towns are very much aware of the greater world outside and feel pressure from other groups. Anticipating the 2002 Olympic Games in Utah, the city council of tiny La Verkin, near Zion National Park, met in July 2001 to pass an anti-United Nations ordinance, prohibiting the city from supporting the UN or putting the insignia on city property. Residents oppose the UN as contrary to God, family, and country, everything La Verkin stands for. Two-thirds of arid Utah is owned by the federal government, and some residents fear that UN policies could influence land use. Councilman Al Snow, who proposed the ordinance, said, "Oh, I imagine that every time you stand up for freedom, you're a radical, aren't you? But . . . when you stand up for freedom, God is there with you." Many Utahns favor pulling out of the UN. When Utah Attorney General Mark Shurtleff told the La Verkin City Council members that their anti-UN law failed to uphold the rights of citizens who favored feeding starving children and promoted nuclear disarmament, La Verkin moderated its ordinance. Flying the UN flag on the

City Hall flagpole and taxation of La Verkin for stationing UN troops were still forbidden. Not every resident agreed with the ordinance; Eliot Hill noted, "All this does is make us look like a bunch of kooks."[31]

These examples reveal the dividing line between LDS and U.S. culture. Although Mormons seem very American, they also attempt to draw a moral boundary that they choose not to cross. On the other side of the line, non-Mormons are just as likely to rebuff Mormons. One outside observer quipped that a man who didn't drink, didn't smoke, and didn't swear could not be trusted. Other outsiders draw the line along the Christian/non-Christian boundary. A survey of 500 Utah and California clergy surveyed by FAIR, the Foundation for Apologetic Information and Research, determined that only 6 percent considered Mormons Christian.[32]

Mormons are accustomed to meeting various kinds of exclusion and disparaging comments. Meredeth Brooks, a Mormon student, planned to attend the Summer Christian Fellowship, a nondenominational evangelical group at Dartmouth College in New Hampshire. She was told that her religious beliefs prevented her from participation. Unfortunately, she accidentally received an e-mail from the Summer Christian Fellowship advising leaders how to respond to her, quoting the book of Galatians, "if any one is preaching to you a gospel contrary to that which you received, let him be accursed." Brooks responded that she was a Christian and that "It's rather bigoted of the SCF to be exclusionary based on their fundamentally wrong and naive categorization of my religion." At issue here are the contradictory desires of the Summer Christian Fellowship to be doctrinally pure while welcoming all people. The dispute embarrassed Dartmouth College, which prides itself on tolerance. In the same vein, Linda Ellison, a student at the Harvard Divinity School, found little tolerance there. She was shocked by the "derogatory comments about Mormons that other students felt completely free to share with her, not only before but also after they learned about her religious background."[33]

Small incidents such as this are characteristic of the skirmishes along the boundary with the wider world. A church as foreign as the Church of Jesus Christ of Latter-day Saints, with its checkered history, continues to irritate others. As the Church tries to manage its public face and to build bridges with other groups, tensions flare. Leaders encourage service and support. Skilled professionals smooth over potential conflicts. But in many places, the Church is felt as an oppressive presence. Making peace with the larger community continues to be a serious issue.

THE INTELLECTUAL
ACTIVITIES OF RECENT
YEARS

Do not yield your faith in payment . . . for the recognition and
acclaim of the world.

—*Boyd K. Packer*, 1981

Intellectuals in the Church want either to explore their religious culture
and work out the implications of their beliefs, confirming the faith, mar-
shaling evidence to support its claims, or to resist the culture out of unbe-
lief or resentment, wanting to criticize and undermine the faith. Both
positions present problems for the General Authorities who feel they
should define acceptable beliefs. Leaders have simplified the message to
facilitate rapid Church expansion, leaving both intellectual camps hungry
for complexity and nuance. Along with the poles of belief and doubt are
those of authoritarian control versus free expression. Church leaders
assert their authority over doctrine, establishing and regulating institutions, fixing the boundaries of orthodoxy. Intellectuals submit or rebel.

In the believing camp, much of Mormon intellectual activity takes the
form of defending the faith against doubters. Articles, books, and pamphlets, published mostly in Utah and appealing to Mormon audiences,
rebut critical hypotheses or assemble evidence to prove the miraculous
nature of the work. They react to criticism that in the nineteenth century
came from the East and England, augmented by local dissidents who
wanted to modernize Mormon thinking. In the twentieth century, the University of Utah, once an LDS institution, but becoming increasingly secular, became a site of oppositional thinking. The university housed and
graduated several astute critics whose writing and teaching gave traditional town-gown conflicts a religious bent. Local critics Jerald and Sandra
Tanner, disaffected Salt Lake Mormons, have opposed the Church for

thirty years through their Utah Lighthouse Ministry. They consider the Church to be based on a fraud and have reprinted rare documents through their own newsletters and publications to discredit its foundations.[1] In the last half of the twentieth-century, evangelical critics have led the attack on Mormonism in the name of a more traditional Christianity. To all of these attacks, believing intellectuals mount defenses, creating an atmosphere of constant debate and cultural tension.

Because LDS faith is based on supernatural events that occurred comparatively recently such as the translation of the gold plates and the revelations to Joseph Smith, Mormon history has always been controversial. With the critics constantly challenging the accuracy of the founding stories, apologists have tried to write faith-promoting history. Traditionally, faithful historians have tidied up the record, quashed embarrassing episodes, and overlooked leaders' flaws. New generations of Mormon historians, committed to their religion but trained professionally, have argued for a candid confrontation of good and bad facts. Much of their revisionist scholarship has made its way into mainstream accounts, but conservatives still put faith first.[2]

Controlling belief is difficult in the Church. In line with their do-it-yourself theology, believing Mormons differ on a broad range of issues. Many Mormons find the finer points of Mormon history and theology stimulating and worth discussion, although most Mormons are uninterested and unconcerned. Some resent discussion, feeling that exploring problems is a needlessly disruptive exercise. "When the Prophet speaks, the debate is over," they say.[3]

Nevertheless, the Church has a lively intellectual life that is of great importance in understanding Mormonism. The Church has always had standout thinkers who have debated major issues of doctrine and policy. On the conservative side, Apostle Bruce R. McConkie, author of the encyclopedic *Mormon Doctrine*, defined orthodox belief for many Mormons for two generations.[4] Liberals include Eugene England and Richard Poll.

A microcosm of the diverging styles can be seen in a celebrated showdown between England, a provocative thinker who studied English literature at Stanford, and McConkie, a lawyer and doctrinaire General Authority. In 1979, England, then associate director of Brigham Young University's Honors Program, spoke to students on lifelong education. He used the Mormon doctrine of eternal progression as an example and, citing God as a model, said that humans could experience the joys of learning forever. In England's view, God was ever increasing in glory and knowledge. England believed this idea, extrapolated from Joseph Smith's funeral sermon for King Follett, was perfectly orthodox.[5]

In the summer of 1980, however, Elder Bruce R. McConkie gave an address at Brigham Young University titled "The Seven Deadly Heresies." His first heresy was that God is progressing in knowledge. God was, McConkie asserted, absolute, perfect, and, therefore, not improving. England, confused by this development, discovered in further research a way to reconcile this apparent contradiction by thinking of God in separate spheres, perfect in respect to us, while still progressing within some realm beyond ours.

England wrote to Elder McConkie explaining this interpretation just before leaving for London for a semester abroad. He received McConkie's long response weeks after a copy of the letter had been circulating in the United States. McConkie noted that he wrote "in kindness and in plainness and perhaps with sharpness." He rehearsed scriptural and historical arguments against God progressing in knowledge. He told England to cease speaking on the topic and urged him to be "faith promoting" and "in harmony with that which comes from the head of the Church."

> It is my province to teach to the Church what the doctrine is. It is your province to echo what I say or to remain silent. You do not have a divine commission to correct me or any of the Brethren. The Lord does not operate that way. If I lead the Church astray, that is my responsibility, but the fact remains that I am the one appointed with all the rest involved so to do. . . .
>
> I advise you to take my counsel on the matters here involved. If I err, that is my problem; but in your case if you single out some of these things and make them the center of your philosophy, and end up being wrong, you will lose your soul.[6]

England did not speak on the issue again until 1989 when he published an extended disquisition harmonizing the conflicting statements that God is all knowing and still progressing.[7] His article quoted Church leaders defending the distinction of spheres. The McConkie-England disagreement revealed the division between theological conservatives and liberals within the believing camp and, in a larger sense, the tension between authoritarian control versus free expression.

Richard Poll dramatized the difference between liberal and conservative believers in his essay "What the Church Means to People Like Me."

Poll described two familiar types of Mormons using Book of Mormon images. "Iron Rod" Mormons—an image from a dream of Lehi—are admonished to find their way through the murk of life by strict obedience to the commandments. Holding on to the iron rod is not easy, but every step is clearly defined. The "mind and will of the Lord" may be obtained on any question with guidance from the Scriptures, modern prophets, and the Holy Ghost. "Liahona" Mormons, on the other hand, who are named for the compass that worked on faith and guided Lehi's family through the wilderness, feel their way along with occasional divine help. Although Liahonas lack full knowledge and certitude, they see enough to function with purpose. Poll thought that basic temperament divided the camps. Iron Rodders see a questioning attitude as imperfect faith; Liahonas feel that people without questions have closed minds. Iron Rodders see the Lord involved in all details of life; the Liahonas are more apt to see people, even the Lord's prophets, struggling alone at times, employing the God-given gift of agency as they can. Both Iron Rodders and Liahonas, Poll concludes, are useful to the Church's work.[8]

Poll noted that following the brethren is a practical, Iron Rod idea. Authoritarianism is pragmatic, and the institutional emphasis on compliance tends to put Iron Rodders in presiding positions. But he, a Liahona, saw in the Church an impressive ability to accommodate changing realities. Church members, having forgotten their past or never having known it, learn a very selective, idealized history. "To the extent that the oracles from the past are perceived as unchanging, the processes of change—of continuous revelation—within the church today are likely to be resisted, overlooked, or rationalized." Poll thought it risky and counterproductive to substitute myth for historical truth. The selective embellishing, revising, and forgetting of aspects left the members vulnerable. He believed efforts to deny dissonance stemmed not from doctrine but from the personal characteristics of leaders and followers.[9]

Most believing intellectual Mormons are probably Liahonas. One of these, a university professor, shares Poll's unwillingness to commit to myth. "Where does [my scientific training] leave me? The same as I am with respect to a lot of things, with an open mind. So many people stand up in church and say, 'I know.' There are very few things in this life I know for sure. In science you never assume you have the final word on anything. Later information may not undo it, but it will reinterpret and extend it further." He spoke to the benefits of the Church from observation. "My testimony is that following these teachings has proven to be beneficial. I have seen humble people grow to giants by participating in the church."[10]

The Iron Rod mentality has welcomed the standardization of materials. By submitting all Church publications to review by a central committee, doctrine and history have been homogenized, simplified, and regularized. Since the 1970s, committees have established consistency in Church practice and teaching. To further regularize teaching, Church magazines published by the semi-independent Church auxiliaries such as the women's Relief Society were discontinued, not because of objectionable content, but because they represented their own organizations. The magazines were succeeded by "correlated" periodicals for adults, young people, and children. After the 1960s, lesson manuals were assigned to central lesson-writing committees to assure consistency and orthodoxy.

Although correlation tended to contain inquiry, in 1972, intellectual life expanded as never before. Leonard J. Arrington, raised a potato farmer in Idaho who later studied economics and history at the University of North Carolina in Chapel Hill and taught at Utah State University in Logan, was named Church Historian, the first (and only) professional historian to hold the office. A strong leader and bridge-builder, Arrington had organized the Mormon History Association in 1965, providing LDS historians with a forum and opportunity for dialogue. Arrington had earlier gained access to the Church archives, open to few, to work on the dissertation that became his respected book *Great Basin Kingdom: An Economic History of the Latter-day Saints, 1830–1900.* In this rational telling of the LDS story, Arrington depicted Brigham Young as the master planner of a desert economy.

Because of the historical department's productivity, the issues of definition, control, and selective inclusion rose early. As Arrington writes in his memoir, some leaders were uncomfortable with the human details included in published letters from Brigham Young to his sons. When a new history, *Story of the Latter-day Saints,* by staffers James Allen and Glen Leonard was published in 1976, one or two members of the Quorum of the Twelve objected to the volume's "absence of inspiration." Ezra Taft Benson, then president of the Twelve, criticized LDS historians for humanizing leaders and for underplaying "revelation and God's intervention in significant events." Arrington's department received a long memo asserting that *Story of the Latter-day Saints* was a secular history lacking sufficient spiritual aspects and citing too many anti-Mormon books. All historical publications, the critique said, should be routed through the Correlation Committee to be corrected for fact, tone, and impact. Arrington concluded that the leaders wanted pages filled with scriptural allusions, nothing controversial.

The Church authorities were faced with a dilemma. They were bombarded with questions from members and media about historical materials they had no time to read, yet the studies, written by Historical Department staffers and carrying the official or semi-official authority of the Church, were unsatisfactory. To ease the tension, Arrington and his associates were moved to Brigham Young University in 1980 and renamed the Joseph Fielding Smith Institute for Church History. By then Arrington's staff had written hundreds of articles and about thirty books and long manuscripts.[11] Arrington was released as Church Historian in 1982 and replaced by a General Authority.

The difficulties of the Leonard Arrington era pointed out the serious intellectual problem: Who speaks for the Church? Leaders are uneasy when researchers apply their tools to the hallowed old stories. Shouldn't the stories just be accepted? Shouldn't the tone continue worshipful? Shouldn't the Mormon story be shielded from embarrassing details? This problem climaxed with Arrington's plan to produce a sixteen-volume history for the Church's 150th anniversary in 1980. Sixteen faithful scholars were engaged and set to work. The plan was moving along well, with contracts signed, research progressing, and even some volumes completed before leaders, deciding that the Church could not be represented by these scholars, cancelled the series. Several of the books were published but not under official auspices. The ultimate conclusion was that the leaders, not the scholars, speak for the Church, and writings by historians must be considered as independent work.

With limited opportunity to publish through the Church, scholars have found other outlets. One locus is Signature Books, a Salt Lake City publishing house inspired by the cancellation of the sixteen-volume series. Founded by George D. Smith, a wealthy Mormon, Signature expanded the scope of Mormon history by supporting unfettered historical inquiry. Encompassing a wide range of history, fiction, and personal essays, Signature has released a title a month for more than twenty years, or 4,000 pages a year. The staff aims to enhance the "opportunities for expression by scholars and writers within the local community." Smith claims to publish "responsible historical research," even as some conservatives call Signature an "anti-Mormon press."[12]

Signature sees itself as partly in competition with Deseret Book, the long-standing, Church-owned publishing house. Deseret Book publishes inspiring, faith-promoting works for popular and semi-popular audiences, but in recent years it has expanded into more academic realms. In 1989, Deseret Book began publication of *The Papers of Joseph Smith*, an ambitious series that sought to reproduce all of the Prophet's writings and dictations with scholarly annotations. With First Presidency approval, the project later expanded to include some thirty-six researchers and staff. When completed, the Papers staff is expected to produce about twenty-four volumes "stuffed with more than 5,000 documents related to Smith, including journals, diaries, correspondence, discourses, written histories and legal cases."[13]

Deseret Book also co-publishes with FARMS, the Foundation for Ancient Research and Mormon Studies, a group devoted to defending the faith and authenticating the Book of Mormon. FARMS was founded in 1979 by John Welch and John Sorenson to coordinate the publication of Book of Mormon research. FARMS employs some full-time research scholars and has published the work of more than one hundred BYU faculty members. Books, articles, and reprints are churned out, making the research widely available. The founding motto "By study, and also by faith,"[14] comes from LDS scripture, showing the preferred stance for the LDS scholar. Some Mormons consider FARMS too apologetic, but the depth of the research in support of the Book of Mormon has made its work popular.[15]

Despite its good intentions, FARMS' was too successful in broadcasting its message and in raising funds. To assure Church control, an effort began to situate it under the BYU administration, and in 1995, Brigham Young University and FARMS formalized their relationship. President Gordon B. Hinckley observed that FARMS "represents the efforts of sincere and dedicated scholars. It has grown to provide strong support and defense of the Church on a professional basis."[16] In 2001, FARMS was absorbed under a new research entity, ISPART, the Institute for the Study and Preservation of Ancient Religious Texts, engaged in such ecumenical projects as working with Islamic and Catholic scholars to publish ancient documents.

The appetite for intellectual activity extends to a series of independent or semi-independent intellectual journals that boast small but loyal followings. *Dialogue: A Journal of Mormon Thought*, a quarterly founded by

Eugene England and G. Wesley Johnson, began publication in 1966 to provide an outlet for investigations of Mormon culture. *Dialogue*'s appearance reinvigorated *BYU Studies,* Brigham Young University's flagship journal, founded in 1959. *BYU Studies,* a "multidisciplinary" academic journal, is dedicated to the correlation of "revealed and discovered truth" and to the belief that the "spiritual and intellectual can be complementary and fundamentally harmonious avenues of knowledge." The editors believe that "faith and reason, revelation and scholarly learning, obedience and creativity are compatible." The *Journal of Mormon History,* begun by the Mormon History Association in 1974, followed by the *John Whitmer Historical Association Journal* in 1980, organized by Community of Christ scholars, foster research in all aspects of Mormon history. The Mormon History Association's annual Tanner Lecture, given by a non-LDS professional historian with strong credentials, infuses the field with new energy.[17]

Sunstone, founded in 1975, provides an arena of lively discussion as well as a magazine of features and news. *Sunstone* sponsors annual forums to discuss Mormon thought and experience, and "the rich spiritual, intellectual, social and artistic qualities of Mormon history and contemporary life." Symposia are held in several cities. As the magazine celebrated its quarter century of existence, the editor noted that its "expansive, chaotic ventures have been tempered by pragmatic, stone hard realities. Its Mormon trek has been a wild, twisting, high-speed quest that kept its company wondering and a little fearful about what was next." *Sunstone* continues to celebrate and disseminate Mormon experience, scholarship, and art.[18]

Exponent II, a "modest but sincere newspaper," an unofficial voice of LDS women, began in 1975. Inspired by the rediscovery of the *Woman's Exponent,* an independent Salt Lake publication running from 1872–1914, the quarterly, published in Boston, discusses women's issues. The first issue stated, "*Exponent II,* poised on the dual platforms of Mormonism and Feminism, has two aims: to strengthen the Church of Jesus Christ of Latter-day Saints, and to encourage and develop the talents of Mormon women. That these aims are consistent we intend to show by our pages and our lives."[19] This feminist newspaper, like a long letter from a dear friend, encourages submissions from readers and publishes theme issues. Some original workers are still at it.

The activity in LDS-related journals, like the large presses, can be seen as seesaw efforts between the liberal and conservative wings of

Mormondom. The role of belief in historical inquiry, the interpretation of Scripture, the nature of God, the place of women and blacks, and so on, are debated vigorously.

One of the recurring issues is the definition of orthodoxy. What is normative Mormonism? In an effort to set up a hierarchy of basic Mormon beliefs, LDS sociologist Armand Mauss proposed a "scale of authenticity," an operational construct to give weight to potentially conflicting and changing LDS teachings. That such a scale would be useful suggests the complexity of potential beliefs. His first category, "Canon Doctrine," includes doctrines and texts that the prophets have presented to the Church as received by direct revelation and that have been accepted by the sustaining vote of the membership. Canon Doctrine consists of the standard works of the Church, and material added to them: the Bible, the Book of Mormon, the Doctrine and Covenants, and the Pearl of Great Price.

Mauss's second category, "Official Doctrine," includes statements from the First Presidency, Church lesson manuals, and magazines and other publications. Their content is official doctrine when presented but may change over time. The third category, "Authoritative Doctrine," includes all other talks, teachings, and publications of other authorities on doctrines and scriptures. "Popular Doctrine," the lowest or least authentic category, includes folklore, common beliefs, and unofficially circulating prophecies. Mauss warns against canonizing doctrines not explicitly included in the standard works and advocates patience and care in passing judgment on doctrine. "It is not blind faith that is required of us but only that we seek our own spiritual confirmation before questioning official instruction."[20]

The avalanche of opinion, much of it speculative, rushing from the many Mormon-related publication outlets, has made the Mormon image impossible to control. An attempt to manage the evidence and alter the past led to the most dramatic incident in recent years. In 1980, Mark Hofmann, a young premed student and LDS documents dealer, announced that he had found the [Joseph] Smith family Bible. This 1668 Cambridge edition of the King James Bible, purportedly belonging to Joseph Smith's sister Katharine Smith Salisbury, turned out to contain a treasure. Two of the Bible's pages, partly stuck together with glue, held a folded sheet of paper appearing to be a famous lost Church document, the Anthon transcript. In 1828, Joseph Smith had copied some hieroglyphs from the Book of Mormon gold plates for Martin Harris to take to Professor Charles

Anthon at Columbia University in New York City to be verified as authentic ancient writing. Hofmann showed the document to various people who thought it was genuine, and then to Church officials who hailed the miraculous find.

Hofmann was incredibly deft at finding Church-related documents. In 1981, he sold to the Church a copy of a blessing purportedly given by Joseph Smith to his son Joseph Smith III, conveying the right of succession as president and prophet. The lack of any contemporaneous succession statement had led to uncertainty after Smith's death, and this blessing filled the void. Hofmann also found a letter claiming to be from Thomas Bullock to Brigham Young, dated 1865, accusing Young of destroying the Joseph Smith III blessing. Church leaders publicized some purchases; others were quietly locked away.

Hofmann successfully sold many important items in and beyond the Mormon market. But he turned out to be very different from the mild collector he seemed to be. He was in fact an expert forger. Well versed in early Church history and Joseph Smith lore, he constructed false documents, ingeniously meeting standards of historical authenticity. The Joseph Smith III blessing and Thomas Bullock letter were both forgeries. So was a letter collector Steven F. Christensen bought from Hofmann in 1984 and donated to the Church, the so-called "Salamander Letter," supposedly from Martin Harris to W. W. Phelps, dated 1830, outlining an alternate, magic-filled account of the origin of the Book of Mormon. According to the document, a white salamander rather than the Angel Moroni delivered the golden plates, contorting the Church's founding story. The *Deseret News* published the text after Hofmann leaked the contents.[21]

Hofmann's run lasted for four lively years. His documents had been rigorously authenticated, but suspicions eventually arose, and by 1983, a few experts were sure that some were fraudulent. Hofmann then exercised another remarkable skill. To prevent the discovery of his schemes, he made bombs that killed two people, including Christensen, and with another bomb, intended for a third victim, he accidentally injured himself. In 1987, after a trial and plea bargain, he admitted responsibility for the two deaths and his many forgeries and was imprisoned for life.[22]

Although Hofmann's activities left a cloud over Mormon studies for years, the forgeries generated intense scholarship about Mormon origins. Ironically, the Church, in having to deal with so many damaging disclosures became more open. Press conferences were held and new finds published.

To make available historical documents, a publishing alliance was eventually struck between the Church Archives and *BYU Studies*. By 1992, Deseret Book published a second edition of *Story of the Latter-day Saints*, the book that had once caused a firestorm. Church leaders appeared to have relaxed their strict control of the past.[23]

Still, Church authorities were guarded about scholarly Mormon inquiry. In 1989, Apostle Dallin H. Oaks urged that people without authority be disregarded when speaking on religious doctrines, commandments, ordinances, and practices. These "alternate voices," he warned, could be found in magazines and journals and heard at lectures, symposia, and conferences. He warned members against them and against engaging in disputation. The world needed "not more scholarship and technology but more righteousness and revelation."[24]

Most hearers interpreted Oaks's "alternate voices" to mean the unofficial LDS journals and presses. In 1991, two weeks after the Sunstone Symposium in Salt Lake City where there were talks concerning the temple and problems of missionary work in South America, the Church issued a statement, signed by the First Presidency and the Twelve, deploring the "bad taste and insensitivity of these public discussions of things we hold sacred." Some topics had been discussed in the press "in such a way as to injure the Church or its members or to jeopardize the effectiveness or safety of our missionaries." The statement called this discussion "inappropriate."[25]

Vern Anderson, the AP reporter who closely followed the standoff during these years, noted that this was the highpoint of the Church's friction with the "tiny but vocal intellectual community." The private censure that followed the public rebuke underscored the "growing tension between an authoritarian hierarchy and an informal network of members pressing for unfettered historical and doctrinal inquiry." Symposium speakers were called in for interviews. Mormon leaders themselves declined to be interviewed, but a spokesman offered a dictionary definition of unacceptable dissent as "conflict, discord, strife, objection, protest, rebellion, contradiction, or to differ, disagree or oppose," and noted that members whose behavior fit these parameters subjected themselves to "the possibility of church discipline," formal or informal to "safeguard the purity, integrity and good name of the church." The editor of *Sunstone* apologized for any offense, saying that he believed that "open and honest examination" helped to strengthen the Church.[26]

This movement to contain "alternate voices" turned publishing in the unofficial press (*Sunstone, Dialogue, Exponent II*), as well as speaking at public events that such groups sponsored, into renegade activities. Teachers at Brigham Young University and in the Church Education System were discouraged, though not forbidden, from participation, marginalizing these publications.[27]

Instead, leaders encouraged daily study of the LDS scriptures, an effort that gained momentum after the Church published a revised and enhanced version of the canon. In 1979, a new edition of the Bible and a Bible dictionary were published, followed two years later by a "triple combination"—Book of Mormon, Doctrine and Covenants, and Pearl of Great Price. These standard works came with notes, maps, topical guides, and cross references, showing broad scholarly energy. President Spencer W. Kimball, who gave the original committee its charge, said the goal was to "assist in improving doctrinal scholarship throughout the Church."[28]

The renewed emphasis on scripture study, especially the Book of Mormon, led the Church away from speculative theology. The freewheeling General Conference addresses of earlier years, elaborating unique LDS doctrines, were gradually replaced with a basic Christian message downplaying denominational differences. Several LDS intellectuals, however, hungering for the old days, pressed forward in the speculative tradition. In 1990, Margaret Toscano, a graduate student in Hebrew at the University of Utah, and her husband, Paul Toscano, a Salt Lake City attorney, published *Strangers in Paradox: Explorations in Mormon Theology,* in which they speculated on a feminist theology for Mormonism. Was there room for God the Female in the Mormon Godhead? In several well-publicized talks, Paul Toscano called for the worship of a female Deity. He said that Mormons already worshiped a holy woman. Riding the crest of the Mormon feminist movement, Toscano condemned the bland, correlated church he called "McMormonism" and urged feminist intellectuals not to be intimidated.[29]

Toscano's outspoken talks led to trouble. Mormons who published or spoke to large audiences were disciplined. In 1993, Toscano and five other well-known intellectuals were tried in separate, local Church courts. Most had published articles in *Sunstone* that were cited in the charges. Five, including Toscano, were excommunicated; the sixth was disfellowshipped; they became known as the "September Six." Church leaders denied charges of a purge, but the timing seemed remarkable. The fallout moved beyond the small sphere of concerned intellectuals and was widely reported in the national press. Far from possessing the vibrant intellectual tradition members recognized, the Church was portrayed as repressive and vindictive.[30]

Excommunication is a heavy and painful punishment for Mormons. It is, according to non-Mormon scholar Melvyn Hammarberg, an "emotionally potent identity-defining and boundary-maintaining instrument." One bishop said that 90–95 percent of his rare disciplinary courts involved sexual sins in all their varieties, but cases of apostasy received the most attention and most involved women. About a dozen high profile cases of discipline and resignation from the Church took place in the early 1990s, and in 2002, another six "intellectuals," deemed guilty of writing or talking about positions considered injurious to doctrine, were cut off. Lavina Fielding Anderson, of the first group, titled the conflict "the orthodoxy wars." The Church held these councils, as Hammarberg quoted from the official handbook, to "preserve the doctrinal purity of the Church," defining apostates as those who "repeatedly act in clear, open, and deliberate public opposition to the Church or its leaders" or "persist in teaching as Church doctrine information that is not Church doctrine after being corrected by their bishops or higher authority." In practice, apostates are not punished for beliefs, but for publicly opposing the Church, by publishing or speaking out. After her excommunication for apostasy, Anderson wrote to the first presidency. "I still love the Church and wish to be part of it. I am still attending my meetings, reading the Scriptures, holding family prayers, and participating in daily family devotional. I do not feel angry or bitter. My hope is for reconciliation and a healing of this breach." She would be welcomed back if she recanted her former views and actions.[31]

Some Mormon intellectuals resent it when a few dissenters appear to represent the whole intellectual community. Susan Easton Black, then Brigham Young University's Associate Dean of General Education and Honors, organized a 1996 collection of essays from LDS intellectuals on reasons for their belief. In the preface, Noel Reynolds, president of FARMS, countered media reports representing Mormon dissidents as "the thinking Mormons who know the inside story." Said Reynolds, "The overwhelming majority of LDS academics and intellectuals are active, faithful Latter-day Saints who find these detractors to be driven by a secret hate for a goodness they cannot understand or enjoy on their own terms."[32]

Much of the conflict between leaders and scholars stems from the definition of authority. Iron Rodders would like all authority in the hands of the Brethren, the higher Church authorities, whereas Liahonas see individual choice and personal revelation as key. When members seem to follow the strange gods of other movements, there is concern. In an unpublished but widely discussed talk in 1993, Elder Boyd K. Packer listed as dangerous adversaries, "the gay-lesbian movement, the feminist movement, and the ever-present challenge from the so-called scholars or intellectuals."[33] Packer's use of the phrase "so-called" cast suspicion on all intellectuals.

Despite the tension, the General Authorities need intellectuals. By the 1990s, most of the Apostles and many of the Seventies had graduate degrees, suggesting the importance of education. When critics try to undermine Church belief and practice, authorities do not object to—and many welcome—apologists' responses. Criticism still drives the apologists' research agenda. Much of the writing about Joseph Smith is still directed at *No Man Knows My History*, Fawn Brodie's journalistic biography of Smith published in 1945. Stanley P. Hirshson's *The Lion of the Lord*, a biography of Brigham Young based largely on negative eastern newspaper reports, led leaders to charge Leonard Arrington with writing *Brigham Young: American Moses*, published in 1985. When Brent Lee Metcalf published a 1994 collection of essays critical of The Book of Mormon, FARMS amassed an army of scholars to refute every essay in a 550-page book review. The evangelical assault on Mormonism seen in the film *The God Makers* and the Presbyterians' denial of Mormons as Christian, finds its most scholarly expression in *The New Mormon Challenge*.[34] One LDS scholar welcomes the anti-Mormon books. "They keep us on our toes."[35]

Still, a few believing scholars are eager for the Church to set its own research agendas, a sign of scholarly maturity. They want believers to write of problems they devise themselves rather than reacting to the work of others. This involves rising above the orthodoxy wars to engage national and international themes. From an intellectual point of view, believing scholars have transcended the old style that admits of no blemishes in the Church's past and now include all aspects of the Mormon story in their histories, but they have not yet managed to place that story in a larger context. Only gradually are Mormon scholars beginning to pose questions with universal interest. Amid the contention and discouragements, there are reasons to believe Mormon intellectual life will flourish.

An often-quoted scripture, "the Glory of God is intelligence," supports the divinity of mental activity.[36]

Because of the emphasis on obedience, submission, and service, Mormon intellectuals may appear unduly docile and oppressed to outsiders. But under the surface of Mormon culture is a world brimming with intellectual activity. Some Mormons, under the influence of modern rationalism, question the Church's beliefs. In the name of scientific objectivity they dispute the old stories and object when Church leaders constrain critical thought. Other Mormon thinkers, while submitting to authority, write books defending the faith and exploring their religion. These camps, ever divisive, will doubtless continue the debate for years to come.

THE CITY OF ZION

The most ambitious desert civilization the world has seen.
—*Marc Reisner*, 1986

Marc Reisner, in his poetic book *Cadillac Desert*, describes coming on Utah during a winter night flight through frigid air and thin moonlight. He saw emptiness, no forests, no pastures, no lakes, no rivers; there was no fruited plain. He saw uninhabited distance, a lot of emptiness. Then the landscape heaved upward.

> We were crossing a high, thin cordillera of mountains, their tops already covered with snow. The Wasatch Range. As suddenly as the mountains appeared, they fell away, and a vast gridiron of lights appeared out of nowhere. It was clustered thickly under the aircraft and trailed off toward the south, erupting in ganglionic clots that winked and shimmered in the night. Salt Lake City, Orem, Draper, Provo: we were over most of the population of Utah.

> That thin avenue of civilization pressed against the Wasatches, intimidated by a fierce desert on three sides, was a poignant sight. More startling than its existence was the fact that it had been there only 134 years, since Brigham Young led his band of social outcasts to the old bed of a drying desert sea. . . . Within hours of ending their ordeal, the Mormons were digging shovels into the earth beside the streams draining the Wasatch Range, leading canals into the surrounding desert which they would convert to fields. . . . Without realizing it, they were laying the foundation of the most ambitious desert civilization the world has seen.[1]

Salt Lake City is the capital of Mormondom. Here are the leaders of the Church, many of them descended from pioneer families. Here are the iconic buildings, holy places to Church members—the grey-granite Salt Lake temple with its six thrusting steeples topped by a gold angel, the black-roofed, oval tabernacle shaped like half an egg lying on the ground, the skyscraper that houses the bureaucracy.

But Church members now number less than half of the city's population, and those outside the fold sometimes distrust and resent the minority institution that dominates the city. The politics of Salt Lake City speak volumes about the relationship between Mormons and everyone else, not only in the polarized city of Salt Lake, but in the United States at large. The tensions, the collaborations, the negotiations are often spelled out most legibly in the city beside the salty lake.

Salt Lake City is the most durable of the Church's Zions. The Tenth Article of Faith states that "Zion will be built upon this (the American) continent." After the exodus from Nauvoo, Illinois, in 1846, Salt Lake became the place for the Saints to gather. It remains the most religiously homogeneous large city in North America. The size of Providence, Rhode Island, Salt Lake stands unshadowed by larger metropolises. It's the only show around. Historian Gary Wills once mentioned that it was the nation's only holy city.[2]

Salt Lake City could not be founded today. The development required an open, thinly settled frontier with few inhabitants. In 1847, the advance party of 150 men and a few women reached the Salt Lake Valley, finally out of the mountains through which they had slaved with ax and shovel. Brigham Young, low with mountain fever, arrived on July 24 and confirmed that this was indeed the place to settle. Harriet Snow, seeing the wasteland that was her new home, said to her husband Lorenzo, "We have traveled fifteen hundred miles to get here, and I would willingly travel a thousand miles farther to get where it looked as though a white man could live."[3] But she stayed. The 24th of July, commemorating the pioneer arrival, is Utah's biggest holiday. From 1846 to 1869, thousands of families like the Snows crossed the plains and mountains to the arid Great Salt Lake basin in covered wagons and on foot, hoping to find a place so barren and undesirable that no one would bother them.

If Nauvoo was the city of Joseph Smith, Salt Lake was the city of Brigham Young. This carpenter, with little formal schooling or experience in administration, was a colonizing genius. When the first pioneers arrived, the Great Salt Lake Valley was a level strip of land fifteen or twenty miles wide and twenty to forty miles long between the Wasatch Mountains and the Great Salt Lake. The valley had little rain and timber, but creeks were dammed, irrigation ditches dug, land cleared, corn planted, and the wilderness blossomed. Cooperation and discipline united the people. By the 1870s the land boasted tall trees, profitable farms, and acres of peach orchards in a huge Mormon empire. Salt Lake City, the command post, was a thriving city.[4]

Four days after his arrival, Brigham Young walked the area, planning the city, waving his hand toward a central ten acres for the temple. Wilford Woodruff noted that the city was "laid out into lots of 10 rods by 20 [each] exclusive of the streets & into Blocks of 8 lots each, Being 10 acres in each block & one & a quarter in each lot." Streets were to be eight rods wide, so that an ox team could turn around, with a twenty-foot wide sidewalk on each side. Each house was to be built in the center of its lot, twenty feet from the front; four public squares, ten acres each, were set aside.[5] Salt Lake was a planned city anchored by the temple.[6]

Mormons, fresh from England and Scandinavia, poured into the city. More than 300 wagon trains, 10,000 wagons in all, brought people to Utah over the next twenty-two years. H. H. Bancroft described this moving city of Mormon immigrants, as a "migration without parallel in the world's history." The settlers traveled by ship to New Orleans, then 700 miles up the Mississippi and 500 more up the Missouri to Nebraska, where the wagon trains set off. To help indigent converts, the Church set up a Perpetual Emigrating Fund, advancing travel costs to be repaid later. In its thirty-seven-year existence, the fund spent several million dollars in cash and donated equipment and services to bring poor converts to Zion.

After the Transcontinental Railroad was completed in 1869, converts could travel from Liverpool, England, to Ogden, Utah, in just twenty-four days instead of the old three to five-month trip. No wonder that the pre-1869 arrivals are considered the real pioneers. By 1887, more than 85,000 immigrants and thousands of their uncounted children had made the journey. After their arrival, they were often sent out to one of the 500 pioneer colonies founded by the Saints, along "the Mormon corridor" from Colorado to California, from Canada to Mexico. Young was determined that the Saints would live "free and independent" of outsiders, or "Gentiles." This self-sufficiency policy encouraged local industries, most of them short-lived. A co-operative store for Church members opened in

1869 so that Church members could participate in trade and ownership and to hinder "profiteers" from charging exorbitant prices. The flagship store of the Zion's Cooperative Mercantile Institution, known as ZCMI, wholly owned by Church people, opened for business on Salt Lake City's Main Street on April 1, 1876. The façade was of fashionable cast iron. The newspaper proudly announced, "To say that the place looks splendid does no more than do it justice, as it compares in many points probably with any store on the continent."[7]

This closed economy was a point of friction in the Church's relationship with the outside world. The outside trade issue resolved itself gradually but especially after Utah's statehood in 1896 when outside merchants entered the city in great numbers and took over the economy. In 2001, the Church sold ZCMI to Meier and Frank and Company.[8]

From early days, the Mormons have gotten along fairly well with the Catholics and Jews, groups sharing the experience of discrimination. Protestants who led the nineteenth-century anti-Mormon crusades have been less compatible. As of 2003, Mormons constituted 48 percent of the city, Catholics 9 percent, and Protestants 8 percent. The second largest group at 19 percent were "nones," people without a religious affiliation, although they might well be religious. In Utah as a whole, Mormons are 57 percent of the population.[9] All but Mormons qualify as "Gentiles" in this city, polarized along the Mormon/Gentile line. Gentiles feel a heavy Mormon hand exercises power whenever it chooses. Mormons do not understand why their wide smiles and offerings of fresh bread and cookies set people's teeth on edge. The Mormons want the city to reflect its heritage, and the Gentiles want a city as diverse as other American cities.

Salt Lake City mayor Rocky Anderson, a former Mormon, thinks that the city would be a better community if people on both sides could break out of their isolation. City government tends to be run by non-Mormons, democrats. State government, however, reflects the majority Latter-day Saint population in the state and is largely conservative and Republican. James E. Shelledy, the former editor of the *Salt Lake Tribune*, complained, "The fact is we live in a quasi theocracy. . . . Eighty per cent of officeholders are of a single party, ninety per cent of a single religion, ninety-nine per cent of a single race, and eighty-five per cent of one gender." Church leaders have issued public assurances that it is alright to be a democrat, but Church members vote heavily Republican. The strength of the dominant religion provokes non-Mormons to move from indifference to opposition.[10]

But to say that Utah is Mormon and conservative does not do justice to the degrees and nuances of difference. The Republican Party is divided between those who control the party and an outspoken far right that decries even their leaders as republicans in name only. On the whole, the right-wing group, although Mormon-dominated, is farther from the official stands of the Church than are the democrats. The Church supports public education, whereas the far-right wing of the Mormon-dominated Utah legislature attacks it, calling for tax credits for home-schoolers and support for private schools. The Church opposes abortion, except for cases of rape, incest, or the mother's life. The far right opposes abortion, period. On gun rights, another emotional issue, the Church declares that there is no place for guns at schools, and leaders have publicly opposed the unlimited availability of guns. Yet ultra-conservatives vehemently support the right to carry hidden weapons. The Church condemns child abuse and neglect, but conservative republicans want to limit the state's right to intervene in abuse cases, in the name of family sanctity.[11]

Because of its frontier mentality and perhaps because of its beleaguered history, Utah has permissive gun standards. The state has 42,000 people with permits to carry guns and has ordered all state offices, parks, hospitals, and college campuses to remove gun bans in compliance with the law allowing for concealed weapons. The universities have banned guns on occasion for the security of important visitors, and officials would like to extend the ban. Utah's attorney general, however, threatens fines and lawsuits to enforce the law permitting concealed weapons, noting that there is plenty of evidence that "more guns equals less crime." This is the classic Utah encounter between conservative individualists and moderates. Two-thirds of all citizens, according to a *Deseret News* poll, favor banning guns from schools and day-care centers. Many would go much further.[12]

Utah Republicans as a whole are somewhat more conservative than national republicans. A survey found Utahns close to the median on most issues like spending for national defense versus national programs, national health care, and the death penalty but considerably more conservative on "moral issues" such as abortion, gay rights, government-sponsored open space, and doctor-assisted suicide. Compared to the state, Salt Lake City is more moderate.

The election in 2004 demonstrated these complex political factors. Utah went more solidly for George W. Bush for president than any other state. Ironically, at the same time, Senator Harry Reid, D-Nevada, one of five Mormons serving in the Senate, rose to minority leader of the U.S. Senate, the highest post held by a Church member. Utah governor, Republican Jon Huntsman, Jr., decisively defeated Scott Matheson, Jr., in all but three Utah counties, one of them Salt Lake, continuing the twenty-year tradition of a Republican in the state house. Both candidates came from respected political families. Matheson is the son of the last Democratic Utah governor and the brother of U.S. representative Jim Matheson. Huntsman, who out-campaigned and outspent his opponent, is the son of the senior Jon Huntsman, an industrialist and philanthropist who provides Church president Gordon B. Hinckley with a corporate jet for his travels. The candidates agreed on many issues, but Huntsman supported tax breaks for private school education, backed the state constitutional amendment toughening Utah's ban on same-sex marriage, and focused on jobs and the economy. After the election, he vowed to look at the state's moribund tax code, simplifying taxes, giving breaks to small business, and matching other states' economic incentives. He said the state lived in "splendid isolation" to economic realities and that he would look at the restrictive liquor laws as part of an aggressive campaign to boost Utah's image and its economy. He wanted to play up the people's work ethic and entrepreneurial spirit and the educated, tech-savvy work force. He predicted big changes.[13]

Another deep tension in the divided city came to light during Salt Lake City's newspaper wars between the Church-owned *Deseret News* and the critical, Gentile-owned *Salt Lake Tribune*. One has long spoken for the Church, the other for the opposition. The *Tribune*, begun in 1871 by Mormon dissidents, had been owned since 1902 by silver magnate and U.S. senator Thomas Kearns and four generations of his descendants, now the McCarthy family. The *Tribune* is the most powerful non-LDS institution in the state. In 1997, the family and other owners agreed to a profitable stock swap, exchanging the paper and some voting stock in the cable giant Tele-Communications Inc., or TCI, for TCI common shares. TCI had been founded in part with money from the *Tribune* in the 1950s. The paper's management would remain the same, and the family would buy the paper back in a few years.

In the course of events, TCI was acquired by AT&T, which did not want the newspaper, but any sale was complicated by the joint ownership of the Newspaper Agency Corporation, which has printed both the *Tribune* and the *News* for fifty years, an economic collaboration. The papers share presses, circulation crews, and advertising staff. The McCarthy family wanted to buy the *Tribune* back, but the *News* had to approve the sale, making the business fight a religious issue. An AT&T memo summed up the dispute: "Family wants to buy assets back. NAC [the press operations] not transferable . . . . Church will not consent because it hates family . . . . Family may not have the dollars."[14]

In 2000, AT&T divested itself of the *Tribune* selling to a Denver operation, MediaNews Group Inc., for $200 million. The horrified McCarthy family tried to stop the sale, not wanting to lose the paper, fearing Media-News would soften *Tribune* editorial criticisms of the Church. But neither federal judge nor the Federal Trade Commission saw any reason to block the sale. After months of litigation, the courts ruled the sale valid, saying the McCarthys knew the risk of losing the paper when they agreed to the stock deal. The *Deseret News*, in the meantime, was happy with new owners at MediaNews who supported their plan for morning publication, a plan the *Tribune* had opposed. MediaNews promised to "serve all of Utah and be beholden to no one." As their president Dean Singleton noted, "We view this as business people. . . . They (the McCarthys) view this as a generations war against the Mormon church. That's the difference."[15]

Tribune readers watched the paper closely, fearing that the critical edge would disappear. Singleton predicted rosy futures, increased circulation and advertising for both papers. He acknowledged the cultural divide in Salt Lake and pledged that the *Tribune* would bridge it, not make it wider. "It has been a 'them-and-us' situation. The *Tribune* is now committed to being a newspaper for all cultures."[16]

In a later chapter of the ongoing conflict, publisher Singleton disapproved of the *Tribune*'s handling of the case involving Elizabeth Smart, the kidnapped Mormon teenager. Two reporters sold salacious and inaccurate information to a supermarket tabloid, offending the family and their sympathizers. The reporters were reprimanded, but many thought the punishment insufficient. Singleton swept into town, apologized to the family, fired the reporters, and moved out the *Tribune*'s long-time editor, James E. Shelledy.[17]

Until this incident, the divided city had been united by the Smart case. The Smart family, beautiful, talented, prosperous, and virtuous, would seem to have been insulated from the evil forces of the world. Yet their home was invaded and their daughter stolen away by a homeless eccentric, the self-styled street preacher Brian David Mitchell, castigated by both the

LDS Church, which had long since excommunicated him, and by the Gentile community, which considered him representative of the regressive, deluded, fundamentalist aspects of Mormonism at its worst. Both the LDS and Gentile communities condemned this mystical deviant, but Singleton's action seemed to side with the LDS community.

The city as a whole enjoyed the spotlight turned on Salt Lake during the three-week period when the 2002 Winter Olympic Games visited Salt Lake City, but the tensions of Mormons with the world at large were frequently exposed by reporters filing their stories. The media coverage before and during the Games illustrates how other this place was considered to be. Even as Utah tried to redefine itself as a modern metropolitan center with supreme ski resorts and spectacular natural beauty in contrast to the older straight-laced, Puritanical Mormon image, the news stories still opened with jokes about polygamy, the Church's dubious Christianity, and the problems of getting alcohol. Lawrence Wright, in a long piece in *The New Yorker*, described the Church in faint praise as "a young well-scrubbed, and ingratiating religion." A hundred years ago, he noted, this had been "the most persecuted creed in America." Now it was "perhaps the country's most robust religion."[18] His piece made frequent forays into plural marriage and the Mountain Meadows Massacre, the skeletons in the Mormon closet.

Long before the Games actually commenced, the Salt Lake Olympic Committee was discredited for bribing members of the International Olympic Committee and their families, an extortion organizers understood as the price for hosting the Games. The bribes were medical operations, jobs, and stipends for young people. The scandal exposed, the SLOC leaders resigned and a new committee rose under Mitt Romney, the Massachusetts head of Bain, Ltd., and a turnaround specialist who had challenged Ted Kennedy for a Massachusetts senatorial seat. The Mormon Romney, who took over the scandal-plagued Games, noted that Utah had let the country down, and he vowed to stage a great event.[19]

Early on, two able and well-known apostles, Neal A. Maxwell and Robert D. Hales, were assigned to coordinate Church-Olympic relationships. The Church commissioned books and planned advertising and proselytizing efforts for interested visitors. Later, leaders drew back from this aggressive plan seen as unsuitably turning the Games into a missionary campaign. The Church vowed to be good hosts. Even so, Romney was plagued by comments about the Mormon Games or the Mo-lympics. To show the wide support in the city, he put fifteen non-Mormon boosters into a publicity picture with flutes of champagne. The *London Evening Standard* noted before the Games that "with their unconditional welcome and unprecedented global visibility, the Mormons cannot lose."

Church Public Affairs sent out press kits, urging reporters to look beyond the idea that those odd Mormons "party too little and marry too much." The press coverage was usually favorable. Matt Lauer of NBC's "Today" show called members "honest, hardworking people with exceptional family values." Canadian Gary Mason reported on the clean-cut, nice people who combine charity and industry. He thought that the LDS nature of the town was bound to come through, and if the "Mo-lympics" managed to be successful and safe, they would certainly reflect positively on the Church.[20]

Utah's smoking bans were not much of an issue, but the state's restrictive liquor laws, seen as the Church forcing the Word of Wisdom on unbelievers, were inhibiting. Local people know how to pay a modest admission fee to bars designated "private clubs," or visiting the many full-service restaurants with no restrictions and substantial wine lists. Alcohol is easily come by in Park City, thirty-eight miles from Salt Lake City, site of many Olympic activities. Mayor Anderson had hoped that alcohol might flow more freely during the Games, but the Church opposed liberalizing Utah's laws, sternly noting that "the impact on society from the abuse of alcohol, in terms of pain, sorrow, misery and lost lives, is incalculable," and that "existing alcohol laws are supported by a majority of Utah citizens." A secured eight-block square with the Olympics Medals Plaza featured free high-profile entertainment—and hot chocolate.[21]

As the Olympics approached, *New York Times* writer George Vecsey, an Olympic watcher, just hoped that the event could take place without any terrible problems. "Good luck, Salt Lake City," he wrote. "I hope we remember you for a thousand years as competent, conventional and safe. No surprises. A few smiles, a few cheers, a few medals, a nice little Osmond Family Olympics."[22]

The Games themselves went better than could have been hoped. As the Olympics receded into history, the local people were satisfied. The city, especially the mountain venues, provided a beautiful backdrop. The volunteers were cheerful from first to last. The security was effective. The Church kept its word and held its tongue. Some journalists found the Church less weird than expected. Mitt Romney, who inherited the Games at a low point and turned them around said, "It was more wonderful, more significant than we ever imagined." Romney, unpaid, reaped great personal success, jump-starting his stalled political career. He returned to Boston, was elected governor of Massachusetts, and looms as a presidential contender.[23]

Critics admitted that the city had blossomed with unexpected life and beauty but expected it soon to return to its "poky old self." Others were more positive. George Vecsey wrapped it up: "Make no mistake, these were Mormon Games, no matter how much that aspect was played down. There was almost no overt proselytizing, but . . . the people of Utah were sportsmanlike toward visitors and athletes from all countries. . . . I'll have good memories of seeing friends, and of the thoughtful planning and capable people who took care of us. Thank you, Salt Lake City."[24]

The Olympic coverage paid little attention to Salt Lake's economic ills. The city suffers as shopping life moves south out of the downtown where the temple, tabernacle, and Church headquarters are located. The declining inner-city malls need expensive reinvention, and people question the future. One commentator suggested that efforts to save the downtown were doomed. He suggested that the city had always been an important religious center and the downtown should develop like the Vatican. More beautiful Church buildings and gardens would make more sense than expecting people to shop and dine there. He saw in the struggle to maintain the downtown the underlying division between the Saints and Gentiles, "an intractable, fundamental, historic and economic reality."[25]

How to deal with the two retail malls that the Church purchased is a major planning issue. In 2003, the Church brought in city planner Ronald Pastore to oversee redesign and redevelopment. He was optimistic about Salt Lake City. As the Church proceeded with plans for a $500 million downtown redevelopment, Mayor Rocky Anderson criticized the secretive planning process and feared that a new massive mall would not meet the city's needs. He liked the idea of town houses on the street front and gardens in back and additional necessities such as grocery and drug stores to provide a mix of food, beverage, entertainment, retail stores, and housing, but he wanted a ground level walking, traditional downtown setting with smaller, cut-up blocks and less enclosed retail.[26]

A group attempting to heal the city's religious and cultural fractures is the "Alliance for Unity," a group of eighteen business, political, religious, and media leaders who search for common ground. In September of 2001, the group gathered at the State Capitol to read a statement aiming "to help people cross boundaries of culture, religion, and ethnicity to better understand and befriend one another." Catholic bishop George Niederhauer hoped that religious understanding would spread and affect the way groups talk about each other in closed rooms. Mormon apostle M. Russell Ballard advised members to reach out to neighbors of other cultures. President Hinckley has also addressed bias and bigotry. "We must not be clannish." We can "cherish our method of worship without being offensive to others." After a year of talking and lunching, Alliance members decided to teach civility and tolerance in the schools.[27]

The drive for civil harmony was disrupted by a protracted fight over the use of a single-block walkway in downtown Salt Lake City. Temple Square, home to the Salt Lake Temple and the Visitors' Centers, was expanded to the east when the Church reacquired the grand old Hotel Utah in 1987. This posh empire hotel was refurbished as the Joseph Smith Memorial Building to house restaurants, offices, a theater, and a genealogical library. To consolidate its property, in 1999, the Church bought from the city a block of public street between the building and Temple Square, paying $8.1 million for it and closing it to traffic. The Church landscaped the strip and opened a gate from Temple Square into what became Main Street Plaza. Brides have their pictures taken there with the temple in the background. Twenty-four hour public access was allowed by way of a public easement, but the Church required "suitable" behavior—no smoking, sunbathing, bicycling, distributing anti-LDS literature, and "engaging in any illegal, offensive, indecent, obscene, lewd or disorderly speech, dress, or conduct."[28]

Security guards restrained the behavior of pamphleteers who flock to Salt Lake City during conference time to carry signboards and give out leaflets attacking the Church. The enraged demonstrators took their protest to court, but the local courts upheld the Church's right to impose restrictions on the Plaza's use. The American Civil Liberties Union of Utah appealed this ruling to the 10th Circuit United States Court of Appeals in Denver, which overturned the decision. The three Denver judges voided the restrictions on the Main Street Plaza on the grounds that the city had retained an easement that required opening the one-block stretch to pamphleteers and smokers. The judges spoke of the marketplace of ideas in religion being a hallmark of American society and that to restrict activities in public places infringed on free speech. Local ACLU leader Dani Eyer agreed. "People who have problems with a religion have a right to offer alternative views near the seat of that religion's power. 'It is as it ought to be.'" This opinion left the city and the Church in a quandary of conflicting territoriality. The Church owned the land, which they had purchased with the idea of controlling behavior. The city retained the easement, which the judges said required free speech.[29]

Public opinion split along religious lines. Opened as a place for solitude and contemplation, the two-acre plot became a symbol of the local power struggle. The Church hinted that additional funds for the easement might be available. Mayor Anderson refused to give up the easement but began to talk of limiting restrictions to a couple of "protest zones," with controlled noise, placards of limited size, leaflet distribution, and "other peaceful individual expressive activities." He called it an olive branch, giving the Church 95 percent of what it wanted. The Church rejected the plan as no compromise at all. Stephen Pace, a local resident, noted that no recent issue compared to the conflict that "dramatically and unnecessarily picked at the scab" of the "pretty iffy" 150-year church/state relationship.[30]

Meanwhile, the plaza protesters became popular media figures. Kurt Van Gorden, the Baptist preacher from Southern California, kept on trying to save Mormons by handing out pamphlets to passersby during his monthly trips to Salt Lake City. "I'm sure I'm a pain to the Mormon Church," he admitted, "But do they see how much of a pain they are to the Constitution and American citizens?" Van Gorden noted that "The persecuted have now become the persecutors in what they've been doing to people like me, in trying to prevent me from the free exercise of my beliefs." Lonnie Pursifull, another plaza preacher, said he knew he was an unpopular person, but "I'm not in this for popularity." Pursifull preaches to atheists and homosexuals as well as Mormons. "We go and show them their sin and then we show them a way out—faith in Jesus Christ. . . . If we just went there and bashed them and trashed them, we wouldn't be doing them no good."[31]

When the situation was about as tense as could be, Mayor Anderson agreed to give up the easement entirely in exchange for two acres of land, worth almost $100,000, on Salt Lake's west side, to be used as a community center for the underprivileged. Utah's Alliance for Unity, which had been fidgeting at the edges of the dispute calling for civility, stepped in to raise $5 million to build the community center.[32]

The swap of easement for land was consummated on 28 July 2003 with a six to zero positive vote by the City Council. Councilwoman Nancy Saxton abstained, regretting that the options for LDS believers and nonbelievers to coexist had been closed off. "The lines are drawn," she said. "That part of

Main Street is really totally private." The Church won't put up signs or gates, but pedestrians will feel their power to do so. The Unitarian Church and the ACLU swiftly filed suit against the city for giving up the easement.[33]

As land divides the city and state, so does liquor. When the Utah Department of Alcoholic Beverage Control prepared an extensive restructuring of the state's liquor laws, the director gave it to the Church to review before the public hearing. Church officials refused to comment on the proposed changes but indicated that they would not oppose the legislation if it remained intact. Although tacit Church support was necessary to pass the bill, citizens nevertheless resented that no other entity had an advance look. The *Tribune* denounced this as bad public policy, saying an open process with the widest possible public debate from the beginning would be preferable to the appearance of advance veto power. The ACLU demanded copies of all documents, believing that "democracy dies behind closed doors." Critics thought the Church had hijacked the democratic process, preventing the input of others.[34]

Nothing shows the state of Mormon relationships with American culture better than the conflicts in Salt Lake City. Friendly, vigorous, happy Mormons make every effort to open their arms to the world, and yet no one dislikes Mormons more than the "Gentiles" who live among them. They see the Church as backward, clannish, and repressive. Since the end of polygamy in the nineteenth century, Mormons have wanted to assimilate into American culture. They volunteer, they contribute, they are law-abiding, and yet they are resented. Despite gestures of good will on both sides and efforts to accommodate one another, tension remains. Although tolerance and kindliness will reign on the surface, the deep-seated aversions emerge again and again. Noel de Nevers, a Gentile Mormon watcher, suggests that non-Mormons have three options—to retreat, to resist, or to relax. For himself, he chooses the last option and notes the advantages: besides local cultural and educational opportunities, he always has something to talk about.[35]

THE CHURCH AT ONE HUNDRED AND SEVENTY-FIVE

Mormonism is a new religious tradition.

—Jan Shipps, 1985

In 2005, the Church celebrated Joseph Smith's 200th birthday on December 23, 1805, and the 175th anniversary of the organization of the Church on April 6, 1830. As the juxtaposition of the anniversaries makes clear, Smith was just twenty-five years old when he organized the Church. Nothing known of him or the circumstances gave reason to expect much from the fledgling movement, yet at the April 2005 General Conference speakers noted the Church had grown over the past decade by three million members to more than twelve million. Five hundred new stakes (dioceses) and 4,000 new wards and branches (congregations) had been organized. The number of operating temples had grown from forty-seven in 1995 to 119 in 2005 with three more to be dedicated during the year. The membership of student-age young people enrolled in the Church Education System had doubled to about 400,000. The Perpetual Education Fund, which had begun with "nothing but hope and faith," had assisted nearly 18,000 young people in twenty-seven countries, helping them to prepare for better employment. The Book of Mormon, printed in eighty-seven languages in 1995, was available in 106 languages in 2005, and fifty-one million copies had been distributed in that decade. Thousands of new chapels had risen as well as the immense Conference Center in Salt Lake City. Sermons preached during the conference were broadcast to nearly 5,800 venues in eighty nations and translated into seventy-five languages. An estimated $641 million had been distributed worldwide through "humanitarian efforts," often in collaboration with other religious groups.[1]

A new general presidency of the Primary, the organization for teaching children, was installed. The new president, Cheryl C. Lant, the mother of nine children, had studied early childhood development at Brigham Young University and was the co-founder and co-owner, with her husband, of a private school for children and the developer of a phonics-based beginning reading program. She was therefore a working mother who had extended her mothering reach beyond her own children both in her school and in her congregation.

Eight new men were called to the First Quorum of the Seventy to serve until age seventy when they would be retired as emeriti. Six were from Utah and Idaho, the other two from Brazil and Mexico. Of the four new General Authorities called to the Second Quorum of the Seventy for a shorter period, two were from Utah and one each from Korea and Germany. Thirty-seven Area Seventies, leaders who continued their real-world jobs while administering the affairs of multiple stakes locally, were released from their duties while another thirty-eight were called to fill the ranks. The new group had greater international representation with seven from the United States, six from Mexico, three from the Philippines, two each from Argentina, Brazil, Chile, and Peru, and a good sprinkling from other countries: Nicaragua, Ecuador, Guatemala, and Honduras from Spanish-speaking countries, Germany, England, the Netherlands, Latvia, and Norway from Europe, and Australia and New Zealand from the southern hemisphere.[2]

From this position of strength, Church members prepared to celebrate Joseph Smith's bicentennial with a year of conferences, books, exhibitions, films, and local events. During the thirty-eight and a half years of his life, Smith established the Church's guiding principles and practices, built cities and temples, launched a massive missionary program, and produced over 800 pages of scripture. Church members have long held that Smith, considered by many a fraud or a religious fanatic, is not properly appreciated. Mormons hope that talking about him will win respect for his considerable achievements. As one historian said, "We live in an unbelieving age. But Joseph Smith comes along and renews the belief that God will intervene and speak to people. . . . That gives us a basis for believing and hoping that God is actually intervening in the church as a whole, but even more so in our own lives."[3]

2005 marked the tenth anniversary of the First Presidency of the Church with Gordon B. Hinckley, Thomas S. Monson, and James E. Faust in office. Hinckley has been hailed as a builder of temples and chapels, of innovative charitable programs, and of steering a steady course through the problems of modern life. In his decade-long administration, leaders stressed emphasis on the family; the number of operating temples, which will total 130 when those announced are completed; technical improvements allowing widespread travel and broadcasting via satellite; emphasis on Jesus Christ; technical improvements on FamilySearch, the Internet genealogy program that provides online access to more than a billion names; good media attention; wide distribution of the Book of Mormon in many languages; the Perpetual Education Fund; gifts of food, clothing, and supplies around the world; the growth of the Church outside the United States; the building of the Conference Center; and the restoration of historic sites.[4]

There were also problems faced by the Church in this triumphant decade. Many of the achievements have their opposite side: the weakening of the family, seen specifically in figures on divorce and abuse and urgent warnings against gambling and pornography; the problems of exponential growth, and the problems of poverty and lack of education. In 2005, three important indicators were down: the number of children, the baptismal rate, and the number of missionaries, all reflecting shrinking rates of growth. The total number of missionaries was down when it had been 51,000 in 2004 and 61,000 the year before. These figures represented a combination of higher qualifications for potential missionaries and for the people they would like to baptize, as well as a demographic reduction in the number of available young men and women. New children of record—the number of members added by births—were down 587 to 98,870, reflecting a lower birthrate among Mormons. Convert baptisms, which have hovered at 300,000 annually for some years, were down 1,684 from the year before to 241,239. The speedily growing Church is slowing down.[5]

Also interesting are the confrontations with other groups. The Church does very well as a monolith but frequently suffers in a larger context.

1. Officials of the state of Illinois, discovering that earlier state residents had expelled Mormons and killed the Church's founder in the 1840's, moved to apologize for the act. The resolution draft asked the Mormons for their "pardon and forgiveness," but Illinois lawmakers edited the language that implicated them in acts they had not committed and instead voted for a fainter "official regret."[6]

2. When Mormons made their Tabernacle on Temple Square available to evangelical Ravi Zacharias, as part of a network of 100 evangelical churches trying to improve relations with the Mormons, this "historic occasion" included an apology by Richard Mouw, president of Fuller Theological Seminary in California, who confessed that evangelicals had sinned against Latter-day Saints. "We've often seriously misrepresented the beliefs and practices of members of the LDS faith. . . . We've told you what you believe without first asking you." "Let me state it clearly. We evangelicals have sinned against you." Other evangelicals "expressed dismay" at Mouw's statement. "[Mouw] was wrong. He had no business. And it will hurt," said evangelicals in response, calling the comments "insensitive," "inaccurate," and "ignorant." Mouw eventually apologized, saying "I am deeply sorry for causing distress in the evangelical community," but "I make no apology for wanting to foster gentle and reverent dialogue with Mormon friends."[7]

3. Joshua Cohen prefaced an obituary for LDS historian Hugh Nibley with a statement unimaginable considering it was about a religious group in a newspaper for a general audience.

> From the earliest age, I was taught to be respectful of the beliefs of others, tolerant of their traditions though they might differ from my own. Then I met the Mormons.
>
> I hate the Mormons. I hate that, like a McDonald's Fish Filet, they're the same everywhere. From Utah to Ukraine, I've seen them in their suits, with their Elder-name tags and fluoridated grins. I hate them for their quick American friendliness, a geniality without depth. Above all, I hate them because they pulled off what I've always wanted to do: They invented a religion, and made [a lot] of money in the process.[8]

So has it always been. There is something in people that balks at the Mormons. In the last few decades there has been a steady stream of books identifying the problems of the Church and prophesying their fatal effect. Observers, outsiders, insiders, and "insider—outsiders," study Church literature, interview Mormons, and come up with judgments about the Church's progress in the modern world. There have been at least a dozen such books written since 1960. The Church is large enough, offbeat enough, and successful enough to attract attention. Most of the books offer a diagnosis in their conclusions about the pitfalls the Church will surely stumble into. Yet somehow the Church adapts and moves on.

The older books presented problems that seemed insurmountable at the time. When journalist William J. Whalen published *The Latter-day Saints in the Modern Day World: An Account of Contemporary Mormonism* (1964) he saw a church numbering two million "riding the crest of popularity." Still, he foresaw an emerging conflict between the increasing higher education of the members and a religion of miracles, revelation, and questionable doctrines. He noted as prime issues the priesthood denial to black members and the Book of Mormon's claim to historical authenticity. How could well-educated Mormons accept beliefs so distant from modern rationalism?

After forty years, the Book of Mormon's historicity provokes heated debates, but many educated members still accept its veracity. The 1978 revelation expanding the priesthood to include people of all races reduced racial pressures. As to education squelching religiosity, Mormons cite a 1984 study by BYU professors Stan Albrecht and Tim Heaton in the *Review of Religious Research* finding that LDS Church members become more religiously active with increased education, the opposite of what is found in most churches.[9] A follow-up study, parsing fields of study, might temper those results. Still, Whalen would find many highly educated Mormons active in the Church.

Twenty years later, academics Robert Gottlieb and Peter Wiley, in *America's Saints: The Rise of Mormon Power* (1984), reflected the political paranoia of their time. Alarmed by the Church's power to convert, organize, and mobilize new members and to control critical voices, they saw sinister potential in the Church's corporate power and expanded influence.

Gottlieb and Wiley noted the programmatic changes of the late 1950s, revising the curriculum, simplifying, economizing, and centralizing the whole institution. Ending their narrative in 1983, Gottlieb and Wiley feared that conservative Ezra Taft Benson, a cabinet member under President Dwight D. Eisenhower, might become Church president, further narrowing Mormon lives. But the authors later acknowledged that the Church had escaped ruin. President Spencer W. Kimball lived on, delaying Benson's rise to power. The appointment of moderates Dallin Oaks and Russell Nelson as apostles diluted the conservatism.[10] When Benson did become President in 1985, he did not take the Church to the far right but emphasized reading the Book of Mormon.

John Heinerman, an anthropologist and Mormon, and Anson Shupe, a sociologist and a Methodist, took on related issues in *The Mormon Corporate Empire* (1985), seeing duplicity throughout Mormonism. The vastly wealthy, anti-democratic, authoritarian Church with its partisan political influence, sexism, and censorship, had an insensitive bureaucracy. The writers observed member infiltration into power positions in the government, military, and business worlds, preparing for the millennial day when the nation was at risk and the Mormons took control, reshaping American society and democratic institutions, and freezing out other religions. "The LDS Church's goals have not mellowed," they insisted. "The Church . . . still rejects religious pluralism."[11]

Documenting the wealth of the Church, the authors estimated by 1983 the Church held $1 billion in stocks and bonds and had an annual income of $207 million. They estimated the Church's total assets then at $7.9 billion. They urged the Church to open its books to avoid the appearance of evil.[12]

The writers feared that the Church might be planning to take over the U.S. government. In truth, rescuing the American nation used to be a regular topic of discussion among Mormons who thought the Church would have to step in when the "Constitution hung by a thread," but no one mentions it now, speaking instead of tolerance, cooperation, and acceptance. Heinerman and Shupe's dire predictions seem no closer now than when written.

The concern for power continued in the most recent outsider critique, *Mormon America: The Power and the Promise* (1999). Journalists Richard N. and Joan K. Ostling broke new ground in aiming at readers in and out of the Church, presenting a "candid but nonpolemical overview" about the "subculture's colorful history, unique beliefs, and penchant for secrecy, its lifestyle and finances, its place in the religious and secular world today" and the future. The Ostlings concentrated on present-day issues, reporting on hidden activities about hierarchy and riches. Updating the work of Heinerman and Shupe, they estimated a financial empire worth $25 to $30 billion in the late 1990s, for which they credited tithing donations along with savings from much unpaid volunteer labor.[13]

Church leaders do not answer criticism about their vast financial empire. They downplay assets, reporting that suggested holdings are exaggerated. Most are revenue-consuming, rather than revenue-producing, they say. The chapels and temples, and the three expensive branches of Brigham Young University, produce no income. Roger Clarke, who manages the money, will say only that Church members are generous, that all building expenses are paid out of current revenues, and that the accumulating reserves, enough to operate the Church for several years, have never been touched. Clarke notes two of Hinckley's reasons for keeping the financial situation quiet: he does not want the members to think the Church has unlimited funds, which it actually does not; and he does not want to dishonor the widow's mite, the sacrifice of the poor.[14] Change is unlikely. Other book writers, including a few life-long members and a group of sympathetic outsiders, have also offered extended analyses of the Church. Their books are more likely to describe an institution that Mormons recognize.

Armand L. Mauss, a believing Mormon and a sociologist, in his book *The Angel and the Beehive: The Mormon Struggle with Assimilation* (1994), traced an undulating assimilation arc from 1900. According to Mauss, persecution and repression kept Mormons in isolation in their western redoubt until the turn of the century when the end of polygamy and statehood allowed assimilation to begin. By 1950 or so, Mormons had entered mainstream America with an unrivaled patriotism, living the American Dream. Thanks to the conservative turn in American culture after World War II, the Church in the 1950s was typical of the grassroots thinking of the nation. Except for the race issue, all major institutional and doctrinal accommodations to mainstream America had been achieved. David O. McKay, the Mormon president in the 1950s and 1960s, was known for patriotism, liberal thinking, and conciliation. Church members still considered themselves peculiar because of belief in Joseph Smith's visions, the Book of Mormon, and living prophets, but the Church had attained a degree of assimilation impossible in the nineteenth century.[15]

At this point, according to Mauss, it was as if someone said, "enough!" Assimilation was eroding Mormon identity. As geographic boundaries were eliminated, Mormons reached into their bag of cultural peculiarities to find traits to mark their boundaries and to encourage a retrenchment mentality. Mormons reversed the assimilationist trend by emphasizing claims to continuous revelation through modern prophets, families, temple work, missionary work, and religious education. Genealogical work was computerized at enormous cost, and local genealogical libraries were widely dispersed. The proliferation of convenient new temples decentralized and democratized temple attendance. Some old exclusive, millenarian, and eschatological doctrines were down played as obedience to modern prophets, and the Book of Mormon as a witness for Christ was stressed. This emphasis on distinctive Mormonism became noticeable by the 1960s.[16]

The leaders taught a new and strict obedience in contrast to seeking a universal good understandable to everyone. Some interpreted the injunction to "Follow the Brethren" to mean unquestioning obedience. They added corollaries to underscore the point: "When our leaders speak, the thinking has been done" and "When the Prophet speaks, the debate is over." These dicta are contrasted with the Church's steady devotion to "free agency," the right of people to make their own decisions and Joseph Smith's often-quoted statement, "I teach them correct principles, and they govern themselves."

This shift back to some aspects of old-style Mormonism took place against the cultural change of the Civil Rights Movement, an expansion of tolerance, a general loosening of traditional morality, and substance abuse. Mauss saw the Mormons retreating to old ways, building Church identity against the world. The correlation movement, he believed, sharpened this new identity while simplifying and homogenizing the work of the Church. This minimalizing of Mormonism made it maximally adaptable, a transportable model manageable by new members and plainly visible to visitors everywhere. The General Authorities also said they instituted these "course corrections" because the Church had become over-programed and over-regimented. The new motto was "reduce and simplify."[17]

Mauss regretted that simplification eliminated broader cultural programs—dances, plays, speech festivals, choral programs, and sports tournaments—but the back-to-basics trend helped to assimilate the large numbers of new converts and freed up women from heavy Church responsibilities. Mauss wondered whether minimalization had impoverished Mormonism's cultural experience.[18]

Jan Shipps, a non-Mormon professor of history emerita at Indiana University-Purdue University at Indianapolis, traced a similar and complementary arc. An "inside-outsider," she argued that Mormonism was not traditionally Christian but a new religious tradition of its own. Surveying the Mormon image since 1960 in her memoir-like collection of updated essays, *Sojourner in the Promised Land: Forty Years Among the Mormons* (2000), Shipps observed that the Mormons' appearance as model Americans was achieved against the radical image of pot-smoking, flag-burning, hairy-faced radical youth. Next to them, Mormons appeared neat, modest, virtuous, family-loving, conservative, and newly appealing patriotic people. The contrast between the clean-cut Mormons and the scruffy hippies moved the Mormon image from the earlier quasi-foreign, alien style to the super-American portrait of the late 1960s and early 1970s, when they became "more American than the Americans."[19]

But, according to Shipps, visibility bred contempt. Suddenly Church members began to seem more dangerous than the Christian Scientists, Jehovah's Witnesses, and Seventh-day Adventists, the other three indigenous American "cults." Exposure led to the creation of anti-Mormon materials such as the film *God Makers: the Mormon Quest for Godhood,* which proposed to unmask the secrets of Mormonism.[20]

In discussing women and history, Shipps concluded that women's lives in the Church had become passive whereas men's had scarcely changed. Because of this change, she doubted that Mormon women would be allowed to interpret their own history, a potentially dangerous subject. Mormon women intellectuals' interpretation of the Mormon past threw the conservative present into question. Organizationally, Mormon women had lost much of their autonomy during the twentieth century, and this fact had to be played down. Shipps saw the enthusiasm for a Mother in Heaven among some Mormon women as a thwarted effort to develop a feminist theology.[21] Shipps's reading of the situation rang true for older Mormon women intellectuals, the second-wave feminists, but their daughters, more inclined to make the most of the present, are free of this past.

These short reviews indicate the potential and adaptability of this sprawling church. Despite predictions of fatal flaws, the Church avoided destruction and evaded some serious challenges. Because the lumbering organization is fast on its feet, some criticisms now seem dated. Others are still cogent. Will the Church with its hidden books avoid major financial scandals? Will the Church's extreme image-consciousness backfire? Will challenges to the Book of Mormon persuade members? These questions continue to engage observers.

Writers on Mormonism have said that the Church cannot deal with the forces of modernity. A primitive faith such as this is expected to wither in the face of science and modern skepticism. The authoritarian priesthood hierarchy is out of step with America democracy, and the lack of openness and free debate should alienate educated members. Contradictions such as these seem likely to doom the Church to irrelevance or debilitating internal conflict.

And yet the Church has grown and prospered. Modernity has not stopped Mormonism from thriving. Educated members have learned to live with the clash with modern rationalism; there are always issues, but none are fatal. The concealment of Church finances rarely arouses insider fears because the Church record of responsible management is long and reassuring. Church power poses no significant threat to the nation. On the contrary, Mormons feel their Church has little influence in most arenas of power outside the Rocky Mountain states.

Critics have suggested that the Church proselytizes to amass revenue through tithing funds. But those who work with new members recognize that conversion is a long-term, high-risk investment. New converts are modest in possessions, socially marginal, and poor in spirit. They cost the Church rather than providing revenue. The American Church provides major financial support for Latter-day Saints in other countries. More to the point is the question if the United States can bear the cost of this world-wide Mormon empire. The answer depends on the strength of the American economy.

On the other hand, after exponential growth, the numbers are slowing. Judging from current conversion rates, the Church is not likely to meet Rodney Stark's high-end prediction of 265 million members by 2080, and even the lower reaches of sixty million seem optimistic. Two reasons for slower growth are the emphasis on retaining members and the emphasis on gathering potential members through media outlets rather than knocking on doors. Television ads gather in people to be taught, but a much lower percentage joins the Church. Slower growth causes Mormons to reconsider their self-congratulation. How will the Church deal with diminished yields, when members have become accustomed to expecting major growth? Members are embarrassed by this change of fortune, but with fewer new people to socialize and fellowship, the Church may be able to mature and enrich its existing programs, consolidating gains.

How will the Church deal with inner tensions such as intellectual freedom, democracy in Church government, and above all, gender issues, which affect so many individuals and families? Although women's roles have been predicted to be the next major tension, feminism offers little threat to the Church. Feminist issues are too American to sway an international Church, and the number of feminists is too small even in the United States. More important, new opportunities for involvement and development have quietly opened opportunities to women. The Church is coming to grips with new women, women with career ambitions, even as domestic women are nurtured.

The gender tension of the future will continue to be the preferential treatment for men. The Church has more difficulty retaining men than women, and because they make up the center of the organization, they are the center of attention. The Church has invested too much energy in establishing the family as the unit of priesthood organization, firmly fixing the female as the angel of the hearth and the male as family leader, to diminish male roles. However, modifications occur. Although leaders react dramatically and negatively to social change at first, they usually accommodate in the long run. Change in policy is possible without changing scriptural directives.

Marriages are changing. More serious female careers among devoted members are spurring tolerance and acceptance of strong women. In cooperative marriages, couples share work and child care. Imaginative planning of schooling and work schedules allows partners equal opportunities to develop their talents. Economic circumstances often require that women contribute to household expenses, and as in pioneer families, women pull their own weight. Families with two working parents benefit from the Mormon congregational community—a modern version of the proverbial village rearing the child.

Further difficulty among women lies along the single/married line as the many devoted single women work out their destinies in this married church. They have to make professional decisions while still looking for priesthood holders to marry, hoping to be mothers. More accept the new model of the Mormon single woman who builds a productive life in the professional world rather than languishing in sorrow. This model holds that a woman can thrive and contribute although unmarried, mothering part time. The acceptance of alternative models of the good woman seems obvious to the world at large; within Mormonism it is a breakthrough.

As a final stage of assimilation into American life, Mormons are entering the American power structure. Centered and disciplined, devoted to education and self-improvement, Mormons do well in finance, business, and law. Matured by their mission experience, they rise in the nation's institutions. The deepening pool of talent in the professions, the corporations, and the governments sparks occasional concern about a "Mormon Mafia," successful Mormons who offer their fellow believers a leg up.

So far Mormons have shown less interest in philanthropy and community involvement. Mormons have devoted their off-hours and spare money to Church programs, but this pattern may change as they grow in professional influence. More Mormons are moving into performance, scholarship, and the arts. The high level of cultural accomplishment has been virtually eliminated in individual congregations, but drama, dance, and music continue to be valued. In a vital, artistic world, members busily scribble novels, shoot films, and compose and record music in classical and popular genres. Significantly, many do well with the growing Mormons-only market. Although the Church has not turned out any Shakespeares or Mozarts, there are Scarlattis and Charles Brockden Browns. The arts flourish in Salt Lake City, and Mormons find places in other areas. Concerts, dramas, and art exhibitions by Mormon artists and performers are increasingly common, as are film festivals and pools of artistic patronage.

The combination of an encompassing theology and tightly woven community life give Mormons a fundamental confidence that holds up well in emergencies. They come together naturally when disaster strikes. Their belief in the goodness of God enables them to cope with losses. They are a long way, however, from developing the tolerance and sensitivity that Church leaders have been preaching; blunders arise out of the energy the Church generates.

The Church offers its members the opportunity to participate, to organize, to carry out programs, to work together, and to serve and be served in a vital community, all of which brings satisfaction and personal development. The theology provides meaning and direction for life. Lay leadership means that everyone has a place and can be a leader. The prophetic tradition of living leaders who interpret God's will for His children gives confidence about the future. Clear direction comes from the Book of Mormon and other Latter-day scriptures, purporting to be the word of God. The Church's plan of salvation, which spans a premortal world to life beyond the grave, promises eternal relationships and happiness. In times of suffering, Mormons can retreat to their holy places in the temple, leaving their troubles behind. Altogether, the Church produces good-hearted, cheerful people who can be rallied to a good cause. The question is whether these strengths will enable Mormondom to surmount the obstacles it faces in a pluralistic and often hostile world.

CHRONOLOGY

1820   Joseph Smith's first vision.
1827   Joseph Smith received gold plates at Hill Cumorah.
1830   The Book of Mormon published.
        Joseph Smith organized "Church of Christ" in Fayette, New York.
1836   The Kirtland Ohio Temple dedicated.
1842   Articles of Faith published.
        The Female Relief Society organized.
1844   Joseph Smith and brother Hyrum killed by a mob while in jail in
            Carthage, Illinois.
1846   The Nauvoo Temple dedicated.
        Mormon pioneers left Nauvoo.
1847   Brigham Young became Church's second president.
        The pioneers arrived in Great Salt Lake Valley.
1852   Plural marriage publicly announced.
1857   U.S. President James Buchanan ordered an army to Utah to put
            down a rebellion. Army arrived peacefully the next year,
            staying until 1861.
        The Mountain Meadows Massacre in southern Utah.
1862   Federal law defined plural marriage as criminal bigamy.
1877   Brigham Young died, age seventy-six. John Taylor became
            Church's third president in 1880.
        The St. George (Utah) Temple dedicated.
1882   The Edmunds anti-polygamy bill, defining polygamous living as
            unlawful cohabitation, made law, disenfranchising those in
            polygamous marriages.

1884   The Logan (Utah) Temple dedicated.
1887   The Edmunds-Tucker Act became law, disincorporating the
         Church, dissolving the Perpetual Emigrating Fund, abolishing
         female suffrage, and confiscating Church property.
       President John Taylor died "in exile," age seventy-eight,
         succeeded in 1889 by Wilford Woodruff, fourth president.
1888   The Manti (Utah) Temple dedicated.
1890   President Wilford Woodruff issued the "Manifesto" discontinuing
         plural marriage. "Official Declaration—1" in the Doctrine and
         Covenants.
1893   The Salt Lake Temple dedicated.
1896   Utah entered U.S.A. as state.
1898   President Wilford Woodruff died, age ninety-one, succeeded by
         Lorenzo Snow, fifth president.
1901   President Lorenzo Snow died, age eighty-seven, succeeded by
         Joseph F. Smith, son of Hyrum Smith, sixth president.
1917   President Joseph F. Smith died, age eighty, succeeded by Heber J.
         Grant, seventh president.
1919   The Laia Hawaii Temple dedicated.
1923   The Alberta Temple in Cardston, Canada, dedicated.
1927   The Mesa Arizona Temple dedicated.
1929   The Mormon Tabernacle Choir began weekly network radio
         broadcasts.
1945   President Heber J. Grant died, age eighty-eight, succeeded by
         George Albert Smith, eighth president.
1951   President George Albert Smith died, age eighty-one, succeeded by
         David O. McKay, ninth president.
1954   Church announced Indian Student Placement Program.
1955   The Swiss Temple dedicated.
1956   The Los Angeles California Temple dedicated.
1958   The New Zealand Temple dedicated.
       The London Temple dedicated.
1960   Harold B. Lee began correlation plans.
1961   First non-English speaking stake organized in The Hague,
         Netherlands.
       Language Training Institute begun at Brigham Young University.
1962   First Spanish-speaking stake created in Mexico.
1964   LDS Pavilion opened at New York's World Fair.

Oakland California Temple dedicated.

1966   First stake organized in South America, São Paulo, Brazil.

Granite Mountain Records Vault dedicated.

1970   President David O. McKay died in Salt Lake City, age ninety-six,
         succeeded by Joseph Fielding Smith, tenth president.

First Asian stake organized in Tokyo, Japan.

First African stake organized in Transvaal, South Africa.

Relief Society, financially independent since inception, stopped
         fund-raising activities and turned assets over to priesthood
         leaders.

Monday named Family Home Evening.

1971   Church magazines consolidated.

Genesis Group for LDS African Americans organized.

1972   Church-wide sports tournaments and dance festivals discontinued.

Church Historical Department organized, Leonard J. Arrington,
         church historian.

Ogden and Provo, Utah, Temples dedicated.

President Joseph Fielding Smith died in Salt Lake City, age ninety-
         five, succeeded by President Harold B. Lee, eleventh president.

1973   First stake on mainland Asia organized in Seoul, Korea.

President Harold B. Lee died in Salt Lake City, age seventy-four,
         succeeded by President Spencer W. Kimball, twelfth president.

1974   Church College of Hawaii became BYU–Hawaii.

The Washington, D.C., Temple dedicated.

1975   President Kimball announced organization of First Quorum of the
         Seventy.

Church auxiliary conferences discontinued.

Brigham Young University celebrated 100th anniversary.

1976   At General Conference, Joseph Smith's Vision of the Celestial
         Kingdom and Joseph F. Smith's Vision of the Redemption of
         the Dead accepted as Scripture, first addition to Doctrine and
         Covenants since 1890.

Doctrine and Covenants sections 137 and 138 added.

First Presidency published statement against abortion.

Missouri's 1838 order to exterminate Mormons rescinded by Gov.
         Christopher S. Bond.

Adney Komatsu, of Hawaii, was first ethnic Japanese and former
         Buddhist to become a Seventy.

First Presidency spoke against proposed Equal Rights Amendment to the U.S. Constitution, "which could indeed bring them far more restraints and repressions. We fear it will even stifle many God-given feminine instincts."

1977 Yoshihiko Kikuchi is first Japanese-born man in First Quorum of Seventy.

1978 The First Presidency announced revelation making worthy men of all races eligible for priesthood; the revelation was made "Official Declaration—2" in the Doctrine and Covenants.

Genealogical plan to extract names from records announced.

Emeritus status announced for General Authorities due to age or infirmity, excluded First Presidency and the Quorum of the Twelve.

Language Training Center became Missionary Training Center, training all missionaries.

First Presidency allowed women to pray in sacrament meetings.

São Paulo Brazil Temple dedicated.

1979 *Ensign* magazine published first counselor N. Eldon Tanner's statement, "When the prophet speaks the debate is over."

1,000th stake of the Church created in Nauvoo, Illinois.

Church published new 2,400-page LDS edition of the King James Version of the Bible.

Apostle Gordon B. Hinckley, chair of the Special Affairs Committee, tells stake presidents in Missouri and Illinois how to conduct LDS anti-ERA campaign.

Sonia Johnson excommunicated for public criticism of Church and support of ERA.

1980 U.S. and Canadian members began consolidated meeting schedule in three-hour Sunday block.

Church celebrated 150th anniversary.

The Tokyo and Seattle Temples dedicated.

1981 Plans to build nine smaller temples announced.

Angel Abrea became first Hispanic Latin American sustained in First Quorum of Seventy.

Church published new edition of the Triple Combination (Book of Mormon, Doctrine and Covenants, and Pearl of Great Price).

Network of 500 satellite dishes for stake centers outside Utah announced.

Jordan River Temple dedicated.

1982   Church membership reached five million member mark.

Subtitle "Another Testament of Jesus Christ" added to Book of Mormon.

Leonard J. Arrington released as church historian.

First Presidency to pay all costs of meetinghouse construction.

ERA defeated.

1983   Gordon B. Hinckley paid Mark Hofmann $15,000 for an alleged Joseph Smith letter about his treasure digging.

Temples in Atlanta, Georgia; Apia, Samoa; Nuku'alofa, Tonga; Santiago, Chile; Papeete, Tahiti; and Mexico City dedicated.

1984   Genealogical Facilities Program announced for local chapels.

First general authorities called for limited terms to Quorums of Seventy.

Temples in Boise, Idaho: Sydney, Australia; Manilla, Philippines; Dallas, Texas; Taipei, Taiwan; and Guatemala City dedicated.

The Church organized the 1,500th stake, 150 years after first stake created in Kirtland, Ohio.

1985   Temples in Freiberg, Germany; Stockholm, Sweden; Chicago; Johannesburg, South Africa; and Seoul, South Korea dedicated.

President Spencer W. Kimball died in Salt Lake City, age ninety, succeeded by President Ezra Taft Benson, thirteenth president.

1986   Temples in Lima, Peru; Buenos Aires, Argentina; and Denver, Colorado dedicated.

Church membership reached six million.

Seventies Quorums in stakes disbanded.

First Presidency issued statement opposing legalization of gambling.

1987   Documents dealer and forger Mark Hofmann imprisoned after a plea bargain admitting responsibility for the bombing deaths of two people and forgery.

Church-owned Hotel Utah in Salt Lake City remodeled as the Joseph Smith Memorial.

The Church's Genealogical Department renamed the Family History Department.

Frankfurt Germany Temple dedicated.

1988   First stake in West Africa organized in Nigeria.

Michaelene P. Grassli, general Primary president was first woman
    to speak in general conference in 133 years.

100 million temple endowments for the dead completed.

1989   Brigham Young University contracted with Macmillan Publishing
    Company for the *Encyclopedia of Mormonism*.

Second Quorum of the Seventy created for temporary
    appointments of general authorities.

100th stake in Mexico created.

Payment of ward and stake budget assessments discontinued.

Las Vegas Nevada and Portland Oregon Temples dedicated.

First Navajo general authority George P. Lee excommunicated.

Eli Lilly pharmaceutical company confirmed Utah's highest
    national per capita use of Prozac.

1990   Church headquarters to pay all operating expenses for local
    congregations.

Helvecio Martins of Brazil, first black general authority, sustained
    to Second Quorum of Seventy.

Chieko Nishimura Okazaki sustained as first counselor in general
    presidency of the Relief Society, first non-Caucasian counselor
    in Mormon history.

Temple ceremony modified.

Toronto Ontario Temple dedicated.

Four LDS chapels in Chile burned protesting arrival of U.S.
    president George H. W. Bush.

1991   Gordon B. Hinckley said praying to our "Mother in Heaven" is
    inappropriate.

500,000th full-time missionary called.

Provo-Orem ranked as America's "most-livable metropolitan
    area" by *Money* magazine.

General Authorities issued statement against *Sunstone* symposium
    as offensive and in bad taste.

Membership in Church reached eight million.

Encyclopedia of Mormonism, prepared by editors at Brigham Young
    University, published by Macmillan.

1992   Relief Society marked 150th anniversary.

Lino Alvarez (first Mexican general authority), Augusto A. Lim
    (first Flipino general authority), and Kwok Yuen Tai (first

Hong Kong Chinese general authority) called to the Second Quorum of the Seventy.

1993   San Diego California Temple dedicated.

Apostle Boyd K. Packer listed three major threats: gay-lesbian movement, the feminist movement, and the challenge from "so-called scholars or intellectuals."

BYU terminated five junior professors. Media reports questioned school's academic freedom.

Joseph Smith Memorial Building, formerly Hotel Utah, dedicated.

Excommunication of five of the "September Six" for heresy.

1994   President Ezra Taft Benson died in Salt Lake City, age ninety-four, succeeded by President Howard W. Hunter, fourteenth president.

Orlando Florida Temple dedicated.

First Presidency issued statement against legalization of same-gender marriages.

Church active in defeating lottery initiative in Oklahoma.

2,000th stake in the Church, the Mexico City, Mexico, Contreras Stake, created.

1995   Bountiful Utah Temple dedicated.

The Church reached nine million members.

President Howard W. Hunter died, after less than a year in office, succeeded by President Gordon B. Hinckley, fifteenth president.

The International Olympic Committee decreed 2002 Winter Olympics in Salt Lake City.

"The Proclamation to the World on the Family" issued.

President Hinckley interviewed by CBS TV host Mike Wallace on show *Sixty Minutes*.

The Church released logo emphasizing primacy of Jesus Christ in the Church's theology.

Local LDS leaders urged to use toll-free telephone number to report cases of child abuse.

Wallace B. Smith, president of RLDS church (later Community of Christ) announced W. Grant McMurray as his successor, ending succession of Joseph Smith's descendants as presidents since 1860.

Presiding Bishop Merrill J. Bateman announced as new president of Brigham Young University.

1996   A 150th anniversary reenactment of the Nauvoo exodus began two years of commemoration of pioneer wagon train migration.

The Church announced that the majority of members live outside the United States.

President Hinckley announced construction of large new assembly hall.

Hong Kong and Mount Timpanogos Utah Temples dedicated.

Latter-day Saint Charities, a non-profit corporation to deliver aid around the world announced.

1997   St. Louis Missouri and Vernal Utah Temples dedicated.

Correlation of the Priesthood and Relief Society curriculum announced.

Mormon Trail Wagon Train entered Salt Lake City, 150 years later, after ninety-three days on the trail.

1998   Construction of thirty smaller temples announced.

Preston England and Monticello Utah Temples dedicated.

President Hinckley appeared on the Cable News Network (CNN) television show, "Larry King Live."

Church offered $8 million for a block of Main Street between Temple Square and the Church Administration Building. City Council approved in 1999.

1999   Temples in Anchorage, Alaska; Colonia Juarez, Chihuahua Mexico; Madrid, Spain; Bogota, Columbia; Guayaquil, Ecuador; Spokane, Washington; Columbus, Ohio; Bismarck, North Dakota; Columbia, South Carolina; Detroit, Michigan; Halifax, Nova Scotia; Regina, Saskatchewan; Billings, Montana; Edmonton, Alberta; and Raleigh, North Carolina, were dedicated.

The rebuilding of the Nauvoo Temple, destroyed in 1848, announced.

A gunman opened fire in the Church Family History Library, killing three and wounding four.

FamilySearch Internet Genealogy Service, a free website, launched. Three billion hits the first year.

Mormon Tabernacle Choir celebrated seventy years continuous radio broadcasting.

President Hinckley dedicated reconstructed monument honoring 120 people killed in the Mountain Meadows Massacre of 1857.

The First Presidency reaffirmed "strict political neutrality for the Church."

Premiere concert of the Mormon Tabernacle Choir, the Temple Square Chorale, and the orchestra performed at Temple Square.

Documentary "American Prophet: The Story of Joseph Smith" made national debut on PBS.

Larry King interviewed President Hinckley, the Rev. Robert Schuller, and Archbishop Desmond Tutu.

The First Presidency reaffirmed counsel to stay home rather than immigrate to United States.

2000 Temples in St. Paul, Minnesota; Kona, Hawaii; Albuquerque, New Mexico; Louisville, Kentucky; Palmyra, New York (built on former 100-acre farm of Joseph Smith, Sr.); Fresno, California; Medford, Oregon; Reno, Nevada; Memphis and Nashville, Tennessee; Cochabamba, Bolivia; San Jose, Costa Rica; Montreal, Quebec; Fukuoka, Japan; Adelaide and Melbourne, Australia; Suva, Fiji; Baton Rouge, Louisiana; Oklahoma City, Oklahoma; Caracas, Venezuela; Houston, Texas; Birmingham, Alabama; Santo Domingo, Dominican Republic; Recife and Porto Alegre, Brazil, were dedicated as well as nine more in Mexico alone: Ciudad Juarez, Hermosillo Sonora, Oaxaca, Tuxtla Gutierrez, Villahermosa, Tampico, Merida, and Veracruz.

Boston, Massachusetts, Temple, the 100th operating temple in the Church dedicated.

100,000,000 copy of the Book of Mormon, first published in 1830, printed.

Church reached eleven million members with a predominance of non-English speakers.

The 21,000-seat Conference Center in Salt Lake City dedicated.

2001 The Freedman's Bank Records, a genealogical resource for African Americans, released.

Media urged to use correct, full name—The Church of Jesus Christ of Latter-day Saints, avoiding use of "Mormon Church."

Perpetual Education Fund announced.

Temples in Montevideo, Uruguay; Winter Quarters, Nebraska; Guadalajara, Mexico; Perth, Australia; Columbia River, Washington, dedicated.

American Family Immigration Center opened at New York City's Ellis Island with family history records extracted from microfilm by Church members.

Ricks College renamed Brigham Young University–Idaho.

2002   Salt Lake City hosted the 2002 Winter Olympic Games.

Temples in Snowflake, Arizona; Lubbock, Texas; Monterrey, Mexico; Cambinas, Brazil; Asuncion, Paraguay; Nauvoo, Illinois; The Hague, Netherlands, Temples dedicated. The temples in Freiberg, Germany, and Monticello, Utah, Temples were rededicated after remodeling.

First missionary training center in Africa opened in Ghana.

Attempts to buy Martin's Cove, Wyoming, failed.

Three census databases, the 1880 U.S. Census, the 1881 Canadian Census, and the 1881 British Census added to the Church Family Search Internet site.

Temple recommends valid for two years instead of one.

Missionary farewells, homecomings, and open houses discontinued.

Standards for missionary worthiness raised.

2003   Church began satellite training meetings.

Mormon Tabernacle choir celebrated seventy-five years of network broadcasting.

Apia Samoa Temple destroyed by fire and then rebuilt.

2004   Accra, Ghana, Copenhagen Denmark, and Manhattan, New York, Temples were dedicated.

Anchorage Alaska Temple and São Paulo Brazil Temples rededicated.

Illinois House of Representatives passed a resolution regretting Saints' expulsion in 1846.

Eighth Quorum of Seventy created.

Doubleday published trade edition of Book of Mormon.

A seismic retrofit of the historic Tabernacle began.

Note: Entries gathered from the annual *Deseret News Church Almanac*, from the chronology of D. Michael Quinn, *The Mormon Hierarchy: Extensions of Power* (Salt Lake City: Signature Books, 1997), newspapers, a list compiled by Matthew K. Heiss of the Church Archives, the *Deseret News*, and other sources.

NOTES

PREFACE

1. Sir Richard F. Burton, *The City of the Saints: And Across the Rocky Mountains to California* (New York: Harper and Brothers, 1862), 203.
2. Sydney E. Ahlstrom, *A Religious History of the American People* (New Haven: Yale University Press, 1972), 508.
3. Jan Shipps, *Sojourner in the Promised Land: Forty Years Among the Mormons* (Urbana: University of Illinois Press, 2000), 246–48, locates the division between the churches in the meaning of the word "restoration;" "Mormons' Cousins in Missouri on New Path," *Salt Lake Tribune*, (19 January 2002); Jan Shipps, "How Mormon Is the Community of Christ?" *The John Whitmer Historical Association Journal: 2002 Nauvoo Conference Special Edition*, 195–204.
4. Carrie A. Moore, "Ex-RLDS Church Revising Its Image," *Deseret News* (24 May 2003); Steve Brisendine, "Community of Christ on Unfamiliar Ground After Leader's Resignation," *Daily Herald* (12 February 2005); Heather Hollingsworth, "Community of Christ Names New Leader," *Kansas.com* (7 March 2005).
5. On Strang, see Roger Van Noord, *King of Beaver Island: The Life and Assassination of James Jesse Strang* (Urbana: University of Illinois Press, 1988); on the Godbeites, see Ronald W. Walker, *Wayward Saints: The Godbeites and Brigham Young* (Urbana: University of Illinois Press, 1998).
6. Kathryn M. Daynes, *More Wives Than One: Transformation of the Mormon Marriage System, 1840–1910* (Urbana: University of Illinois Press, 2001); Sarah Barringer Gordon, "The Mormon Question: Polygamy and Constitutional Conflict in Nineteenth-Century America," ed. Thomas A. Green and Hendrik Hartog, *Studies in Legal History* (Chapel Hill: University of North Carolina Press, 2002).

7. Gordon B. Hinckley, interview by Larry King, on *Larry King Live*, 8 September 1998.

8. Several of the cases involved professors at the Church-owned Brigham Young University. See Bryan Waterman and Brian Kagel, *The Lord's University: Freedom and Authority at BYU* (Salt Lake City: Signature Books, 1998).

9. Mark P. Leone, *Roots of Modern Mormonism* (Cambridge, MA: Harvard University Press, 1979), 7.

10. Gustav Niebuhr, "Adapting 'Mormon' to Emphasize Christianity," *New York Times* (19 February 2001); "Church Should Be Called by Its Revealed Name," *LDS Church News* (17 February 2001); "Proper Church Name Usage Reaffirms Centrality of Christ," *LDS Church News* (3 March 2001); "The Church of Jesus Christ of Latter-day Saints Disputes Media Use of 'Fundamentalist Mormon,'" statement of The Church of Jesus Christ of Latter-day Saints, quoted by www.ldstoday.com (10 April 2005).

CHAPTER ONE

1. For Mormonism generally, see Jan Shipps, *Mormonism: The Story of a New Religious Tradition* (Urbana: University of Illinois Press, 1985); on Joseph Smith, see Richard L. Bushman, *Joseph Smith and the Beginnings of Mormonism* (Urbana: University of Illinois Press, 1984); on Mormonism's place in American religious history, see Martin Marty, *Pilgrims in Their Own Land: 500 Years of Religion in America* (New York: Penguin USA, 1985).

2. Chad Phares, "Church Now Fourth Largest in United States," *News from the Church* (10 April 2005).

3. Laurie Goodstein, "Conservative Churches Grew Fastest in 1990's, Report Says," *New York Times* (18 September 2002); Peggy Fletcher Stack, "LDS, Evangelicals Nation's Fastest Growing Churches," *Salt Lake Tribune* (18 September 2002); Carrie A. Moore, "LDS Meeting Challenges of Diversity," *Deseret News* (4 October 2002); "LDS Church Statistics," *Deseret News* (6 April 2003); "2004 Annual Report," *Church News* (16 April 2005); Rodney Stark quoted in Coke Newell, *Latter Days: A Guided Tour Through Six Billion Years of Mormonism* (New York: St. Martin's Press, 2000), 223.

4. "Trend of Decelerating Church Growth Continues," *Newsletter of Cumorah.com* (6 April 2002); "LDS Church Statistics," *Deseret News* (6 April 2003).

5. Rodney Stark, "Modernization and Mormon Growth: The Secularization Thesis Revisited," ed. Marie Cornwall, Tim B. Heaton, and Lawrence A. Young, *Contemporary Mormonism: Social Science Perspectives* (Urbana and Chicago: University of Illinois Press, 1994), 14–15, 22.

6. See D. Michael Quinn, "Plural Marriage and Mormon Fundamentalism," *Dialogue: A Journal of Mormon Thought* 31:2 (Summer 1998), 1–68.

7. Patricia S. Norwood, "Translation Work Taking Book of Mormon to More People in More Tongues," *News From the Church* (9 February 2005); Carrie A. Moore, "Doubleday Book of Mormon is On the Way," *Deseret Morning News* (11 November 2004).

8. George Will, quoted in R. Laurence Moore, *Religious Outsiders and the Making of Americans* (New York: Oxford University Press, 1986), 43.

9. Susan Buhler Taber, *Mormon Lives: A Year in the Elkton Ward* (Urbana, University of Illinois Press, 1993), 101.

10. Doctrine and Covenants 20:77–79 1981; Book of Mormon Moroni 4:3, 5:2 1981.

11. Gordon B. Hinckley, "A Chosen Generation," *Ensign* (May 1992), 69.

CHAPTER TWO

1. For Joseph Smith among the visionaries, see Richard Lyman Bushman, "The Visionary World of Joseph Smith," *BYU Studies* 37:1(1997–98), 183–204. Mormonism in the context of enthusiastic religion is discussed in Nathan O. Hatch, *The Democratization of American Christianity* (New Haven: Yale University Press, 1989), 113–22.

2. Joseph Smith, History 1:15–19, 25, The Pearl of Great Price 1981.

3. On the First Vision, see Milton V. Backman, Jr., *Joseph Smith's First Vision: The First Vision in Its Historical Context* (Salt Lake City: Bookcraft, 1971). For emerging significance of the First Vision, see James B. Allen, "Emergence of a Fundamental: The Expanding Role of Joseph Smith's First Vision in Mormon Religious Thought," *Journal of Mormon History* 7(1980), 43–61. For the First Vision in Mormon verse and song, see Richard H. Cracroft, "Rendering the Ineffable Effable: Treating Joseph Smith's First Vision in Imaginative Literature," *BYU Studies* 36:2(1996–1997), 93–116.

4. "Wentworth letter, 1842," *Papers of Joseph Smith*, 1.

5. Dean C. Jessee, ed. *The Papers of Joseph Smith, Volume 1, Autobiographical and Historical Writings* (Salt Lake City: Deseret Book Company, 1989), 430–31.

6. Joseph Smith, History 2:1–72, The Pearl of Great Price 1981.

7. On Joseph Smith's death, see Dallin H. Oaks and Marvin S. Hill, *The Carthage Conspiracy: The Trial of the Accused Assassins of Joseph Smith* (Urbana: University of Illinois Press, 1979).

8. William W. Phelps, adapted from Joseph Swain, "Redeemer of Israel," *Hymns of the Church of Jesus Christ of Latter-day Saints* (Salt Lake City: The Church of Jesus Christ of Latter-day Saints, 1985), 6.

9. Gordon B. Hinckley, interviewed by Mike Wallace, *60 Minutes* (7 April 1996).

10. Joseph Smith, *History of the Church of Jesus Christ of Latter-day Saints* (Salt Lake City: Deseret News, 1949), 5:215.

11. Jon Krakauer, *Under the Banner of Heaven: A Story of Violent Faith* (New York: Doubleday, 2003); Michael Janofsky, "Kidnapping Case Puts Mormons on Defensive," *New York Times* (24 March 2003); Peggy Fletcher Stack, "Revelation: Is It Divine Inspiration or Delusion?" *Salt Lake Tribune* (22 March 2003).

12. There is some debate over the authorship of the "Articles of Faith." Smith signed his name to the letter in which they were first included, but some have argued that his follower Orson Pratt drafted the articles. See David J. Whittaker, "The 'Articles of Faith' in Early Mormon Literature and Thought," *New Views of Mormon History: A Collection of Essays in Honor of Leonard J. Arrington*, ed. Davis Bitton and Maureen Ursenbach Beecher (Salt Lake City: University of Utah Press, 1987), 63–92.

13. Joseph Smith, *History of the Church*, 4:535–541, The Pearl of Great Price 1981.

14. Alma 42:5, 42:16, Book of Mormon 1981.

15. Susan Buhler Taber, *Mormon Lives* (Urbana: University of Illinois Press, 1993), 23, 35.

16. Doctrine and Covenants 130:2 1981.

17. On the Word of Wisdom and Mormon health generally, see Lester E. Bush, Jr., *Health and Medicine Among the Latter-day Saints: Science, Sense, and Scripture* (New York: Crossroad, 1993). On the Word of Wisdom and Mormon identity, see Jan Shipps, *Mormonism: The Story of a New Religious Tradition* (Urbana: University of Illinois, 1985), 109–29.

18. Michelle Nevada, "Bread for Thought," *Arutz Sheva: IsraelNationalNews.com* (31 January 2003).

19. Daniel Yee, "Utah Reached Goal of 12% Smoking Rate," *Chicago Sun-Times* (11 November 2004); Gordon B. Hinckley, interviewed by Larry King, *Larry King Live* (8 September 1998); James E. Enstrom, "Health Practices and Cancer Mortality among Active California Mormons," *Journal of the National Cancer Institute*, 81:23(6 December 1989), 1807–14; "Utah Ranked No. 4 in Health," *Daily Universe* (23 January 2003).

20. Scott Williams, Corissa Jansen and Ana Caban, "Some Churches Try to Revive Traditional Tithing Support," *Milwaukee Journal Sentinel* (25 December 2001); Gordon B. Hinckley, interviewed by Larry King, *Larry King Live* (8 September 1998).

21. Taber, *Mormon Lives*, 14.

22. Figures estimated by Bishop Richard Lyman Bushman in 2003, recalling the 1970s and 80s.

23. www.providentliving.com provides information for self-reliance.

24. Taber, *Mormon Lives*, 149.

25. Larry E. Dahl and Donald Q. Cannon, eds., *Teachings of Joseph Smith* (Salt Lake City: Bookcraft, 1997), 55.

26. Lutheran Church Missouri Synod, "Are Mormons generally regarded as Christians, and how do their beliefs differ from those of the Missouri Synod?" Q & A Internet site, www.lcms.org/cic/mormon.html.

27. Daniel H. Ludlow, ed., *Encyclopedia of Mormonism* (New York: Macmillan Publishing Company, 1992), 941; David L. Paulsen, "The Doctrine of Divine Embodiment: Restoration, Judeo-Christian, and Philosophical Perspectives," *BYU Studies*, 35:4(1995–96), 6–94. A thorough discussion of the criticisms is Stephen A. Robinson, *Are Mormons Christian?* (Salt Lake City: Bookcraft, 1991). A nuanced discussion of the stakes involved is Jan Shipps, *Sojourner in the Promised Land: Forty Years Among the Mormons* (Urbana: University of Illinois Press, 2000), 335–57.

28. For Mormon views of Scripture, Philip L. Barlow, *Mormons and the Bible: The Place of the Latter-day Saints in American Religion* (New York: Oxford University Press, 1991). On the Joseph Smith translation, see Robert J. Matthews, *'A Plainer Translation': Joseph Smith's Translation of the Bible, A History and Commentary* (Provo: Brigham Young University Press, 1985). "Church Releases the Scriptures: CD-ROM Standard Edition 1.0," *LDS Church News Release*, 20 December 2001.

29. The literature on the Book of Mormon is vast. A place to begin is the two-dozen entries on the Book of Mormon in volume one of Daniel H. Ludlow, ed., *Encyclopedia of Mormonism*, 4 vols. (New York: Macmillan, 1992). A book of critical essays is Dan Vogel and Brent Lee Metcalfe, eds., *American Apocrypha: Essays on the Book of Mormon* (Salt Lake City: Signature Books, 2002). The first non-polemical treatment by a non-Mormon press is Terryl L. Givens, *By the Hand of Mormon: The American Scripture that Launched a New World Religion* (New York: Oxford University Press, 2002). On Joseph Smith and Book of Mormon translation, see Richard L. Bushman, *Joseph Smith and the Beginnings of Mormonism* (Urbana: University of Illinois Press, 1984), 79–113.

30. Exceptions to this rule include Thomas F. O'Dea, *The Mormons* (Chicago: University of Chicago Press, 1957), 258-65; Paul C. Gutjahr, *An American Bible: A History of the Good Book in the United States, 1777–1880* (Stanford: Stanford University Press, 1999), 151–58; Carrie A. Moore, "Book of Mormon on Heavy-Hitter List," *Deseret News*, 10 July 2003.

31. The arguments for and against the Book of Mormon as a nineteenth-century cultural production are reviewed in Givens, *By the Hand of Mormon*, 117–84.

32. Ezra Taft Benson, "Flooding the Earth With the Book of Mormon," *Ensign* 17 (November 1988), 4; see Doctrine and Covenants 84:54–58 1981; Noel B. Reynolds, "The Coming Forth of the Book of Mormon in the Twentieth Century," *BYU Studies*, 38:2(1999), 6–47.

33. Answers to the questions of Claudia L. Bushman, 2001.

34. Answers to the questions of Claudia L. Bushman, 2001.

35. For studies of Latter-day Saint wards, see Susan Buhler Taber, *Mormon Lives: A Year in the Elkton Ward*, 170–71; Jan Shipps, Cheryll L. May, and Dean L. May, "Sugar House Ward: A Latter-day Saint Congregation," James P. Wind and James W. Lewis, *American Congregations: Volume 1, Portraits of Twelve Religious Communities* (Chicago: University of Chicago Press, 1994) 293–348; and Ronald W. Walker, "'Going to Meeting' in Salt Lake City's Thirteenth Ward, 1849–1881: A Microanalysis," in Bitton and Beecher, *New Views of Mormon History*, 138–61.

36. Taber, *Mormon Lives*, 11.

37. Taber, *Mormon Lives*, 276.

38. Taber, *Mormon Lives*, 184.

39. Taber, *Mormon Lives*, 178.

40. Shipps, May, and May, "Sugar House Ward," 343.

41. Gustav Niebuhr, "New Leader of Mormons Takes Joy In Changes," *New York Times* (23 July 1995).

42. Gordon B. Hinckley, interviewed by Mike Wallace, *60 Minutes* (7 April 1996); Gordon B. Hinckley, interviewed by Larry King, *Larry King Live* (8 September 1998).

43. William J. Whalen, *The Latter-day Saints in the Modern Day World: An Account of Contemporary Mormonism* (New York: The John Day Company, 1964), 291.

44. *The Deseret Morning News Church Almanac* (Salt Lake City: Deseret Morning News, 2005), 29–51; John L. Hart, "Two more Quorums are Created; Now Eight," *Church News* (7 May 2005).

45. Dan Harrie, "State Continues to Keep Church Off Staffing List," *Salt Lake Tribune* (14 January 2003).

46. Gordon B. Hinckley, interviewed by Mike Wallace, *60 Minutes* (7 April 1996); Gordon B. Hinckley, interviewed by Larry King, *Larry King Live,* (8 September 1998).

CHAPTER THREE

1. "Member Spotlight: The Bryant Family," *Provo 8th Ward Newsletter* (July 2001).

2. Stacy Wismer, "Students Feel Compelled to Marry Early," *BYU NewsNet* (12 June 2002).

3. Gordon B. Hinckley, interviewed by Mike Wallace, *60 Minutes* (7 April 1996).

4. David C. Dollahite, ed., *Strengthening Our Families: An In-Depth Look at the Proclamation of the Family* (Provo: School of Family Life, Brigham Young University, 2000) was prepared as a course text. The large book compares every element of the proclamation on the family with social scientific research.

5. The Proclamation, signed by the First Presidency and Council of the Twelve Apostles, is available at www.lds.org.

6. Gordon B. Hinckley, *Teachings of Gordon B. Hinckley* (Salt Lake City: Deseret Book, 1997), 209.

7. "Family Proclamation is a Beacon of Light," *Church News*, 24 November 2001.

8. Susan Buhler Taber, *Mormon Lives: A Year in the Elkton Ward* (Urbana: University of Illinois Press, 1993), 26.

9. Adriana C. Olson, "Chadwick Tells BYU to Forget Cinderella," *BYU NewsNet* (7 May 2002).

10. Elaine Jarvik, "Living Single in a State of Matrimony," *Deseret News* (15 December 2002); "The Changing American Family," *The New York Times* (18 May 2001).

11. David O. McKay, *Family Home Evening Manual* (Salt Lake City: Church of Jesus Christ of Latter-day Saints, 1965), iii. McKay was quoting James Edward McCulloch, *Home: the Savior of Civilization* (Washington, D.C.: The Southern Co-operative League, 1924), 42; Harold B. Lee, *Strengthening the Home* (Salt Lake City: The Church of Jesus Christ of Latter-day Saints, 1973), 7; *Church News* (3 February 2001).

12. Taber, *Mormon Lives*, 306, 310.

13. Sharon Haddock, "Family-Help Program Touted," *Deseret News* (20 August 2002); Jason Swensen, "Resolve to Hold Family Home Evening," *Church News* (28 December 2002).

14. Tim B. Heaton, Kristen L. Goodman, and Thomas B. Holman, "In Search of a Peculiar People: Are Mormon Families Really Different?" ed. Marie Cornwall, Tim B. Heaton, and Lawrence A. Young, *Contemporary Mormonism: Social Science Perspectives* (Urbana and Chicago: University of Illinois Press, 1994), 88–89.

15. Carrie A. Moore, "Statistics Offer Good and Bad News for LDS," *Deseret News* (11 August 2002).

16. Richard N. Ostling, "Survey: Religion Matters to Many Teens," *nashuatelegraph.com* (24 February 2005); Yonat Shimron, "Mormon Teens Cope Best," *newsobserver.com* (13 March 2005); Jonah King, "About Three U.S. Teenagers in 10," *The Baptist Standard* (7 November 2004); Elaine Jarvik, "LDS Teens Tops in Living Faith," *Deseret Morning News* (15 March 2005).

17. Bill Dedman, "Proportion of Married Americans Drops Slightly in New Census," *Boston Globe* (6 June 2002); Elyse Hayes, "Census Bucks Utah's 'Norms,'" *Deseret News* (4 June 2002).

18. Mary Morley, *BYU NewsNet*, 3 April 2002.

19. "Utah Tax Burden Highest in West," *The Daily Herald* (5 Aug 2001); "Nation's Largest Share of Big Homes Belongs to Utah," *The Daily Herald* (7 August 2001); Lesley Mitchell, "Utah's High Rate of Foreclosures Concerns HUD," *Salt Lake Tribune* (29 April 2003).

20. "Utah Leads Bankruptcy Parade," *USA Today.com* (23 August 2002); Michael Vigh, "Con Artists Find LDS Easy Prey," *Salt Lake Tribune* (18 January 2003); Pat Reavy, "Big Scams Fleece LDS Flocks," *Deseret News* (17 January 2003).

21. Taber, *Mormon Lives*, 304–5.

22. Carrie A. Moore, "Statistics Offer Good and Bad News for LDS," *Deseret News* (11 August 2002); Hilary Groutage Smith, "Mormon Home Life is Likened to Evangelical Sects," *The Salt Lake Tribune* (11 August 2002).

23. "Family Services Web Site Reaches out to Unmarried Birth Mothers," *LDS Church News Release* (31 October 2001).

24. Sarah Jane Weaver, "He Understands Love," "First Presidency: 'We Honor Adoption,'" *Church News* (24 November 2001).

25. "Bishops' Wives Tell It Like It Is," *MeridianMagazine.com* (15 April 2002).

26. Taber, *Mormon Lives*, 304.

27. On Brigham Young's family, see Dean C. Jessee, "A Man of God and a Good Kind Father: Brigham Young at Home," *BYU Studies* 40:2(2001), 23–53. On Joseph Smith's family, see Todd Compton, *In Sacred Loneliness: The Plural Wives of Joseph Smith* (Salt Lake City: Signature Books, 1996). On nineteenth-century Mormon plural marriage families, see Jessie L. Embry, "Mormon Polygamous Families: Life in the Principle,"ed. Linda King Newell, *Publications in Mormon Studies* (Salt Lake City: University of Utah Press, 1987).

28. Kathryn M. Daynes, *More Wives Than One: Transformation of the Mormon Marriage System 1840–1910* (Urbana: University of Illinois Press, 2001), 114–15.

29. Kimball Young, *Isn't One Wife Enough?* (New York: Henry Holt & Co., Inc., 1954), 411.

30. D. Michael Quinn, "Plural Marriage and Mormon Fundamentalism," *Dialogue* 31:2(Summer 1998), 1–68, provides excellent sketches of various groups.

31. Martha Sonntag Bradley, *Kidnaped From That Land: The Government Raids on the Short Creek Polygamists* (Salt Lake: University of Utah Press, 1993), 182–95.

32. Charlie LeDuff, "A Holdout Polygamist, 88, Defies the Mormons," *New York Times* (23 February 2002); Quinn, "Plural Marriage," 6.

33. LeDuff, "Holdout Polygamist."

34. Janet Bennion, *Women of Principle: Female Networking in Contemporary Mormon Polygamy* (New York: Oxford University Press, 1998), viii, 5.

35. Bennion, *Women of Principle*, 6, 9, 64–66, 72, 86–87.

36. "Dormant Polygamy Issue Spotlighted by Smart Case," *The Olympian* (17 March 2003); Jon Krakauer, *Under the Banner of Heaven: A Story of Violent Faith* (New York: Doubleday, 2003).

37. Bennion, *Women of Principle*, 17, 29, 34, 145, 151–53.

38. Mary Batchelor, Marianne Watson, and Anne Wilde, *Voices in Harmony: Contemporary Women Celebrate Plural Marriage* (Salt Lake City: Principle Voices, 2000).

39. Batchelor, et al., *Voices in Harmony*, 5, 41, 70.

40. Batchelor, et al., *Voices in Harmony*, 78-83, 90–93.

41. "Polygamist Jailed for Child Rape," *BBC News* (28 August 2002).

CHAPTER FOUR

1. "Members Worldwide Hear Proceedings Live," *Church News* (12 October 2002); Peggy Fletcher Stack, "End of Missionary Farewells Brings Relief, Disappointment," *Salt Lake Tribune* (12 October 2002).

2. "This Isn't a Time for Spiritual Weakness," *Church News* (12 October 2002); "Time Has Come to Raise Missionary Standards," *Church News* (18 January 2003); "Preparation: 'We need vibrant, thinking, passionately devoted missionaries who know how to listen to, and respond to the . . . Holy Spirit.'" *Church News* (1 February 2003).

3. Robert Ratish, "Two Missionaries Arrested in Tourist Ascent," *Bergen County* (NJ) *Record* (13 March 2002).

4. "Missionary Couples Needed in the World," *Church News* (27 October 2001).

5. "Volunteer Efforts, Contributions Offer Hope to Others," *Church News* (15 June 2002).

6. "Local Doctor, Wife Answer a Higher Call," *Fairbanks* (AK) *News-Miner* (2 July 2001); number of missions from *Church News* (26 February 2005).

7. Quoted in Wallace Turner, *The Mormon Establishment* (Boston: Houghton Mifflin Company, 1966), 90.

8. Richard O. Cowan, *The Church in the Twentieth Century* (Salt Lake City: Bookcraft, 1985), 283–86; Brent L. Top, "A Lengthening Stride, 1951 Through 1999," *Out of Obscurity: The LDS Church in the Twentieth Century* (Salt Lake City: Deseret Book, 2000), 29–30; Tad Walch, "Missionary Gaffes Good for a Laugh," *Deseret News* (8 March 2003).

9. "First 54 Missionaries Enter First Training Center in Africa," *Church News* (25 May 2002).

10. Spencer W. Kimball, "When the World Will Be Converted," *Ensign* (October 1974), 8; ed. Edward L. Kimball, *The Teachings of Spencer W. Kimball* (Salt Lake City: Bookcraft, 1982), 550; "Advice to a Young Man: Now Is the Time to Prepare," *New Era* (June 1973), 8–9.

11. "E-Mail Again Allowed for LDS Missionaries," *Salt Lake Tribune* (10 January 2002).

12. Eastern States Mission, *Elders' Reference* (Brooklyn, New York: the Church of Jesus Christ of Latter-day Saints, 1913), 35–36, quoted in Robert E. Lund, "Proclaiming the Gospel in the Twentieth Century," *Out of Obscurity: The LDS Church in the Twentieth Century* (Salt Lake City: Deseret Book, 2000), 227–28; *The Uniform System for Teaching Families* (Salt Lake City: The Church of Jesus Christ of Latter-day Saints, 1973), A-1, quoted in Robert E. Lund, "Proclaiming the Gospel," 232–33.

13. *Instructions for the Discussions* (Salt Lake City: Church of Jesus Christ of Latter-day Saints, 1986), 1, quoted in Robert E. Lund, "Proclaiming the Gospel," 234; Doctrine and Covenants 50:14 1981.

14. Peggy Fletcher Stack, "LDS Missionaries to No Longer Use Memorized Lessons," *Salt Lake Tribune* (18 January 2003); Adam C. Oson, "Preach My Gospel Being Launched in Missions Worldwide," *News of the Church* (10 February 2005).

15. Luke 10:1; Keith Parry, "The Mormon Missionary Companionship," ed. Marie Cornwall, Tim B. Heaton, and Lawrence A. Young, *Contemporary Mormonism: Social Science Perspectives* (Urbana: University of Illinois Press, 1994), 183–84.

16. Parry, "Missionary Companionship," 186–88.

17. Peggy Fletcher Stack, "Thousands of Mormon Girls Pine While Their Sweethearts Serve," *Salt Lake Tribune* (18 March 2002).

18. William A. Wilson, "Powers of Heaven and Hell: Mormon Missionary Narratives as Instruments of Socialization and Social Control,"ed. Marie Cornwall, Tim B. Heaton, and Lawrence A. Young, *Contemporary Mormonism: Social Science Perspectives* (Urbana: University of Illinois Press, 1994), 216; William A. Wilson, "On Being Human: The Folklore of Mormon Missionaries," *Sunstone* 22 (June 1999), 44–60.

19. Wilson, "Powers of Heaven and Hell," 215.

20. Wilson, "Powers of Heaven and Hell," 213–14.

21. Gordon Shepherd and Gary Shepherd, "Sustaining a Lay Religion in Modern Society: The Mormon Missionary Experience,"ed. Marie Cornwall, Tim B. Heaton, and Lawrence A. Young, *Contemporary Mormonism: Social Science Perspectives* (Urbana: University of Illinois Press, 1994), 163–64, 175–76.

22. Shepherd and Shepherd, "Sustaining a Lay Religion," 165–74.

23. Quoted in Richard N. and Joan K. Ostling, *Mormon America: The Power and the Promise* (San Francisco: Harper, 1999), 210; Shepherd and Shepherd, "Sustaining a Lay Religion," 174–75; Gordon B. Hinckley, "Some Thoughts on Temples, Retention of Converts, and Missionary Service," *Ensign* (November 1997), 52.

24. Shepherd and Shepherd, "Sustaining a Lay Religion," 177; Carrie A. Moore, "Sunstone Looks at Missions Gone Awry," *Deseret News* (9 August 2002).

25. Helen Ubinas, "Hartford Missionaries Overcome Rejection; But Are Human, Too," *Hartford* (CT) *Courant* (9 July 2001).

26. Genevieve Roja, "Missionaries Give Lesson in Tolerance and Dedication," *San Jose* (CA) *Metroactive News* (26 July 2001).

27. Diane Lewis, "Keeping the Faith," *Garden City* (KS) *Telegram* (11 June 2001).

28. Mike Bockoven, "LDS Missionary Returns with 'Lifetime of Stories,'" *Grand Island* (NE) *Independent* (12 June 2001).

29. Kate Silver, "High on LDS: Two By-the-Book Guys Brave the Mean Streets, Slamming Doors and Strip Teases for One Soul Purpose," *Las Vegas Weekly* (22 August 2002).

30. Susan Buhler Taber, *Mormon Lives: A Year in the Elkton Ward* (Urbana: University of Illinois Press, 1993), 250–51.

31. Taber, *Mormon Lives*, 84.

32. James Lucas, "Mormons in New York City," ed. Tony Carnes and Anna Karpathakis, *New York Glory: Religions in the City* (New York: New York University Press, 2001), 206; Shaun D. Stahle, "Missionary Work at the Ward Level," *Church News* (1 June 2002).

33. Coke Newell, *Latter Days: A Guided Tour Through Six Billion Years of Mormonism* (New York: St. Martin's Press, 2000), 247.

34. John P. Livingstone, "The Simplification and Reduction of Church Curriculum," *Out of Obscurity: The LDS Church in the Twentieth Century* (Salt Lake City: Deseret Book, 2000), 177–78, 190–93.

35. Victor L. Ludlow, "The Internationalization of the Church," *Out of Obscurity: The LDS Church in the Twentieth Century* (Salt Lake City: Deseret Book Company, 2000), 177–78, 221–24.

36. Ludlow, "Internationalization of the Church," 210–13, 218–24.

37. Mark Grover, "The Miracle of the Rose and the Oak in Latin America," *Out of Obscurity: The LDS Church in the Twentieth Century* (Salt Lake City: Deseret Book, 2000), 139–40, 143–46.

38. E. Dale LeBaron, "The Church in Africa," *Out of Obscurity: The LDS Church in the Twentieth Century* (Salt Lake City: Deseret Book, 2000), 177–78, 180.

39. LeBaron, "The Church in Africa," 183, 188; "Ground Broken for Temple in Accra, Ghana," *Cumorah News Service* (22 November 2001).

40. "Church Added to Chilean Census," *Cumorah News Service* (1 December 2001); David Stewart, "Cumorah Project Newsletter" (6 April 2003); Tim B. Heaton, "Vital Statistics," ed. Daniel H. Ludlow, *Encyclopedia of Mormonism*, 4 vols. (New York: Macmillan Publishing Company, 1992), 4:1527, 1532.

41. Lowell C. "Ben" Bennion and Lawrence Young, "The Uncertain Dynamics of LDS Expansion, 1950–2020," *Dialogue*, 29 (Spring 1996), 8; *Church News* (4 July 1998).

42. "The Church and the Chapel: Meetinghouse Construction in the Former Soviet Union," *Cumorah News Service* (15 December 2001).

43. Douglas J. Davies, *The Mormon Culture of Salvation: Force, Grace and Glory* (Aldershot, Great Britain: Ashgate, 2000), 261.

44. "Arizona Republic Looks at Mormons in Mexico," *Arizona Republic* (22 July 2001).

45. David Knowlton, "Thoughts on Mormonism in Latin America," *Dialogue* 25 (Summer 1992), 41–53.

46. Tad Walch, "LDS Surge in Latin America," *Deseret News* (21 March 2003).

47. Jessie L. Embry, *Black Saints in a White Church: Contemporary African American Mormons* (Salt Lake City: Signature, 1994), 122.

CHAPTER FIVE

1. *Church News* (7 October 2000).

2. *Church News* (23 September 2000).

3. "Dedicatory Prayer; 'We dedicate it as being complete,'" *LDS Church News* (2 April 2005).

4. B. H. Roberts, *A Comprehensive History of the Church, Century I*, 6 vols. (Salt Lake: Deseret News Press, 1930), 3:317, n. 19; Howard W. Hunter, "Being A Righteous Husband and Father," *Ensign* (November 1994), 49.

5. Doctrine and Covenants 88:119 1981; on the Kirtland Temple, see Elwin C. Robison, *The First Mormon Temple: Design, Construction, and Historic Context of the Kirtland Temple* (Provo, UT: Brigham Young University Press, 1997). The recent rebuilding of the Nauvoo Temple has produced many books. Among the best are Don F. Colvin, *Nauvoo Temple; A Story of Faith* (American Fork, Utah: Covenant Communications, 2002) and Heidi S. Swinton, *Sacred Stone: The Temple at Nauvoo* (American Fork, Utah: Covenant Communications, 2002).

6. On the Salt Lake Temple, see Richard Neitzel Holzapfel, *Every Stone a Sermon: The Magnificent Story of the Construction and Dedication of the Salt*

Lake Temple (Salt Lake City: Bookcraft, 1992); On Mormon city planning, see C. Mark Hamilton, *Nineteenth-Century Mormon Architecture and City Planning* (New York: Oxford University Press, 1995).

7. "Temple Approved, First Stake Created in German Democratic Republic," *Ensign* (November 1982), 102–3; Thomas S. Monson, "Thanks Be to God," *Ensign* (May 1989), 51. For information on additional temples, see www.lds.org/temples or refer to the annual *Deseret News Church Almanac*.

8. Sheri L. Dew, *Go Forward With Faith: The Biography of Gordon B. Hinckley* (Salt Lake City: Deseret Book, 2002), 176–85.

9. Dew, *Go Forward With Faith*, 325; "State of the State," *Salt Lake Tribune* (29 Sept. 2001).

10. "Get Yourselves Ready: Temple Represents Highest Ordinances of the Gospel," *Church News* (30 June 2001).

11. Susan Buhler Taber, *Mormon Lives: A Year in the Elkton Ward* (Urbana: University of Illinois Press, 1993), 154–55.

12. Moses 5:11, The Pearl of Great Price 1981.

13. Doctrine and Covenants 84:20 1981. The standard sources on the meaning of Latter-day Saint temple worship are James E. Talmage, *The House of the Lord: A Study of Sanctuaries Ancient and Modern* (Salt Lake City: Deseret News, 1912) and Boyd K. Packer, *The Holy Temple* (Salt Lake: Bookcraft, 1980); A rangy, uncoventionally academic treatise is Hugh Nibley, *Temple and Cosmos* (Provo, UT: FARMS, 1986). A convenient summary is Hugh W. Nibley, "Meanings and Functions of Temples," ed. Daniel H. Ludlow, *Encyclopedia of Mormonism*, 4 vols. (New York: Macmillan, 1992), 4:1458–63. See also Alma P. Burton "Endowment,"ed. Daniel H. Ludlow, *Encyclopedia of Mormonism*, 4 vols. (New York: Macmillan, 1992), 2:454–56.

14. "Comments on Temple Changes Elicit Church Discipline," *Sunstone* 14 (June 1990), 59–61.

15. Karen Hoag, "Family Trip Provides Lasting Memories," "Trip Home Continues Unforgettable Story," *Provo Daily Herald* (23 June 2001).

16. Christian Bottorff, "Church May Sell Forest Hills Site to Baptist-affiliated Church," *Nashville Tennessean* (June 30, 2001); Jamie L. Johnson, "Redlands Temple Plans Released, Few Obstacles Expected," *Redlands Daily Facts* (3 July 2001).

17. *Church News* (13 January 2001); *Church News* (7 October 2000).

18. Justin Pope, "SJC Sides with Mormon Temple in Steeple Ruling," *Boston Globe Electronic Publishing, Inc.*, Associated Press (16 May 2001); "High Court Rules in Favor of Steeple for Boston Temple," *Church News* (19 May 2001).

19. Carma Wadley, "Temple Impact Reaches Far," *Deseret News* (30 April 2002); "Rebuilding of Nauvoo Illinois Temple Completed," *ldstoday.com* (6 May

2002); Bill Broadway, "Mormon Temple Rises Again," *Washington Post* (11 May 2002); Larry Furr II, "Nauvoo Temple will be completed in 2002," *Daily Universe* (14 June 2001); Stephen A. Martin, "First Temple Sunstone Placed," *Burlington* (IA) *Hawk Eye* (22 August 2001); *Church News* (2 December 2000).

20. Stephen A. Martin, "Mormon 'Truth' the Focus of Couple's Sermon," *Burlington Hawk Eye* (15 March 2002).

21. Dennis J. Carroll, "Fear of a Mormon Return: Illinois Town's Fundamentalists Feel Threatened by Giant Temple," *San Francisco Chronicle* (29 April 2002).

22. John L. Hart, "750 Million-name IGI Upgraded," *Church News* (9 November 2002).

23. 1 Corinthians 15:29. On genealogy see James B. Allen, Jessie L. Embry, and Kahlile Mehr, *Hearts Turned to the Fathers: A History of the Genealogical Society of Utah, 1894–1994* (Provo, UT: BYU Studies, 1994); 1 Peter 3:19, 4:6; Doctrine and Covenants 128:18; 138:48, 53–54 1981. Several of Joseph Smith's revelations refer to baptism for the dead. See, for example, Doctrine and Covenants 124:29, 33; 127:5–10 1981.

24. Gustav Niebuhr, "Mormons to End Holocaust Victim Baptism," *New York Times* (29 April 1995); Peg McEntee, "Proxy Baptism of Jews Under Review," *Salt Lake Tribune* (10 December 2002); C. G. Wallace, "Mormons, Jews Meet Over Baptizing Dead," *Las Vegas Sun* (10 December 2002); "Mormons Agree, Again, to End Posthumous Baptisms of Jews," *AZCentral.com* (11 December 2002); Mark Thiessen, "Jewish Leaders Flay LDS Baptisms," *DeseretNews.com* (8 April 2005); Peggy Fletcher Stack, "Proxy Baptism Issue is Resolved," *Salt Lake Tribune* (12 April 2005); Chanan Tigay, "Mormons Still Baptizing Dead Jews," *JewishTime.com* (14 April 2005).

25. "LDS Attempt to Microfilm New Zealand Records Upsets Maori Leader," *Auckland* [NZ] *Herald* (28 December 2001); "Mormons Abusing Memory of Deceased Russians—Religious Council," *MosNews.com* (15 April 2005).

26. *Church News* (20 January 2001); "Preserving Records for Family History Research," *Church News* (5 February 2005); Patricia Selman, "Family History Centers Spreading Across the World," *News From the Church* (24 February 2005).

27. *Church News* (3 March 2001); *New York Times* quoted in http://www.ldstoday.com (3 April 2001).

28. John L. Hart, "Freedman's Bank Project Left an Impact on Inmates," *Church News* (24 March 2001).

29. Susan Sachs, "Ellis Island Opens Its Web Door," *New York Times* (17 April 2001); John L. Hart, "Ellis Island Project Is a Bridge Between Families, Countries," *Church News* (21 April 2001).

30. "1880 U.S. Census to be Available on CDs June 1," *Church News* (26 May 2001); Peggy Fletcher Stack, "Just Log On, Take a Stroll Back to the 1880s," *Salt Lake Tribune* (24 October 2002); "Census Site Proves Popular," *Seattle Post-Intelligencer* (4 November 2002).

31. Richard N. Ostling and Joan K. Ostling, *Mormon America: The Power and the Promise* (San Francisco: HarperSanFrancisco, 1999), 191.

CHAPTER SIX

1. Susan Buhler Taber, *Mormon Lives: A Year in the Elkton Ward* (Urbana: University of Illinois Press, 1993), 326.

2. Wallace Turner noted that the Church was everyman's church, except for the African Negro. Turner spent two of his twelve chapters deploring this doctrine. Wallace Turner, *The Mormon Establishment* (Boston: Houghton Mifflin Company, 1966); Armand L. Mauss, "Introduction: Conflict and Commitment in an Age of Civil Turmoil,"ed. Lester E. Bush, Jr., and Armand Mauss, *Neither White Nor Black: Mormon Scholars Confront the Race Issue in a Universal Church*, (Midvale, UT: Signature Books, 1984), 1–8; Armand L. Mauss, *The Angel and the Beehive: The Mormon Struggle with Assimilation* (Urbana: University of Illinois Press, 1994), 116–17.

3. 2 Nephi 26:33, Book of Mormon 1981; Lester E. Bush, Jr., "Whence the Negro Doctrine? A Review of Ten Years of Answers in Bush and Mauss,"ed. Lester E. Bush, Jr., and Armand Mauss, *Neither White Nor Black* (Midvale, Utah: Signature Books, 1984), 202–3.

4. Lester E. Bush, Jr., "Mormonism's Negro Doctrine: An Historical Overview," *Dialogue* 8 (Spring 1973), 11–68; Turner, *Mormon Establishment*, 224.

5. Bush, "Mormonism's Negro Doctrine," 13, 18–19, 26; Elijah Abel, a former black slave and Mormon pioneer, is the case used to support early tolerance. The Genesis Group, an LDS Church-sponsored group for black Church members, has rehabilitated the Abel family grave sites in Salt Lake City and, along with other groups, erected a monument there. Abel was ordained to the priesthood in 1836 by Joseph Smith, Jr. He and his wife Mary Ann arrived in the Salt Lake Valley in 1852. Abel, a carpenter, worked on three temples and remained a member of the Third Quorum of the Seventy until his death in 1884. The Abels, with their eight children, were members in good standing, but Abel's ordination to the priesthood was an anomaly. "New Monument Erected to Honor Elijah Abel Family: Black Pioneer Was Faithful to LDS Church," *Deseret News* (25 September 2002).

6. Bush, "Mormonism's Negro Doctrine," 26.

7. Bush, "Mormonism's Negro Doctrine," 39.

8. Bush, "Mormonism's Negro Doctrine," 40–41; Joseph Fielding Smith, *The Way to Perfection* (Salt Lake City: Genealogical Society of Utah, 1949), 43–44.

9. In a popular explication of this doctrine, John J. Stewart proposed that "the circumstances of our birth in this world are dependent upon our performance in the spirit world, just as the circumstances of our existence in the next world will depend upon what use we make of the blessings and opportunities we enjoy in this world." He suggested that neutrality in the preexistence was punished by being born a Negro. Thus Negroes were marked to show inferiority and cursed to prevent Cain's posterity from bearing the priesthood in this life. Professor Stewart quoted Brigham Young: a black skin "comes in consequence of their fathers rejecting the power of the Holy Priesthood and law of God." Many early speeches and pronouncements supported this interpretation. John J. Stewart, *Mormonism and the Negro* (Orem, UT: Bookmark, 1964), 33–52; Quotation from Turner, *Mormon Establishment*, 230–31.

10. Gary James Bergera and Ronald Priddis, *Brigham Young University: House of Faith* (Midvale, UT: Signature Books, 1985), 299, 301–302; Bush, "Mormonism's Negro Doctrine," 49.

11. Bush, "Mormonism's Negro Doctrine," 43; Jessie L. Embry, *Black Saints in a White Church: Contemporary African American Mormons* (Salt Lake City: Signature, 1994), 54.

12. Diane Urbani, "LDS Man Opening Minds—and Hearts," *Deseret News* (20 January 2003); Darius Gray, "Transcript of Interview," *Utah's African-American Voices* (4 February 2003); Elisa Anderson, "LDS Genesis President: Race A Divine Calling," *Daily Universe* (28 February 2003).

13. Taber, *Mormon Lives*, 103.

14. Eugene England, "The Mormon Cross," *Dialogue* 8(Spring 1973), 78–79, 85.

15. Arthur Henry King, *Arm the Children: Faith's Response to a Violent World* (Provo, UT: BYU Studies, 1998), 46. This selection, "An Account of My Conversion," was first published in 1986 in King's *Abundance of the Heart* (Salt Lake City: Bookcraft, 1986).

16. Lester Bush, "Writing Mormonism's Negro Doctrine: An Historical Overview," *Journal of Mormon History* 25:1(1999), 241.

17. Mark Grover, "The Mormon Priesthood Revelation and the São Paulo, Brazil Temple," *Dialogue* 23(Spring 1990), 40–41.

18. "Official Declaration—2," Doctrine and Covenants 1981.

19. Embry, *Black Saints*, 67; Mary Frances Sturlaugson, *A Soul So Rebellious* (Salt Lake City: Deseret Book, 1980), 68.

20. Leonard J. Arrington, *Adventures of a Church Historian* (Urbana: University of Illinois Press, 1998), 175–77.

21. Arrington, *Adventures*, 179.

22. Armand L. Mauss, "Introduction: Conflict and Commitment in an Age of Civil Turmoil," and "The Fading of the Pharaohs' Curse: The Decline and Fall of the Priesthood Ban Against Blacks in the Mormon Church," ed. Lester E. Bush, Jr., and Armand L. Mauss, *Neither White Nor Black: Mormon Scholars Confront the Race Issue in a Universal Church*, (Midvale, UT: Signature Books, 1984), 1–8; Armand L. Mauss, *The Angel and the Beehive: The Mormon Struggle with Assimilation* (Urbana: University of Illinois Press, 1994), 116–17.

23. John L. Hart, "A Presence in Harlem," "Book of Mormon Became a Comfort," *Church News* (19 May 2001).

24. Marcus Baram, "Mormons on Mission to Lure City Minorities," *New York Post* (21 April 2003).

25. Cardell K. Jacobson, Tim B. Heaton, E. Dale LeBaron, and Trina Louise Hope, "Black Mormon Converts in the United States and Africa: Social characteristics and Perceived Acceptance," ed. Marie Cornwall, Tim B. Heaton and Lawrence A. Young, *Contemporary Mormonism*, (Urbana: University of Illinois Press, 1994), 342–44; Jessie Embry, "Ethnic Groups and the LDS Church," *Dialogue* 25:4(1992), 103.

26. Embry, "Ethnic Groups," 103.

27. Embry, *Black Saints*, 123.

28. Kirsten Stewart, "Student Leader Wants to Bring Change to BYU," *Salt Lake Tribune* (28 March 2002); "Elected," *Sunstone* (April 2002), 78.

29. Embry, "Ethnic Groups," 107; "New Area Authority Seventies," *Church News* (19 April 2003).

30. Carrie A. Moore, "Black Mormons Say Life Better Since 1978," *Deseret News* (25 May 2003); Carrie A. Moore, "Knight & Co. Put Zip in LDS Hymns," *Deseret News* (9 June 2003).

31. Glen Burton, "Living in the Beehive State Still a Challenge for Blacks," *Salt Lake Tribune* (11 January 2004); Lawn Griffiths, "Latter-day Saints Face Race Issue," *East Valley Tribune* (28 February 2005).

32. Doctrine and Covenants 49:24 1981.

33. Ronald W. Walker, "Seeking the 'Remnant': The Native American During the Joseph Smith Period," *Journal of Mormon History* 19(Spring 1993), 1–33.

34. Bruce A. Chadwick and Stan L. Albrecht, "Mormons and Indians: Beliefs, Policies, Programs, and Practices," ed. Marie Cornwall, Tim B. Heaton and Lawrence A. Young, *Contemporary Mormonism: Social Science Perspectives* (Urbana and Chicago: University of Illinois Press, 1994), 295–309; Bruce A. Chadwick, Stan L. Albrecht, and Howard M. Bahr, "Evaluation of an Indian Student Placement Program," *Social Casework* 67:9(1986),

515–24; Genevieve de Hoyos, "Indian Student Placement Services," ed. Daniel H. Ludlow, *Encyclopedia of Mormonism*, 4 vols. (New York: Macmillan, 1992), 2:679–80.

35. On Lee, see George P. Lee, *Silent Courage: An Indian Story: the Autobiography of George P. Lee, a Navajo* (Salt Lake City: Deseret Book, 1987) and George P. Lee, "The Lee Letters," *Sunstone* 13(August 1989): 50–55.

36. Embry, "Ethnic Groups," 104.

37. Embry, "Ethnic Groups," 105, 109–10.

38. Embry, "Ethnic Groups," 105.

39. P. Jane Hafen, "The Being and Place of a Native American Mormon," *New Genesis: A Mormon Reader on Land and Community* (Salt Lake City: Gibbs Smith, 1998), 38; Sarah Theobald, "Legends Learns Art of Balancing Act," *Daily Universe* (28 February 2003).

40. Embry, "Ethnic Groups," 106–7.

41. Jason Swenson, "Nearly 13,000 Attend Historic Hispanic Fireside," *Church News* (14 December 2002); "How Many Mormons?" *Miami Herald* (11 October 2002).

42. James Lucas, "Mormons in New York City," ed. Tony Carnes and Anna Karpathakis, *New York Glory: Religions in the City* (New York: New York University Press, 2001), 196–203, 207, 220.

43. James Lucas, "Mormons in New York City," 205; Jessie L. Embry, "*In His Own Language:*" *Mormon Spanish Speaking Congregations in the United States* (Provo, UT: The Charles Redd Center for Western Studies, 1997), 80, 82–83.

44. Embry, "*In His Own Language,*" 63; Embry, "Ethnic Groups," 107–8; David Rogers, "L. B. Home to First Cambodian Mormon Ward," *Long Beach Press Telegram* (7 March 2005).

45. Carrie A. Moore, "An LDS Church First: Hispanic Devotional," *Deseret News.com* (28 November 2002); Tim Sullivan, "Spanish Christmas Devotional Held at LDS Conference Center," *Salt Lake Tribune* (9 December 2002); Jerry Johnston, "Hispanic Devotional Was Night to Savor," *Deseret News* (25 January 2003); Joe Baird, "Census Panel Member Calls for Changes," *Salt Lake Tribune* (20 August 2002); Jorge Iber, *Hispanics in the Mormon Zion: 1912–1999* (College Station: Texas A & M University Press, 2000), 113, 125, 127, 136.

46. Dawn House, "LDS Church Celebrates Latino Culture," *Salt Lake Tribune* (15 November 2004).

47. Armand L. Mauss, *All Abraham's Children: Changing Mormon Conceptions of Race and Lineage* (Urbana: University of Illinois Press, 2003), 275–76.

48. Moses 7:18 Pearl of Great Price 1981; 4 Nephi 1:3 Book of Mormon 1981.

49. Hugh Nibley, foreword to *Working Toward Zion: Principles of the United Order for the Modern World*, by James W. Lucas and Warner P. Woodworth (Salt Lake City: Aspen Books, 1996), ix–xi; Jessica Poe, "Lecturer Spotlights Life of Hugh Nibley," *BYU NewsNet* (19 March 2003).

50. Jacob 2:19 Book of Mormon 1981; Hugh Nibley, "Approaching Zion," ed. Don E. Norton, *Collected Works of Hugh Nibley*, vol. 9 (Salt Lake City: Deseret Book, 1989), quoted in Phillip Bryson, "In Defense of Capitalism: Church Leaders on Property, Wealth, and the Economic Order," *BYU Studies* 38:3(1999), 90, 93.

51. See Bryson, "In Defense of Capitalism."

52. Bryson, "In Defense of Capitalism," 89–107.

53. Gordon B. Hinckley, "Bold Initiative: Perpetual Education Fund," "Education Fund is New Road to Self Sufficiency," *Church News* (7 April 2001); "Volunteer Efforts, Contributions Offer Hope to Others," *Church News* (15 June 2002).

54. Shauna Ewell, "One Man's Story of the Perpetual Education Fund," *Scroll* [BYU–Idaho] (28 May 2002); Sarah Jane Weaver, "Returning Missionaries to Receive Helping Hand in Developing Lands," *Church News* (14 April 2001); Jason Swenson, "Welding Program Offers Hope, Opportunity to Faithful Mexicans," *Church News* (12 May 2001).

55. Sarah Jane Weaver, "Perpetual Education Fund Helps 5,360," *Church News* (26 October 2002).

56. Lucas and Woodworth, *Working Toward Zion*, 5.

CHAPTER SEVEN

1. Eileen Gibbons Kump, "Sayso or Sense," *Bread and Milk* (Provo, UT: BYU Press, 1979), 71–80.

2. Susan Buhler Taber, *Mormon Lives: A Year in the Elkton Ward* (Urbana: University of Illinois Press, 1993), 321.

3. Taber, *Mormon Lives*, 335.

4. Brigham Young, *Journal of Discourses*, 13:61 (18 July 1869).

5. Jill Mulvay Derr, Janath Russell Cannon, and Maureen Ursenbach Beecher, *Women of Covenant: The Story of Relief Society* (Salt Lake City: Deseret Book Company, 1992); Linda King Newell, "The Historical Relationship of Mormon Women and Priesthood," ed. Maxine Hanks, *Women and Authority: Re-emerging Mormon Feminism* (Salt Lake City: Signature Books, 1992), 44.

6. Sonja Farnsworth, "Mormonism's Odd Couple: The Motherhood-Priesthood Connection," ed. Maxine Hanks, *Women and Authority* (Salt Lake City: Signature Books, 1992), 299–311.

7. Lori G. Beaman, "Molly Mormons, Mormon Feminists and Moderates: Religious Diversity and the Latter Day Saints Church," *Sociology of Religion* (2001), 65–86.

8. Sarah Jane Weaver, "Dantzel Nelson Succumbs at Age 78," *Church News* (19 February 2005); Jason Swenson, "Regal, Faithful Woman Remembered Lovingly," *Church News* (26 February 2005).

9. Joyce W. Williams of Tallahassee, FL in response to questions from Claudia L. Bushman, 2001.

10. Debra Nussbaum Cohen, "Web is Heaven-Sent for Religious Bloggers," *New York Times* (28 March 2005).

11. Kit Warchol, "Panel Questions Women's Role in LDS Church," *The Daily Utah Chronicle* (11 October 2004).

12. Gordon B. Hinckley, interviewed by Larry King, *Larry King Live* (8 September 1998).

13. Eliza R. Snow, "O My Father," *Hymns of the Church of Jesus Christ of Latter-day* Saints (Salt Lake City: The Church of Jesus Christ of Latter-day Saints, 1985), 292; Linda P. Wilcox, "The Mormon Concept of a Mother in Heaven," ed. Maxine Hanks, *Women and Authority: Re-emerging Mormon Feminism* (Salt Lake City: Signature Books, 1992), 5–17. See also Janice Allred, *God the Mother and Other Theological Essays* (Salt Lake City: Signature Books, 1997) and Margaret Merrill Toscano and Paul James Toscano, *Strangers in Paradox: Explorations in Mormon Theology* (Salt Lake City: Signature Books, 1990).

14. Wilcox, "The Mormon Concept of a Mother in Heaven," 16.

15. "Elder Cree-L Kofford Speaks on God's Plan for Men and Women," *BYU News Releases/Devotional* (18 September 2002).

16. James E. Faust, "Becoming Great Women," *Ensign* 16(September, 1986), 16–20; Ezra Taft Benson, *To the Mothers in Zion* (Salt Lake City: Church of Jesus Christ of Latter-day Saints, 1987), quoted in Laurence R. Iannacone and Carrie A. Miles, "Dealing with Social Change: The Mormon Church's Response to Change in Women's Roles," ed. Marie Cornwall, Tim B. Heaton, and Lawrence A. Young, *Contemporary Mormonism: Social Science Perspectives*, (Urbana: University of Illinois Press, 1994), 278–79.

17. Bruce A. Chadwick and H. Dean Garrett, "'Choose ye this day whom ye will serve:' LDS Mothers' Reaction to Church Leader's Instruction to Remain in the Home," ed. Douglas J. Davies, *Mormon Identities in Transition* (London: Cassell, 1996), 166–79.

18. Courtney Black and Maxine Hanks, "Mormon Women Must Be Heard," *Boston Globe* (7 October 2000).

19. Kent Larsen, "Mormon Women's Boston Globe Declaration Yields Debate," *Mormon News* (27 October 2000).

20. D. Michael Quinn, *The Mormon Hierarchy: Extensions of Power* (Salt Lake City: Signature Books, 1997), 396.

21. John Heinerman and Anson Shupe, *The Mormon Corporate Empire* (Boston: Beacon Press, 1985), 144–68; D. Michael Quinn, *The Mormon Hierarchy: Extensions of Power* (Salt Lake City: Signature Books, 1997), 373–408; James Coates, *In Mormon Circles: Gentiles, Jack Mormons, and Latter-day Saints* (Reading, MA: Addison-Wesley Publishing Company, Inc., 1991), 127–33; Barbara B. Smith and Shirley W. Thomas, "Relief Society in the Twentieth Century," *Out of Obscurity: The LDS Church in the Twentieth Century* (Salt Lake City, Utah: Deseret Book Co., 2000), 314–15; Marilyn Warenski, *Patriarchs and Politics: The Plight of the Mormon Woman* (New York: McGraw-Hill, 1978), 181–95; "Historic Discourse—Excerpts," ed. Maxine Hanks, *Women and Authority: Re-emerging Mormon Feminism* (Salt Lake City: Signature Books, 1992), 113–130; Robert Gottlieb and Peter Wiley, *America's Saints: The Rise of Mormon Power* (New York: G. P. Putnam's Sons, 1984), 202–207.

22. Eloise Bell, "The Implications of Feminism for BYU," *BYU Studies* 16 (Summer 1976), 539.

23. "Historic Discourse—Excerpts," ed. Maxine Hanks, *Women and Authority: Re-emerging Mormon Feminism* (Salt Lake City: Signature Books, 1992), 107; This letter, written in 1979, is quoted in *Dialogue* (Fall 1990), 50.

24. Taber, *Mormon Lives*, 219.

25. Peggy Fletcher Stack, "LDS' Parkin Wants 'Global Sisterhood,'" *Salt Lake Tribune* (5 October 2002). Carrie A. Moore, "Relief Society Leaders Sure of Goal," *Deseret News* (28 September 2002).

26. Elyse Hayes, "Women Urged to Serve Others," *Deseret News* (29 September 2002); Peggy Fletcher Stack, "'Simple Acts of Pure Love' Can Change World, LDS Women Told," *Salt Lake Tribune* (29 September 2002); Bonnie D. Parkin, "See With New Eyes," *Church News* (10 May 2003).

27. Taber, Mormon Lives, 73.

28. Catherine Reese Newton, "Every Woman is a Mother Says Sister Dew," *Salt Lake Tribune* (30 September 2001).

29. Taber, *Mormon Lives*, 302–303.

30. Sarah Jane Weaver, "First She Was a Mother, Now She Is a Doctor, Too: Her Children Are Her Greatest Accomplishments," *Church News* (9 September 2000).

31. Stacey Wismer, "High Anxiety Plagues Y Parents in School," *Daily Universe* (12 June 2002).

32. Sarah Jane Weaver, "BYU Names Chair for Sister Hinckley," *Church News* (3 May 2003).

33. Julie A. Dockstader, "'Limitless is your potential, magnificent is your future,'" *Church News* (31 March 2001).

34. D. Michael Quinn, *Same-Sex Dynamics Among Nineteenth-Century Americans: A Mormon Example* (Urbana: University of Illinois Press, 1996), 370–82.

35. From a Public Affairs Shelf Item, approved by the First Presidency and the Quorum of the Twelve, April 18, 1996, quoted in Coke Newell, *Latter Days: A Guided Tour Through Six Billion Years of Mormonism* (New York: St. Martin's Press, 2000), 254.

36. On same-sex marriage, see Quinn, *Mormon Hierarchy: Extensions of Power*, 402–6; and Quinn, "Prelude to the National 'Defense of Marriage' Campaign: Civil Discrimination Against Feared or Despised Minorities," *Dialogue* 33:3(Fall 2000), 1–52; Armand L. Mauss, "On 'Defense of Marriage': A Reply to Quinn," *Dialogue* 33:3(Fall 2000), 53–65; Kevin O'Hanlon, "ACLU, Other Groups Challenge Restriction," *theindependent.com News* (1 May 2003); "Judge Voids Same-Sex Marriage Ban in Nebraska," *New York Times* (13 May 2005).

37. "HRC Announces Endorsements for Senate Campaign 2002," *Human Rights Campaign Press Release* (10 December 2001).

38. David Crary, "Furor Persists Over Boy Scouts' Gay Policy," *Deseret News* (24 June 2001).

39. "Boy Scouts Under Pressure Year After Court Ruling," *Newsweek* (6 August 2001).

40. Camille S. Williams, "Participating in the Public Forum: Why the Scouts Were Right to Ban Gay Activists as Leaders," *Meridian Magazine* (7 May 2002).

41. "Church, Scouts Sued in Sexual Abuse Case," *Deseret News* (31 May 2002); Jim Walsh, "Former Scout Leader Faces Long Prison Term After Molestation Plea," *Arizona Republic* (4 December 2002); Angie Welling, "Lawyer Ready to Fight LDS," *Deseret News* (5 June 2002).

42. "Mormon Church Backs Nevada Bill Against Single-Sex Marriage," *Reno Gazette Journal* (12 September 2002); "Proposition 22 Dominates California Wards' Attention, Divides Members," *Sunstone* (April 2001), 86–92; Janet Elliott, "Gay Marriage, Abortion Bills Get a Hearing," *Houston Chronicle* (17 March 2003); Rebecca Walsh, "LDS Church Shuns Political Fight over Utah's Marriage Amendment," *Salt Lake Tribune* (30 August 2004); Deborah Bulkeley, "Voters Support Marriage Measure," *Deseret Morning News* (3 November 2004).

43. "Proposition 22 Dominates California Wards' Attention, Divides Members," 86–92.

44. Erin Eldridge, *Born That Way?: A True Story of Overcoming Same-Sex Attraction, with Insights for Friends, Families, and Leaders* (Salt Lake City: Deseret Book, 1994).

45. "LDS Assistance Helps AIDS Retreat," *Deseret News* (29 September 2001).

CHAPTER EIGHT

1. Rosemary Pollock, "Academic Explains Why Rumors Show Mormons Protected from Harm," *Mormon News* (22 October 2001); Mary Ellen Robertson, "Still Circling the Wagons: Violence and Mormon Self-Image," *Sunstone* 40:4(April 2002), 64–66.

2. Judy Magid, "Mormon Choir Is, for Some, a Family Event," *Salt Lake Tribune* (8 December 2002).

3. "Members Worldwide Hear Proceedings Live," *Church News* (12 October 2002); Elizabeth Stohlton, "Conference to Be Broadcast in 17 New Countries," *BYU NewsNet* (4 October 2002).

4. Jeffrey P. Haney, "LDS Leader Calls for Faith, Service," *Deseret News* (26 August 2002).

5. "Lartebiokoshi Stake of LDS Holds Conference," *Acrra Mail* (12 November 2002).

6. William Lobdell, "Losing Faith and Lots More," *Los Angeles Times* (1 December 2001); *Church News* (25 November 2000).

7. Lobdell, "Losing Faith."

8. "Welfare Square Dedicated," *LDS Church Press Release* (4 September 2001).

9. Garth Mangum and Bruce Blumell, *The Mormons' War on Poverty: A History of LDS Welfare, 1830–1990* (Salt Lake City: University of Utah Press, 1993), 175, 179, 263–64; Doctrine and Covenants 82:19 1981.

10. Mangum and Blumell, *The Mormons' War on Poverty*, 199, 206–207.

11. Emiko Lowe, "Church Program Aids Poor, Needy," *Daily Universe* (3 July 2001).

12. Lowe, "Church Program Aids Poor," *Daily Universe* (3 July 2001); Lynn Arave, "Deseret Industries; More than a Thrift Store," *Deseret News* (13 August, 2001).

13. Lee Benson, "Warehouse Stockpiles Goodwill," *Deseret News* (10 August 2001); "Services Fact Sheet—2000" (Salt Lake City: The Church of Jesus Christ of Latter-day Saints, 2000); "Welfare Square Dedicated," *LDS Church Press Release* (4 September 2001); Richard Vara, "Mormon Peanut Butter Plant Spreads Efforts to Food Bank," *Houston Chronicle* (7 March 2003); "Measles Deaths in Africa Dropped by Nearly Half Over Five Years," *PR Newswire* (11 March 2005); Paul Sloth, "Churches Join Forces for Humanitarian Aid," *Onalaska Community Life* (25 March 2005); "Humanitarian Service Project Guidelines," *LDS Church News* (2 April 2005).

14. Yonat Shimron, "The Self-reliance Doctrine," *Raleigh* [NC] *News & Observer* (19 March 2003).

15. Shaun D. Stahle, "Of Books and Basketball," *Church News* (26 May 2001); Jed Woodworth, interviewed by Claudia L. Bushman (20 May 2003).

16. *Church News* (9 December 2000); Shaun D. Stahle, "Liberated by Hope: Returned Filipino Missionaries Learn Business Skills to Improve Lives," *Church News* (21 July 2001).

17. Sarah Jane Weaver, "Helping the Poor Help Themselves—and Then Others," *Church News* (21 April 2001); Rosemary Pollock, "Unitus Seeks to Unite LDS Donors and Volunteers with Charitable Work," *Mormon-News* (17 October 2000); Peggy Fletcher Stack, "Daily Bread, LDS Humanitarians Mobilize to Ease Suffering Among Mormons and Their Neighbors Worldwide," *Salt Lake Tribune* (14 October 2000).

18. "'Amen' to a Church-Free Lifestyle: Irreligious Not Uncharitable," *USA Today* (6 March 2002); "Salt Lake City Tops Charity Giving Study," *USA Today* (28 April 2003).

19. http://www.byu.edu/about/factfile/stud-ff4.html#enro; Jeffrey P. Haney, "Y.'s Sober Status Tops List Again," *Deseret News* (21 Aug. 2001); Jesse Hyde, "Y. Keeps 'Stone Cold Sober' Title," *Deseret News* (20 August 2002).

20. Amy K. Stewart, "Official says BYU Goes Beyond Boundaries," *Provo Daily Herald* (4 August 2001); Jeffrey P. Haney, "Y Happy to be a Language 'Flagship,'" *Deseret News* (3 September 2002); "BYU Sends Most Students for International Study," *BYU Press Release* (15 November 2001); Tad Walch, "Y Is Language Hot Spot," *Deseret Morning News* (22 April 2005).

21. Quoted in Richard N. Ostling and Joan K. Ostling, *Mormon America: The Power and the Promise* (San Francisco: HarperSan Francisco, 1999), 251; Kent P. Jackson, review of Bryan Waterman and Brian Kagel, *The Lord's University: Freedom and Authority at BYU* in *BYU Studies* 38(Winter 1999), 177; Keith J. Wilson, "By Study and Also by Faith: The Faculty at Brigham Young University Responds," *BYU Studies* 38(Winter 1999), 157–75.

22. Shaun D. Stahle, "Restoring Kirtland," *Church News* (1 June 2002); David Lewellen, "Restoring Piece of Mormon History in Ohio," *Canton Repository* (10 August 2002); Laurie Williams Sowby, "Kirtland Enjoying Revival," *ucjournal.com* [Utah County, Utah] (6 October 2002); Carrie A. Moore, "LDS Church Planning to Rebuild Smith' Home," *Deseret Morning News* (2 April 2005).

23. Christopher Smith, "BLM Considering LDS Lease," *Salt Lake Tribune* (14 September 2002); "Lease Martin's Cove," *Salt Lake Tribune*, 21 September 2002; Christopher Smith, "Bill on Martin's Cove May Sink Proposal to Compensate Tribes," *Salt Lake Tribune* (5 October 2002); Christopher

Smith, "Utah Bills Still May Linger," *Salt Lake Tribune* (8 November 2002); Lee Davidson, "Hansen's Swan Song," *Deseret News* (10 November 2002); Lee Davidson, "Bennett Calls Cove Bill Dead—For Now," *Deseret News* (14 November 2002); Ted Monoson, "Lease Offered at Cove," *Casper Star Tribune* (18 January 2003); "BLM Proposes Martin's Cove Plan," *Casper Star Tribune* (17 January 2003); Christopher Smith, "Trouble at the Cove," *Salt Lake Tribune* (10 March 2005); Angie Welling and Carrie Moore, "Martin's Cove Suit Filed," *Deseret Morning News* (10 March 2005).

24. C. G. Wallace, "Utah Abuzz Over 1857 Mountain Massacre," *Washington Times* (21 September 2002).

25. John Elvin, "The Madness at Mountain Meadows," *Insight on the News* (15 January 2003); Robert Plocheck, "Religion in the Media: A Look at Recent Books, Magazines and Web Sites," *Dallas Morning News* (17 October 2001).

26. Elvin, "The Madness at Mountain Meadows;" Wallace, "Utah Abuzz;" Emily Eakin, "Reopening a Mormon Murder Mystery," *New York Times* (12 October 2002).

27. Carrie A Moore, "New Facts on Guilt in Mountain Meadows Massacre," *Deseret News* (18 May 2002); Caroline Fraser, "The Mormon Murder Case," *The New York Review of Books* (21 November 2002).

28. Gustav Niebuhr, "Mormons Step Into the Past in Footsteps of Their Ancestors," *New York Times* (22 June 1997); Anne Underwood, "Onward, Mormon Pilgrims," *Newsweek* (28 April 1997); Robert W. Black, "BLM Limits Use of Mormon, Oregon Trails," *Corvallis Gazette-Times* (29 March 2005).

29. "New Palmyra, NY Visitors' Center Opening Coincides With 65th Pageant Performance," Official News Releases from the Church (10 June 2002); Karen Hoag, "Actors Flock to Manti for Mormon Miracle Pageant," *Provo Daily Herald* (8 June 2002); Cindy Lutz, "Smith's Birthday, New Pageant to Draw Tourists," *Daily Gate City* (31 March 2005).

30. Larry Williams, "Companies Make A Profit Cleaning Up Hollywood's Act," *Hartford Courant* (20 September 2002); Dan Kadison, "H'Wood: Don't Cut," *NYPost.com* (23 September 2002); John Anderson, "Questions of Cleaning Up," *Newsday.com* (3 November 2002).

31. C.G.Wallace, "Utah Town Approves Anti-U.N. Ordinance," *Provo Daily Herald* (6 July 2001"; "LaVerkin Ordinance Unconstitutional," *Provo Daily Herald* (20 July 2001); "Anti-U.N. Ordinance Revised," *Provo Daily Herald* (27 July 2001).

32. "Clergy Feel LDS 'Misguided,'" *Deseret News* (4 August 2001).

33. "Dartmouth Club Denies Mormon Student; Says Mormons Aren't Christian," *The Dartmouth*, (13 July 2001); Wendy S. McDowell, "Builder of a

Stronger Bridge Between HDS and Harvard at Large," *Harvard Divinity Bulletin* 30:3(Winter 2001–02), 35.

CHAPTER NINE

1. Ronald W. Walker, *Wayward Saints: The Godbeites and Brigham Young* (Urbana: University of Illinois Press, 1998). See, for example, Newell G. Bringhurst, "Fawn McKay Brodie and Her Quest for Independence," ed. John Sillito and Susan Staker, *Mormon Mavericks: Essays on Dissenters* (Salt Lake City: Signature Books, 2002), 193–214; Jessie L. Embry, "Maurine Whipple: The Quiet Dissenter," ed. Roger D. Launius and Linda Thatcher, *Differing Visions: Dissenters in Mormon History* (Urbana: University of Illinois Press, 1994), 310–18; Obert C. Tanner, *One Man's Journey: In Search of Freedom* (Salt Lake City: Humanities Center, University of Center, 1994); Brigham D. Madsen, *Against the Grain: Memoirs of a Western Historian* (Salt Lake City: Signature Books, 1994); Sterling M. McMurrin and L. Jackson Newell, *Matters of Conscience: Conversations with Sterling M. McMurrin on Philosophy, Education and Religion* (Salt Lake City: Signature Books, 1996); Ephraim E. Erickson, *Memories and Reflections: The Autobiography of E. E. Ericksen*, ed. Scott G. Kenney (Salt Lake City: Signature Books, 1987). Several were members of the "Swearing Elders," an informal discussion group of university academics with some Mormon affiliation. See Thomas A. Blakely, "The Swearing Elders: The First Generation of Modern Mormon Intellectuals," *Sunstone* 10(1986), 8–13. Lawrence Foster, "Career Apostates: Reflections on the Works of Jerald and Sandra Tanner," *Dialogue: A Journal of Mormon Thought* 17(Summer 1984), 34–60; Leonard J. Arrington, *Adventures of a Church Historian* (Urbana: University of Illinois Press, 1998), 63–64; "The Notorious Tanners," *Salt Lake City Weekly* (27 March 2003). Foster brought his earlier article up to date in Lawrence Foster, "Apostate Believers: Jerald and Sandra Tanner's Encounter with Mormon History," ed. Roger D. Launius and Linda Thatcher, *Differing Visions: Dissenters in Mormon History* (Urbana: University of Illinois Press, 1994), 343–652.

2. The literature on Mormon historiography is vast. A good place to start is Ronald W. Walker, David J. Whittaker, and James B. Allen, *Mormon History* (Urbana: University of Illinois Press, 2001).

3. The phrase, often cited in discussions between liberals and conservatives, is attributed to Elaine Cannon and immortalized in N. Eldon Tanner, "The Debate Is Over," *Ensign* (August 1979), 2–3.

4. Bruce R. McConkie, *Mormon Doctrine* (Salt Lake City: Bookcraft, Inc., 1966). On McConkie's far-reaching influence, see Armand L. Mauss, *The*

Angel and the Beehive: The Mormon Struggle with Assimilation (Urbana: University of Illinois Press, 1994), 161-63, 175-76.

5. See Andrew F. Ehat and Lyndon W. Cook, eds., *The Words of Joseph Smith: The Contemporary Accounts of the Nauvoo Discourses of the Prophet Joseph* (Orem, Utah: Grandin Book Company, 1980), 343–361.

6. Bruce R. McConkie to Eugene England, 19 February 1981, unpublished letter available at the University of Utah Library, at ww.myplanet.net/mike/LDS/McConkie_England_letter.html. On England-McConkie generally, see Mark S. Gustavson, "Scriptural Horror and the Divine Will," *Dialogue* 21:1(1988), 71–72; Eugene England, "On Spectral Evidence," *Dialogue*, 26:1(1993), 145–47.

7. Eugene England, "Perfection and Progression: Two Complementary Ways to Talk about God," *BYU Studies* 29(1989), 31–47.

8. Richard D. Poll, *History and Faith: Reflections of a Mormon Historian* (Salt Lake City: Signature, 1989), 1–8.

9. Poll, *History and Faith*, 19, 22–30, 104–5, 129.

10. Susan Buhler Taber, *Mormon Lives: A Year in the Elkton Ward* (Urbana: University of Illinois Press, 1993), 291.

11. Leonard J. Arrington, *Adventures of a Church Historian* (Urbana: University of Illinois Press, 1998), 143–50, 156, 215. On Arrington's tenure as Church Historian, see Davis Bitton, "Ten Years in Camelot: A Personal Memoir," *Dialogue* 16(Autumn 1983), 9–33, and the special issue memorializing Arrington in *Journal of Mormon History* 25:1(1999).

12. The anti-Mormon accusation was most famously made in Stephen E. Robinson, Review of *The Word of God: Essay on Mormon Scripture*, ed. Dan Vogel (Salt Lake City: Signature Books, 1990), in *Review of Books on the Book of Mormon* 3(1991), 312–18; www.signaturebooks.com.

13. Joseph Smith, *The Papers of Joseph Smith*, ed. Dean C. Jessee (Salt Lake City: Deseret Book, 1989); Tad Walch, "Miller Funding Joseph Smith Project," *Deseret Morning News* (5 April 2005).

14. Doctrine and Covenants 88:118 1981.

15. "FARMS Through the Years," *Insights, A Window on the Ancient World* (November 1999–January 2000).

16. *Insights: An Ancient Window*, the Newsletter of FARMS (October 1997), also www.farms.byu.edu/free/about/farmsbyu.html.

17. Front matter in *BYU Studies* 41:1(2002), 193; Front matter in *Journal of Mormon History* 28:1(Spring 2002), iii.

18. Elbert Eugene Peck, "The Origin and Evolution of the Sunstone Species: Twenty-five Years of Creative Adaptation," *www.sunstoneonline.com*.

19. Claudia L. Bushman, "Exponent II Begins," quoted in *Women and Authority: Re-emerging Mormon Feminism*, Ed Maxine Hanks (Salt Lake City: Signature Books, 1992), 86.

20. Armand L. Mauss, "The Fading of the Pharaohs' Curse: the Decline and Fall of the Priesthood *Ban Against Blacks* in the Mormon Church," ed. Lester E. Bush, Jr., and Armand L. Mauss, *Neither White Nor Black: Mormon Scholars Confront the Race Issue in a Universal Church* (Midvale, UT: Signature, 1984), 174–76.

21. Reproductions of the Joseph Smith III blessing and five other Hofmann forgeries can be found in Joseph Smith, *The Personal Writings of Joseph Smith*, ed. Dean C. Jessee (Salt Lake City: Deseret Book, 1984), 223–26, 277–78, 358–59, 565–66, 596–98, 616–18.   .

22. Arrington, *Adventures*, 219–224. There are many books on the Hofmann forgeries, but the work given complete access to diaries of the Mormon leaders involved is Richard E. Turley, Jr., *Victims: The LDS Church and the Mark Hofmann Case* (Urbana: University of Illinois Press, 1992). A historiographical review is David J. Whittaker, "The Hofmann Maze: A Book Review Essay," *BYU Studies* 29(Winter 1989), 67–124.

23. Among the significant research generated by the Hofmann forgeries was a special issue on early Mormonism and treasure-digging in *BYU Studies* 24(1984); D. Michael Quinn, *Mormonism and the Magic Worldview* (Salt Lake City: Signature Books, 1987); John L. Brooke, *The Refiner's Fire: The Making of Mormon Cosmology, 1644–1844* (Cambridge: Cambridge University Press, 1994); and William E. McLellin, *The Journals of William E. McLellin, 1831–1836*, ed. Jan Shipps and John W. Welch (Provo, UT: BYU Studies, Brigham Young University; Urbana: University of Illinois Press, 1994).

24. Elder Dallin H. Oaks, "Alternate Voices," *Ensign* (May 1989), 27.

25. Peggy Fletcher Stack, "LDS Church Decries Sunstone Sessions, Calls Content Insensitive, Offensive," *Salt Lake Tribune* (24 August 1991).

26. Vern Anderson, "LDS Church Turns Up Heat In Feud With Intellectuals," *Salt Lake Tribune* (5 October 1991); "Church Issues Statement on 'Symposia,'" and "Statement," *Sunstone* 15:4(September 1991), 58–59. On symposium speakers being called in for interviews, see Lavina Fielding Anderson, "The LDS Intellectual Community and Church Leadership: A Contemporary Chronology," *Dialogue* 26:1(Spring 1993), 7–64, esp. 36–39.

27. Bryan Waterman and Brian Kagel, *The Lord's University: Freedom & Authority at BYU* (Salt Lake City: Signature Books, 1998), 181–85.

28. On the LDS edition of the scriptures, see Bruce T. Harper, "The Church Publishes a New Triple Combination," *Ensign* (October 1981), 10–19.

29. Margaret Toscano and Paul Toscano, *Strangers in Paradox: Explorations in Mormon Theology* (Salt Lake City: Signature Books, 1990); Paul James Toscano, *The Sanctity of Dissent* (Salt Lake City: Signature Books, 1994), 96.

30. Lavina Fielding Anderson, "The September Six," ed. George D. Smith, *Religion, Feminism, and Freedom of Conscience: A Mormon/Humanist Dialogue* (Buffalo, NY: Prometheus Books; Salt Lake City: Signature Books, 1994), 3–8.

31. Melvyn Hammarberg, "Guilt, Fear, Anxiety and Love: Disciplinary Councils Among Latter-day Saints Today," ed. Douglas J. Davies, *Mormon Identities in Transition* (London: Cassell, 1996), 105–8.

32. Susan Easton Black, ed., *Expressions of Faith: Testimonies of Latter-day Saint Scholars* (Salt Lake City: Deseret Book; Provo, UT: FARMS, 1996), ix–x

33. Boyd K. Packer, "Talk to the All-Church Coordinating Council," delivered 18 May 1993, unpublished, found at www.zionsbest.com.

34. Fawn M. Brodie, *No Man Knows My History: The Life of Joseph Smith, the Mormon Prophet* (New York: Alfred A. Knopf, 1945); Stanley P. Hirshson, *The Lion of the Lord: A Biography of Brigham Young* (New York: Alfred A. Knopf, 1969); Leonard J. Arrington, *Brigham Young: American Moses* (New York: Alfred A. Knopf, 1985); Brent Lee Metcalfe, *New Approaches to the Book of Mormon: Explorations in Critical Methodology* (Salt Lake City: Signature Books, 1993); *Review of Books on the Book of Mormon* 6:1(1994); Francis Beckwith, Carl Mosser, and Paul Owen, eds., *New Mormon Challenge* (Grand Rapids, MI: Zondervan, 2002). On Brodie's influence, see Newell G. Bringhurst, ed., *Reconsidering No Man Knows My History* (Logan: Utah State University Press, 1996). On Arrington's charge, see Arrington, *Adventures of a Church Historian*, 195–208.

35. Michael R. Ash, "The Impact of Mormon Critics on LDS Scholarship," *Meridian Magazine* (28 August 2002).

36. Doctrine and Covenants 93:36 1981.

CHAPTER TEN

1. Marc Reisner, *Cadillac Desert: The American West and Its Disappearing Water* (New York: Viking, 1986), 1–2.

2. For a history of Salt Lake City, see Thomas G. Alexander and James B. Allen, *Mormons and Gentiles: A History of Salt Lake City* (Boulder, CO: Pruett Publishing, 1984); Gary Wills, *John Wayne's America: the Politics of Celebrity* (New York: Simon & Schuster, 1997), 304–5.

3. James A. Little, "Biography of Lorenzo Dow Young," *Utah Historical Quarterly* 14(1946), 98.

4. Leonard J. Arrington, *Brigham Young: American Moses* (New York: Alfred A. Knopf, 1985), 168.

5. Wilford Woodruff Journal, 28 July 1847, published in *Wilford Woodruff's Journal, 1833–1898*, 9 vols., ed. Scott G. Kenney (Midvale, UT: Signature Books, 1983), 3:239.

6. On Salt Lake City's layout, see C. Mark Hamilton, *Nineteenth-Century Mormon Architecture and City Planning* (New York: Oxford University Press, 1995).

7. D. W. Meinig coined the phrase in his classic article, "The Mormon Culture Region: Strategies and Patterns in Geography in the American West, 1847–1964," *Annals of the Association of American Geographers* 55(June 1965), 191–220; Arrington, *Brigham Young*, 169; *Deseret Evening News* (1 April 1876), quoted in "This Week in Church History: 125 Years Ago," *Church News* (24 March 2001).

8. Joseph Fielding Smith, *Essentials in Church History* (Salt Lake: Deseret Book Company, 1972), 443; "This Week," *Church News* (24 March 2001). On ZCMI, see Martha Sonntag Bradley, *ZCMI: America's First Department Store* (Salt Lake City: ZCMI, 1991).

9. Brady Snyder, "'Nones' Now 2nd in Religion Poll," *Deseret Morning News* (1 December 2003).

10. Lawrence Wright, "Lives of the Saints," *The New Yorker* (21 January 2002), 42; Dan Harrie, "Mormon, GOP Link Doomed Democrats," *Salt Lake Tribune* (6 December 2002); Carrie A. Moore, "Mormon Majority Activates Minority: Sociologist Says Non-LDS Religions in Utah Very Strong," *Deseret News* (2 November 2002).

11. Paul Rolly, "Far Right Wing of Utah GOP at Odds with LDS Positions," *The Salt Lake Tribune* (28 April 2002).

12. Timothy Egan, "Utah Colleges Fight to Keep Weapons Out," *New York Times* (25 January 2002).

13. Christopher Smith, "Reid at Pinnacle of Democratic Party," *Salt Lake Tribune* (22 November 2004); Dan Harrie, "Utah's Top Office Stays Republican," *Salt Lake Tribune* (3 November 2004); Paul Foy, "Huntsman Questions State's Strict Liquor Laws," *Daily Herald* (12 November 2004).

14. Felicity Barringer, "Of Church, State and Journalism," *New York Times* (7 January 2001); Michael Vigh, Elizabeth Neff, and Kristen Moulton, "Anatomy of a Newspaper War," *Salt Lake Tribune* (9 June 2002).

15. Paul Foy, "Salt Lake Tribune Publisher Makes Plans to Step Aside," *Provo Daily Herald* (25 July 2002); C. G. Wallace, "Sale of Newspaper Exposes Religious Rift," *Provo Daily Herald* (2 August 2002).

16. "Under New Management," *Salt Lake Tribune* (27 August 2002); "Deseret News Eyes Morning Launch—Again," *Salt Lake Tribune* (28 September 2002); Glen Warchol, "Tribune Owner Sees Bright Future for Utah Papers," *Salt Lake Tribune* (5 December 2002).

17. Glen Warchol, "Smarts to Receive an Apology," *Salt Lake Tribune* (1 May 2003).

18. Wright, "Lives of the Saints," 40.

19. George Vecsey, "For Salt Lake City Chief, Stress the Games and Limit the Damage," *The New York Times* (24 September 2000).

20. Anna Figueroa, "Salt Lake's Big Jump," *Newsweek* (5 September 2001); "The Olympics and Old Glory, *New York Times* (7 February 2002); Laurie Goodstein, "Mormons Project Image as Diverse as Olympics," *New York Times* (26 January 2002); "Eyes of World Look at Church," *Church News* (16 February 2002); Gary Mason, "Canada Press Reporter Looks at Mormons and Olympics," *Edmonton* [Canada] *Journal* (28 January 2002).

21. "Church Submits Additional Testimony on Alcohol Advertising Policy in Utah." *LDS Church News Release* (10 October 2001); Selena Roberts, "Time for the 'Healing' Games," *New York Times* (6 January 2002).

22. George Vecsey, "Given Options Available, a 'Bland Games' Would Be a Winner," *New York Times* (5 February 2002).

23. "Olympics Earn Friends and Respect for Church," *Church News* (2 March 2002); Michael Janofsky, "Games Behind Him, Olympics Leader Considers Political Run," *New York Times* (25 February 2002).

24. Michael Janofsky, "Utah's Changes May Be as Fleeting as Olympic Glory," *New York Times* (25 February 2002); George Vecsey, "Hughes's Effort Helped Elevate These Games," *New York Times* (24 February 2002).

25. Lucinda Dillon Kinkead and Dennis Romboy, "Down Town?" *Deseret News* (9 June 2002); Kinkead and Romboy, "What Awaits Salt Lake Malls?" *Deseret News* (10 June 2002); Steven Flint Lowe, "It's Time to Accept Reality, See Downtown as Religious Center," *Salt Lake Tribune* (3 November 2002).

26. Brady Snyder, "A Bold Vision for Salt Lake Malls," *Deseret News* (22 May 2003); Brady Snyder, "Rocky Isn't Thrilled by LDS 'Huge Mall' Plan," *Deseret Morning News* (1 April 2005).

27. "Community Alliance Issues Call for Tolerance, Diversity," *Salt Lake Tribune* (18 September 2001); Kristen Moulton, "Utah Alliance Looks to Kids for Tolerance," *Salt Lake Tribune* (14 September 2002).

28. Heather May, "Harassment Near Temple Square," *Salt Lake Tribune* (18 September 2002); "LDS Church Regrets Plaza Guard Episodes," *Salt Lake Tribune* (26 September 2002).

29. Rebecca Walsh, "Court Rejects LDS Plaza Rules," *Salt Lake Tribune* (10 October 2002); Michael Janofsky, "Public or Mormon Plaza? Battle Splits Salt Lake City," *New York Times* (27 October 2002); Glenn Warchol, "Conference Protesters Get ACLU Backing," *Salt Lake Tribune* (7 April 2003); "Utah: Restrictions on Church-Owned Property Appealed," *New York Times* (5 June 2001).

30. "Main Street Plaza Proposal," *Deseret News* (7 December 2002); Heather May, "Rocky Plan Fails to End Plaza Battle," *Salt Lake Tribune* (7 Decem-

ber 2002); Debbie Hummel, "Free-speech Dispute Deepens Chasm Between Mormons and Non-Mormons in Salt Lake City," *NJ.com* (8 January 2003).

31. William Lobdell, "Baptist Preacher Defies Mormons on Their Turf," *Los Angeles Times* (1 December 2002); Heather May, "Free Speech, Religion Collide on SLC Plaza," *Salt Lake Tribune* (5 January 2003); Brady Snyder, "Street Preacher on Mission in Salt Lake," *Deseret News* (18 January 2003); "Main Street Plaza Proposal," *Deseret News* (7 December 2002); Heather May, "Rocky Plan Fails to End Plaza Battle," *Salt Lake Tribune* (7 December 2002); Debbie Hummel, "Free-speech Dispute Deepens Chasm Between Mormons and Non-Mormons in Salt Lake City," *NJ.com* (8 January 2003).

32. "A Main Street Solution;" Kristen Moulton, "Alliance Asks Plaza Parties to Play Nice;" and Heather May, "Rocky's Plan Wins Public Support," *Salt Lake Tribune* (12 December 2002).

33. Stephen Speckman, "Main Street Deal Just About Done," *Deseret Morning News* (27 July 2003); "Unitarians to File Plaza Suit," *Deseret Morning News* (4 August 2003); "Plaza Issue is Settled," *Church News* (2 August 2003).

34. Glen Warchol, "Utah Laws on Liquor to Change," *Salt Lake Tribune* (25 January 2003); "Liquor in the Light," *Salt Lake Tribune* (28 January 2003); Glen Warchol, "ACLU Seeking Data Related to Liquor Law Rewrite," *Salt Lake Tribune* (4 February 2003); Jim Dabakis, "Non-Mormons are Boxed Out," *Salt Lake Tribune* (4 February 2003).

35. Richard D. Poll, "Utah and the Mormons: A Symbiotic Relationship," ed. Eric A. Eliason, *Mormons and Mormonism: An Introduction to an American World Religion* (Urbana: University of Illinois Press, 2001), 173.

CHAPTER ELEVEN

1. Twila Van Leer, "LDS Hail a Decade of Great 'Flowering,'" *Deseret Morning News* (3 April 2005); "Mormon Leadership Trio Marks 10 Years in Power," *AZCentral.com* (13 March 2005); "Wonderful Season," *Church News* (9 April 2005).

2. "Leadership Changes Announced at General Conference," *Newsroom.LDS.org* (2 April 2005).

3. Richard Bushman, quoted by Jill Fellow, in "Celebrating the 200th Anniversary of Joseph Smith," *Daily Herald* (27 March 2005).

4. Jennifer Dobner, "President Hinckley: 'A Man for His Time,'" *Salt Lake Tribune* (2 April 2005); "The First Presidency: 1995–2005," *Church News* (12 March 2005).

5. "2004 Annual Report," *Church News* (16 April 2005).

6. Melissa Sanford, "Illinois Tells Mormons It Regrets Expulsion," *New York Times* (8 April 2004).

7. Kristen Moulton, "Evangelical, LDS Find Bit of Common Ground," *Salt Lake Tribune* (15 November 2004); Cory Miller, "Controversy Surrounds Mormonism Comments by Fuller Exec.," *BP* (24 November 2004).

8. Joshua Cohen, "News & Columns," *New York Press* (9 March 2005).

9. Stan L. Albrecht and Tim B. Heaton, "Secularization, Higher Education, and Religiosity," *Review of Religious Research* 26(1984), 43–58.

10. Robert Gottlieb and Peter Wiley, *America's Saints: The Rise of Mormon Power* (New York: G. P. Putnam's Sons, 1984), 10–12, 58–63, 197, 199–200, 209–12, 245, 247, 256–57.

11. John Heinerman and Anson Shupe, *The Mormon Corporate Empire* (Boston: Beacon Press, 1985), ix, 4, 249–50.

12. Heinerman and Shupe, *Corporate Empire*, 109–10, 113–16, 125–26, 252–257.

13. Richard N. Ostling and Joan K. Ostling, *Mormon America: The Power and the Promise* (San Francisco: HarperSanFrancisco, 1999), xxvi.

14. Ostling and Ostling, *Mormon America*, 400; Roger Clarke, public presentation to the NYLDSPA (New York Latter-day Saint Professional Association), New York, NY, 1997; Sarah Jane Weaver, "'A Better Understanding' to Come of World's Visit," *Church News* (2 March 2002).

15. Armand L. Mauss, *The Angel and the Beehive: The Mormon Struggle with Assimilation* (Urbana: University of Illinois Press, 1994), 4, 8–9, 12, 15–16, 22–24, 26, 35, 46–47, 51, 54, 58, 60–61.

16. Mauss, *Angel and the Beehive*, 25, 29, 31–35, 71, 77, 85–88.

17. Mauss, *Angel and the Beehive*, 123, 127, 132, 206, 209, 211.

18. Armand L. Mauss, "Refuge and Retrenchment: The Mormon Quest for Identity," ed. Marie Cornwall, Tim B. Heaton, and Lawrence A. Young, *Contemporary Mormonism: Social Science Perspectives* (Urbana and Chicago: University of Illinois Press, 1994).

19. Jan Shipps, *Mormonism: The Story of a New Religious Tradition* (Urbana: University of Illinois Press, 1985), 148–49; Jan Shipps, "In the Presence of the Past: Community and Change in Twentieth-Century Mormonism," ed. Thomas G. Alexander and Jessie L. Embry, *After 150 Years: the Latter-day Saints in Sesquicentennial Perspective*, (Provo, UT: Charles Redd Center for Western Studies, Brigham Young University, 1983), 28; Jan Shipps, *Sojourner in the Promised Land: Forty Years Among the Mormons* (Urbana: University of Illinois Press, 2000), 98–100.

20. Shipps, *Sojourner in the Promised Land*, 102–3, 106.

21. Shipps, *Sojourner in the Promised Land*, 193–99, 201–2, 385.

INDEX

ABOUT THE AUTHOR

CLAUDIA L. BUSHMAN is Professor of American Studies at Columbia University and the author of *Mormons in America*, *Building the Kingdom: A History of Mormons in America*, and other books and articles. She is the former director of the Delaware Heritage Commission.